BIG JOE McCARTHY

THE RCAF's AMERICAN DAMBUSTER

DAVE BIRRELL

For my Dad,
Dr. John D. Birrell
[RCAF Medical Officer 1941-1945]
who would have liked it.

Front cover 'American Dambuster'-A painting by Mark Postlethwaite [courtesy the artist]
Joe McCarthy in 1944 [courtesy the McCarthy Family]
Back cover Joe McCarthy and his crew at Scampton following the Dams Raid (l-r) Sgt. George (Johnny) Johnson (bomb-aimer), F/Sgt. Don MacLean (navigator), Sgt. Ron Batson (front gunner), F/Lt. Joe McCarthy (pilot), Sgt. Bill Radcliffe (flight engineer), and F/Sgt. Len Eaton (wireless operator)Missing: F/O Dave Rodger (rear gunner) [courtesy Imperial War Museum]
Nose Art Replicas-by Clarence Simonsen [courtesy the artist]
ISBN: 978-1-9087570-5-0

Printed & bound in the UK by PublishPoint, a service from KnowledgePoint Limited.

Contents

Joe McCarthy and his crew at Scampton following the Dams Raid
(l-r) Sgt. George (Johnny) Johnson (bomb-aimer),
F/Sgt. Don MacLean (navigator), Sgt. Ron Batson (front gunner),
F/Lt. Joe McCarthy (pilot), Sgt. Bill Radcliffe (flight engineer),
and F/Sgt. Len Eaton (wireless operator)
Missing: F/O Dave Rodger (rear gunner)
[courtesy Imperial War Museum]

Foreword

The highlight of my twenty-two years in the Royal Air Force has to be the fifty operations in Bomber Command between June 1942 and April 1944. Eighty percent of these trips were as the bomb aimer with F/Lt. Joseph C. McCarthy's crew.

Joe (an American in the Royal Canadian Air Force) was a big man. Only 23 years old, he was already a natural leader. He was big in size, big in personality, with outstanding flying ability. I am sure that this created a confidence in his crew as a whole. In my case, I never thought that, "I wasn't coming back."

I joined his crew at 97 Squadron and we finished our first tour at the end of March 1943. Joe was asked by Guy Gibson if he would join a unique squadron, which he was forming for one special trip. We, as a crew, agreed to join. We were, however, entitled to one weeks leave at this time and my fiancée and I had decided to get married on April 3rd. On arrival at this new squadron one of the first things we were told was there was to be no leave. Joe took us, as a crew, to see Gibson and said we were entitled to one weeks leave and that his bomb aimer was going to get married on that date. We got our leave and I have always been grateful to Joe for making the wedding possible.

The flying with this new squadron was all at low level and once again Joe proved himself both in training and on operations. Whilst I was with him at 97 Squadron we were on a trip to Berlin when we lost one port engine over the target. En-route home, the second port engine failed. He flew us home on the remaining two starboard engines and, crossing the English coast called "Mayday." We were received by Tangmere and as we came into land Joe called "crash stations" for the only time in my experience.

We landed successfully.

On the return from the Dams Raid, due to compass error, we found ourselves over the Hamm railway yards. This was the major distribution point for Ruhr armament production and was extremely heavily defended. Joe's reaction to the flak assault was to fly so low that the guns could not be depressed enough to fire at us.

If he was very serious about his flying, he was equally cheerful and jovial off duty. Quite fond of a drink he could, in service language, "sink a few."

Consideration for your team is a major facet of leadership. This was clearly demonstrated to me in April 1944 when my wife was expecting our first child. Joe took me aside and said, "Gwyn must be worried sick about whether this child is going to have a father and if she will have a husband. You have got to pack it in." I didn't want to leave the crew but he made me realise that I had other responsibilities than flying to war.

In later years he and Alice would join Gwyn and myself at many squadron reunions. There was always time for conversation about post-war life and quiet reflection on times gone by. This strong relationship continued until his death and I delight in the continuing family ties through his son Joe jr.

Over the years Joe McCarthy was my leader and despite being only two years older, my older brother. He became a much admired, lifelong friend.

George 'Johnny' Johnson
28 December, 2011

Introduction

Joe McCarthy was one of about 9000 Americans who joined the Royal Canadian Air Force prior to the United States entering World War II. The most remembered of these is likely P/O John Gillespie MaGEE, author of the classic aviation poem "High Flight" that begins with, "Oh! I have slipped the surly bonds of Earth and danced the skies on laughter-silvered wings." Of the 9000, Joe McCarthy's air force career is clearly the most outstanding, remarkable for the degree of his involvement and for the variety of his challenges and successes.

In his book 'Wings for Victory,' Spencer Dunmore wrote of these Americans, "They were colourful, those volunteers; professionals and playboys, convicted felons and husbands on the run, idealists and mercenaries, kids seeking adventure, youngsters seeking nothing but an opportunity to fly, middle-aged men looking for work; and to all of them, the RCAFs need was their golden opportunity."

Like John MaGEE, Joe loved to fly and 'dance the sky on laughter-silvered wings' and both were undoubtedly, 'kids seeking adventure' and perhaps 'youngsters seeking nothing but an opportunity to fly.' P/O MaGEE was killed in 1941 while serving as a Spitfire pilot with the RCAFs 412 Fighter Squadron. Joe was more fortunate, defying the odds to survive 67 wartime operations as a bomber pilot. As his career progressed, it became clear that his exceptional flying abilities were complemented by a firm sense of duty and outstanding leadership skills.

During an interview recorded following his retirement, Joe remarked of his wartime career,

"That whole time was amazing. The things that we got into and what we did in those times- the stories and the events that happened were fantastic."[1]

Looking back, there is no question that they were. Joe served and flew with extraordinary people and played a significant rôle in numerous extraordinary events.

Big Joe McCarthy, 1944.
McCarthy Family

A tour of operations with 97 Squadron and being awarded the Distinguished Flying Cross was only the beginning. Personally selected by W/C Guy Gibson, Joe trained for and executed his rôle during the Dams Raid, the most demanding tactical air operation of the Second World War. Almost fourteen months of special and varied operations with 617 Squadron followed. These flights included low-level bombing, target marking, amazingly precise high-level bombing, the use of huge, special purpose bombs against critical targets, and clandestine low-level operations to supply the underground forces in occupied Europe.

Through all this, Joe worked closely with and was highly respected by many of the legends of Bomber Command including Guy Gibson, Mickey Martin, and Leonard Cheshire.

Immediately following the war, Joe played a major rôle in the acquisition and testing of numerous exotic German aircraft before returning to Canada and completing an exemplary post-war career with the Royal Canadian Air Force.

Through all of this, as was almost always the case with Bomber Command aircrew, Joe remained self effacing and modest, willing to give the credit to his crew and fellow airmen, and believed that he was just doing his job.

Prologue

Big Joe Goes Home

The three hour crossing from Digby to St. John aboard the Princess of Acadia was a relaxing part of his journey between Greenwood and Virginia. Following a short drive along the south coast of New Brunswick, Joe would be back in the United States following a remarkable career with the Royal Canadian Air Force.

As Joe leaned on the deck railing and gazed out at the Bay of Fundy his thoughts must have focused on the day 27 years earlier when he and his best friend Don Curtin rode the bus from New York City to Ottawa with the hope of joining another country's air force, becoming pilots, and doing what they thought was right; going to war against the Nazis.

Joe would have heard the aircraft approaching from astern on the same track as the ferry and instantly recognized the Argus. It was not unusual for RCAF aircraft to fly over the ferry when they were on patrol or en-route to other duties. As it flew by, the veteran airman who was known for his un-assuming, self-effacing nature likely didn't realise that this was a special flight, both for the air force he had served so well and for him.

The lumbering Argus banked away from the ferry and began a slow turn, disappearing into the haze. Then it flew by again, this time so close to the ship and so low that Joe didn't have to look up as he exchanged waves with his friends in the cockpit. This time he knew that the low-level flypast salute was for him; a final tribute from the Royal Canadian Air Force.

The King at Scampton-27 May 1943 (l-r) Joe McCarthy, King George VI, and Guy Gibson.

Imperial War Museum

Part One

The RCAF Comes Calling

"So why don't we just go over now and get started."

Early years in New York

Joseph Charles McCarthy was born on 31 August 1919 in St. James on Long Island, New York which was at that time a largely rural community. His grandfather served as a Special Deputy Sherriff in the Bronx, influencing the local political scene with a tendency to be a hot-headed Irishman at times. Known to the family as 'Dep,' he was a fancy dresser who owned a bar which he managed in his spare time. Joe's father, Cornelius Joseph, was a clerk. Shortly after Joe was born, the family moved to the Bronx in New York City where Cornelius worked as a book-keeper at the shipyards. Later, he became a New York fireman.

Joe's mother, Eve, died when was he was about eleven years old and his grandmother took over the responsibility of raising Joe and his younger brother Frank.

The family lived in the Bronx but had a summer home on Long Island. It was here that Joe became a strong swimmer and began working as a lifeguard at Coney Island and other beaches in the New York area. He became friends with Don Curtin who was also a lifeguard and together they developed their skills as competitive swimmers.

Competition was fierce between the various swim clubs on Long Island and Joe's talents were in demand. He was encouraged to swim for several different clubs who would pay him to compete as part of their team. It is said that this blue-eyed, blonde Irish boy once swam for the B'nai Brith as part of a synagogue's team. There were other swim teams that were based on ethnic background as well and Joe collected a number of swimming medals that had names on them that were appropriate for whatever ethnic team he was swimming for that day. Apparently Joe was very successful in making extra money by swimming for the highest bidder.

Above: Joe McCarthy (left) with his brother Frank.
McCarthy Family

Left: Joe, likely nineteen years old, with some of his swimming trophies.
McCarthy Family

As well as swimming, Joe played baseball and other sports and at some point, together with Don Curtin, became interested in aviation and started flying at Roosevelt Field. Joe did odd jobs on the field as well to help pay for his flying lessons.

Even during the late 1930s when Joe and Don took flying lessons there, Roosevelt Field had considerable aviation history associated with it. The British dirigible R-34 had landed there in 1919 after the first east-to-west, non-stop trans-Atlantic flight. Then in 1927, Charles Lindbergh departed from Roosevelt Field in the Spirit of St. Louis on the first solo trans-Atlantic flight.

During the 1930s Roosevelt Field was the busiest civilian airport in the United States. Over 400 aircraft were based there with as many as 300 takeoffs and landings per hour. The field featured regular weekend airshows that drew huge crowds to see aerobatics, skydivers and demonstrations of the latest civil and military aircraft. It is not surprising that as young men in their teens, Joe and Don developed a fascination with aircraft and flying after spending time at Roosevelt Field.

When Joe reached twenty years of age he was swimming competitively, learning how to fly, and taking college courses. Three days later on 3 September 1939, the war that many had felt was imminent officially began with Britain's declaration of war against Germany. The following day Sgt. Albert Prince, the first of over 10,000 Canadians who would be killed serving with Bomber Command, died shortly after attacking a German battleship as the pilot of a Blenheim bomber. Canada's declaration of war followed on 10 September.

The Roosevelt Field flightline, circa 1935. At the time this was the busiest and most famous civil aviation airfield in the world.

Joe had likely already been thinking of joining the air force. He may very well have enrolled in college because at that time a university education was often necessary to become a pilot in the American armed forces.

Over the next year and a half Joe made three attempts to join the United States Army Air Corps. During this time the countries of western Europe were being conquered by the Nazis and there was a real threat that Britain would be invaded as well. Even though the United States was neutral, the Air Corps knew that it had to expand but the US military was unprepared for any large scale expansion and organization was lacking. Each time Joe applied he was told that he would hear back from them but he never did. This may have been because of his lack of a university degree.

While continuing to fly at Roosevelt Field, Joe would undoubtedly have heard that the Royal Canadian Air Force was welcoming American flyers and, in fact, actively recruiting them.

Leaving for Canada and the RCAF

During World War I Billy Bishop became Canada's most famous war hero. Officially credited with destroying 72 enemy aircraft, he was the top Allied ace of the war and a recipient of the Victoria Cross. During 1938 Bishop was put in charge of recruiting for the Royal Canadian Air Force. He also helped to create a system for training pilots across Canada and became instrumental in setting up and promoting the British Commonwealth Air Training Plan.

The young Canadian men loved him and flocked to recruiting stations after each of his speeches. Anxiously awaiting his eighteenth birthday, Murray Peden attended a recruiting rally at which Bishop spoke. He recalled, "being exhilarated by the pugnacious speech" but also that he, "exuded as much dignity as daring." Bishop helped sell war bonds, conducted inspection tours, and socialized in the messes with the young pilots. He even appeared in the Hollywood film, "Captains of the Clouds," playing himself pinning wings on the graduates of an RCAF Service Flying Training School class.

Air Marshal Billy Bishop VC.
Royal Canadian Air Force

When war was declared United States President Roosevelt made it clear that although the United States would remain neutral he understood that, "Even a neutral cannot be asked to close his mind or conscience." There was significant opposition to America's involvement in the war, particularly in the Congress, but Roosevelt would do what he could to assist Britain and her Allies.

Billy Bishop recognized the potential of involving Americans in the RCAF and most importantly, the need for instructors to support the huge training plan that Canada would play the major rôle in. His main concern was that the pool of experienced Americans should be tapped as efficiently as possible without violating the American law that stated that recruiting American citizens on American soil to fight in a foreign war was a violation of the Neutrality Act.

Through magazine covers such as this, Clayton Knight inspired thousands of young Americans to become pilots.
Clarence Simonsen

During World War I Bishop became friends with American artist Clayton Knight who had also flown with the Royal Flying Corps. Through his artwork, Knight had become well known in aviation circles throughout the United States.

Bishop contacted his old friend, telling him that, "American boys will want to help Canada as they did in the First War. But this time they must have direction and be screened. We need someone in the States to sort them out before they cross the border." With his broad ties to aviation in the United States, Knight would be key to the public relations involved in Bishop's initiative.

The Canadian Air Staff were thrilled and the so called, 'Clayton Knight Committee' was instructed to immediately direct qualified American pilots to Canada, although in a way that would not upset the American Government.

Office space for the venture was secured in the Waldorf-Astoria Hotel in New York City and soon Clayton Knight was on a tour of American flying schools. One of first stops would have undoubtedly been at nearby Roosevelt Field.

Concerns regarding recruits having to pledge allegiance to the King, something that could result in forfeiture of citizenship for Americans, were removed when the Canadian government passed an Order in Council replacing this "oath" with an agreement to obey RCAF rules and discipline. The Committee continued its work based at the Waldorf-Astoria but soon many of Knight's pilot friends were employed as recruiters and based in other American luxury hotels in San Francisco, Atlanta, Spokane, Los Angeles, Dallas, San Antonio, Cleveland, Memphis, and Kansas City. Of the 8864 Americans who served in the RCAF, about 800 were killed, many while serving with Bomber Command.

So during 1940 anyone involved with flying schools in the United States would have been exposed to the Committee's influence and Joe McCarthy and Don Curtin began to consider the opportunities that were available north of the border.

Don had been working as a cruise director with the Holland America Steamship Company. However the war began limiting the company's activities and Don was laid off. One day in early May 1941, Joe and Don happened to meet in New York. Don suggested that they enlist in the Royal Canadian Air Force.

On 4 May 1941 the decision had been made and Joe and Don climbed aboard a bus that would take them to Canada and careers with the Royal Canadian Air Force.

Joe was not happy that the US was taking a neutral position in the war but regarding his father's motivation, Joe McCarthy Jr. said, *"I believe that was a part of it but I don't think there was just one specific thing; it was all combined: the money; jobs were still scarce at that time, the adventure of flying, trying to help right a wrong. I think that by this time they realised that the US was going to get in the war sooner or later anyway so why don't we just go over now and get started."*[1]

Adventure in the skies.

Royal Canadian Air Force

Part Two

BCATP Training in Canada

"Dad made sure that he wasn't the best guy around so that he wouldn't get stuck with instructor duty."

To Canada to Join the RCAF

'Don and I boarded a bus and headed for Ottawa. We crossed the St. Lawrence River by ferry and the Canada Customs people helped us get a connecting bus to Ottawa. We spent the night at the YMCA and the following morning, 5 May 1941, we proceeded to the RCAF recruiting office. There we were told we would have to come back in six weeks. Don and I responded that we didn't have the money to return again so if the air force wanted us they had better decide that day.'[1]

With that, the officer in charge looked the two young, strong, healthy Americans over, realised that these were ideal prospects, and said, 'Okay.' Enlistment papers were filled out, medical examinations were passed, and Joe and Don were enrolled in the Royal Canadian Air Force Special Reserve with the rank of 'Aircraftman 2nd Class,' Joe receiving the number J9346. Later that day Joe, Don, and thirteen other recruits were on a train headed to 1 Manning Depot in Toronto.

Joe and Don had entered into one of Canada's major contributions to victory in World War II, the British Commonwealth Air Training Plan (BCATP). Referred to as the 'Aerodrome of Democracy' by US President Roosevelt, Canada had an abundance of air training space beyond the range of enemy aircraft, excellent climatic conditions for flying, immediate access to American industry, and relative proximity to the Britain via the North Atlantic.

Canada had been the location of a major recruitment and training organization during the First World War and Britain looked to it again when the war began. To Prime Minister Mackenzie King this major commitment had the advantage of keeping large numbers of

Explaining the British Commonwealth Air Training Plan to recruits.
Royal Canadian Air Force

Canadians at home and avoiding the raising of a large expeditionary force to fight in Europe as had been the case in World War I. Canada agreed to accept most of the plan's costs, but insisted that the British agree that air training would take precedence over other aspects of the Canadian war effort. The British expected that their Royal Air Force would absorb Canadian air training graduates as in World War I, but King demanded that distinct Royal Canadian Air Force squadrons be formed.

The construction of the training schools was a massive undertaking in itself. On the prairies, farmer's fields were transformed into operational schools within a matter of a few months. This involved the levelling of the land and paving of runways, taxiways, and roads, the building of several huge hangars and dozens of other buildings for accommodation, teaching, and providing other services to the young airmen, and the installation of electrical, water, sewage, and other services.

As well, an aircraft construction industry was developed to provide most of the thousands of aircraft that were necessary.

At the plan's peak 94 schools were operating at 231 sites across Canada, 10,840 aircraft were involved, the ground organization numbered 104,113 men and women, and 3000 trainees graduated each month. In total 131,553 pilots, navigators, bomb aimers, wireless operators, air gunners, and flight engineers were graduated.

Joe and Don began their air force career with a four week posting to the Toronto

A British Commonwealth Air Training Plan School under construction.
Royal Canadian Air Force

Manning Depot where they received an indoctrination into air force life. The recruits marched, paraded, cleaned latrines, were vaccinated, and had haircuts in order to make them all as similar as possible. Then the air force could remake them in its own image.

The recruits were also issued with their uniforms which, as the weeks went on, were worn with an increasing sense of pride as the young men found that they were able to cope with the challenges presented to them.

Almost all were assigned to guard duty during their Manning Depot time. This was largely a further introduction to air force discipline; guarding an air force hangar, runway, or aircraft (four hours on, then four hours off) when there was virtually no risk involved to anything. Joe spent some time at Sydney, Nova Scotia performing guard duty.

Following their stint at Manning Depot, Joe and Don proceeded to 1 Initial Training School (ITS) which was also located in Toronto. Here the atmosphere was similar to a post-secondary school as the potential airmen attended classes to study mathematics, navigation, aerodynamics, and other subjects related to aviation. Between classes, there was daily physical training and parade drill under the direction of the school's disciplinary officer. Results at ITS were critical as the grades would determine the student's next posting. Some students would

be considered suitable for flying training and others would be assigned to navigation or wireless schools.

As for the two young men from New York, the flying training they had received at Roosevelt Field likely provided a sound foundation for their ITS studies. Joe and Don were both successful, graduated on 11 August 1941, and were promoted to the rank of Leading Aircraftsman.

The Link Trainer simulator was utilized at the ITS to assess a student's potential for becoming a pilot.
Royal Canadian Air Force

Elementary Flying Training School

The next step for those who qualified for pilot training was a posting to an Elementary Flying Training School (EFTS). Here an eight week course involved all aspects of basic flight and navigation and about fifty hours of flying in single-engined 'primary' training aircraft such as Fleet Fawns, Fleet Finches, de Havilland Tiger Moths, and later in the war, Fairchild Cornells.

Joe and Don were posted to No.12 EFTS at Goderich, Ontario where Joe had his first RCAF flight in Fleet Finch 4695 on 13 August.

The Fleet Finch is a two-seat, tandem training biplane that was produced by Fleet Aircraft of Fort Erie, Ontario. A total of 447 Finches were built, nearly all of them being used as elementary trainers. Finches served at twelve elementary flying training schools in Canada. Like the more widely used de Havilland Tiger Moth, the Finch was equipped with a sliding canopy over the two cockpits for use during winter operations.

Joe soloed just eight days later after only eight hours of instruction and graduated from the course on 26 September.

Sports were an integral part of life on all the BCATP bases. While at 12 EFTS Joe's baseball and swimming skills contributed to the success of the school's teams. Don and Joe participated in one swim meet that was particularly memorable to Gilbert Turner who, in a letter to Joe written in 1968, reminded him of his successes:

Fleet Finch.
Maynard Norby

"Now we go back to Goderich in the summer of 1941. What a summer and so much to remember. One of the highlights was how you boys in that little Station down the road, walloped the swim trunks off the big and cocky Royal Air Force Station, ten times the size of us at a swimming meet at Goderich. I can still see you and your butterfly crawl. We thought you had gone down for good only to have you re-appear half-way down the course." [2]

Joe's reply to his old friend includes an indication that he and his fellow students did not spend every evening working on their courses:

"Your reminiscence of Goderich does stir the dusty bins of old times. As a matter of fact, winning that swimming meet saved our hides as most of the team were confined to barracks for fence jumping the previous night. Both Frank Ball, the C/O, and his deputy, J. Jordan, were elated over the win and promptly cancelled the CB." [3]

Joe (centre) with his trophy-winning baseball team at 12 EFTS.
Standing: Snider, Caldwell, Galbraith, Joe McCarthy, Falkner, unknown, McIntosh
Kneeling: Unknown, Smith, Hunter, Unknown.
The McCarthy Family

Don Curtin (left) and Joe at Goderich-18 September 1941.
The McCarthy Family

Fleet Finches at 12 EFTS in Goderich, Ontario.
Huron County Museum & Historic Gaol

Joe's class at 12 EFTS. Joe is at centre in the third row. Don Curtin is third from the right in the second row.
The McCarthy Family

Fleet Finches at 12 EFTS in Goderich, Ontario.
Huron County Museum & Historic Gaol

Upon graduation from an EFTS, the student pilot's next posting would be to one of the BCATP's 29 Service Flying Training Schools (SFTSs) where they were expected to improve their navigational skills, master instrument and night flying, and participate in formation flying exercises. Most also had to adapt to flying larger, twin-engined aircraft such as the Avro Anson or Cessna Crane. Pilots who were selected to become fighter pilots were posted to an SFTS where the single-engined North American Harvard was flown. All the SFTS aircraft were more powerful and demanding. Upon graduation from an SFTS the pilot would receive the coveted RCAF Wings and were ready to continue their training, generally overseas and with an emphasis on operational wartime flying.

While at an amusement park during his time at Goderich, Joe and his friends met several young ladies from Detroit, Michigan who had come to Canada for the weekend. The group included Alice and her sister. Although the war would interfere with their relationship, Joe and Alice were eventually married.

Joe and Alice at Goderich, Ontario during the fall of 1941.
The McCarthy Family

Service Flying Training School

Avro Anson Mk IIs.

Joe and Don were both posted to 5 SFTS at Brantford, Ontario where they were introduce to the Avro Anson. The decision had been made that they would be bomber pilots rather than fighter pilots. The Anson first flew in 1935 and went on to serve in a wide variety of rôles during the Second World War. Over 11,000 were built and the Anson was still flying with the Royal Air Force in 1968.

It served operationally during the early years of the war as a light bomber and coastal patrol aircraft. During the evacuation of Dunkirk, Ansons were used aggressively to protect the beleaguered British troops. During this operation one Anson was attacked by ten Messerschmitts but somehow managed to shoot down two and damage a third before the action was broken off. However the Anson was severely limited in range, fire-power, and bomb-load and was soon limited to training, transport, and other non-combat rôles.

The Anson Mk I was to be the standard twin-engined trainer for the BCATP. However by May 1940, British production could not keep up with the demand for aircraft in Canada and Federal Aircraft Ltd. was established in Montreal to produce the aircraft. It featured the considerable use of plywood to save stocks of steel and aluminum for other purposes. A total of 1832 Mk II Ansons were built and later in the war, 1069 Mk Vs were manufactured. The Anson played a vital rôle on Canadian training bases.

Anson IIs were primarily used to train pilots to fly multi-engined aircraft. However wireless operators, navigators, and bomb-aimers used the Anson as well. As a training aircraft the aircraft was docile, forgiving, and easy to fly. It developed such a reputation for reliability that it was dubbed 'Faithful Annie.'

Avro Anson Mk. IIs being assembled at the Federal Aircraft Factory in Montreal, Quebec.

Joe's first flight at 5 SFTS was aboard Avro Anson 6758 on 9 October 1941. One of his more memorable experiences at Brantford was the day his map flew out the window and he got lost. With fuel running low and undoubtedly quite embarrassed, he had to land in a farmer's field to ask directions.

During the time that Joe was receiving his flying instruction, the BCATP was still in its growth phase and there seemed to be a never-ending need for instructors. Like virtually all the students, Joe wanted to go onto combat operations overseas. As he was working through his flying training, Joe was carefully looking ahead to what might follow as Joe Jr. relates:

"When Dad went through training he sort of 'faked it' a little bit. He'd heard through the grape-vine that if they knew that you already knew how to fly that your chances of being ploughed back as an instructor when you got through were quite high. So Dad made sure that he wasn't the best guy around so that he wouldn't get nailed for instructor duty." [4]

Wings Parade at a BCATP Service Flying Training School.
Royal Canadian Air Force

On 7 December 1941, as Joe approached the end of his course at Brantford, he heard the news of the Japanese attack on Pearl Harbor and that his country had not only declared war on Japan, but had also entered the European War.

As part of the arrangements made between Canada, the United States, and the Clayton Knight Committee, it had been agreed that should the United States enter the war, the American airmen serving in the RCAF would have the right to transfer to their own armed services. At some point both Joe and Don would have been presented with this option and both made the decision to continue their service with the Royal Canadian Air Force.

Joe and Don both graduated and received their Royal Canadian Air Force wings on 18 December. Of those excited, proud, and happy young pilots who received their wings that day, most would have eventually made their way to operational flying with Bomber Command and it is likely that fewer than one third would have survived. Although Bomber Command suffered grievous losses throughout the war, the most dangerous time was during 1942, 1943, and early 1944.

Joe's Graduating Class at 5 SFTS. (Joe is 11 in the middle row; Don Curtin is 5 in the back row). [5]
The McCarthy Family

A striking example of the loss-rates is that during the RCAFs Halifax operations between March 1943 and February 1944, the average loss each night exceeded six percent of the bombers sent to the target. A tour of thirty operations was required and at this loss rate, the chances of surviving a tour was a mere sixteen percent.

Both Joe and Don were commissioned as Pilot Officers. The customary practice was that commissions were awarded to the top third of the class and the remainder were promoted to the rank of Sergeant Pilot. With this rank they were referred to as 'non-commissioned officers (NCOs)'. Once in Britain, Joe and Don would find that having some pilots and aircrew who were officers and others who were not posed some difficulties.

Everyone in the air force recognized the need for a structured, orderly organization but what many found difficult to grasp was the situation whereby the members of a bomber crew were artificially split by rank and therefore social status when their lives were totally interdependent. It separated those within a crew and within a squadron with social barriers, pay differences, and they even lived in different quarters.

A Sergeant Pilot was clearly in charge of those aboard his aircraft but he could have officers who ranked above him as part of his crew. More common was the situation where the pilot and perhaps his navigator were officers but many of their crew were not.

When Fred Sutherland, who was part of Les Knight's crew on the Dams Raid, was asked about Joe and the relationship between officers and NCOs, he immediately replied,

"Everybody liked Joe McCarthy. I was an NCO, a Sergeant at the time, and he was a Flight Lieutenant but he always came and talked to you as if you were an equal. Some of the other officers didn't do that and it didn't rub very well." [6]

Like almost all of the SFTS graduates, Joe was immediately posted overseas and ordered to report to Halifax, Nova Scotia to sail to Britain. However he was granted a two week pre-embarkation leave that fortunately corresponded with Christmas. Joe returned to New York to spend some special time with his family including his younger brother Frank who he would not see again until after the war.

Frank joined the United States Navy and had his own perilous wartime experiences. Shortly after completing his training, Frank was assigned to the aircraft carrier USS Bunker Hill. The ship sustained major damage in May 1945 after two Japanese kamikaze hits during the invasion of Okinawa. Frank McCarthy was not injured but 389 sailors were killed and 264 were wounded in the attacks. Although badly crippled, the crew managed to keep the ship afloat and sailed her back to the US for extensive repairs. The Bunker Hill was one of the most heavily damaged carriers to survive the war.

Joe, wearing his brand new RCAF wings, with his father and brother Frank in New York (Christmas 1941)
The McCarthy Family

Part Three

Training in Britain for Operations

"We've got all our crew together now and they sure are a swell bunch. I'm getting quite good at flying the kite now too. Mac lets me take over quite a bit especially on the long trips."

Across the Atlantic to an AFU

Late in December 1941 Joe McCarthy reported to No. 1 'Y' Depot, Halifax, Nova Scotia and boarded a ship to cross the Atlantic to a beleaguered Britain. The Battle of Britain had been won and there was no longer an imminent threat of invasion but other than that, there was no sign that the war was going well. The U-Boat threat was very real and must have weighed heavily on the ninety airmen as they left Halifax harbour.

The ship that Joe was aboard became separated from its convoy due to bad weather and they sailed alone for eleven days before docking in Liverpool. It carried more than the young airmen of course and this one was carrying mutton as well. At some point in the voyage the refrigeration broke down, allowing the mutton to spoil. According to Joe Jr., "This is why my father never liked lamb, although there were very few other foods that he did not like."

After disembarking at Liverpool, the ninety airmen proceed by train to the RCAFs 3 Personnel Reception Unit at Bournemouth on the south coast of England where most RCAF aircrew were introduced to wartime life in Britain. Upon their arrival, Joe's group was surprised to find that, despite being separated from their convoy, they had arrived earlier than the airmen on the other ships.

Bournemouth was formerly a restful resort whose up-scale hotels catered to the upper class who came to enjoy its beaches, warm climate, stately gardens, and lush parks. Now war had transformed the town. Joe would have noticed that the beaches were heavily mined and all access to them barred by coils of rust encrusted barbed wire. He would have heard air raid sirens. Bournemouth suffered its share of bombing attacks during the war with more than fifty air raids leaving 219 people dead and 726 injured. Some 250 buildings were destroyed and another 13,590 needed repairs.

Another young airman, J.A. Campbell, described an attack on Bournemouth that took place a few months after Joe was there,

"We were approaching Bournemouth around noon when we heard sirens. The train came to an immediate stop outside the town. Suddenly there was a quick series of sharp explosions and grey-brown mushrooms of dust and smoke appeared toward the town centre. Now we could hear heavy machine-gun fire and as we crowded to the train windows to see, a flight of Focke-Wulf 190s appeared, turned, and took another pass over the town centre. About one minute later several Spitfires shot overhead at tree-top level, heading seaward.

In the time lapse of roughly four minutes a flight of about fifteen Focke-Wulf 190s had come in from the channel at nought feet, pulled up over the park and town centre, dropped a couple of bombs each, and then had shot up the noontime crowd in the park. There was considerable damage and about twenty civilians; including several children; were killed and many more were injured." [1]

As well as the signs of war, Joe would have also been introduced to wartime English breakfasts that featured powdered eggs on a slice of parched toast with a small piece of grease drenched spam and perhaps some brussel sprouts.

The function of the Personnel Reception Centre was to act as a holding unit and prepare the aircrew for more flying training as soon as Advanced Flying Units (AFUs) could make space available. The airmen had their photographs taken and were issued identification cards as well as new flying suits, silk and fleece lined boots, chamois leather gloves, helmets, and goggles.

Joe and Don continued to train together as both began advanced flying training on 25 February 1942 at 12 AFU at Spitalgate in Lincolnshire. They were flying the Airspeed Oxford.

The spacious cockpit of an Airspeed Oxford.

Designed in Britain during the late 1930s, the Oxford was a twin-engined monoplane that was utilized as an advanced trainer. It was used at SFTSs throughout the BCATP and in other rôles such as light transport. The 'Ox-box,' as it came to be known, was a fairly demanding aircraft for a trainer and had a considerably higher accident rate than the Avro Anson and Cessna Crane which were used in a similar rôle at most SFTSs in Canada.

Advanced flying training was designed to improve the pilot's general flying skills and to take him another step towards being ready to fly on operations. The pilots gained experience flying under worse weather conditions than they had been previously permitted to fly in and learned the 'feel' and flying characteristics of a heavier aircraft. For Joe and the other Canadian pilots there was also a need for them to become familiar with flying above the English countryside and in the English weather. This experience would undoubtedly be called upon while returning to a fogged-in airbase following a raid over Germany, possibly with a damaged aircraft.

Opposite: Hampdens of No. 14 Operational Training Unit over the English countryside near Cottesmore.

Imperial War Museum

Joe and Don continued to train together. On 26 March Joe flew for 35 minutes as a passenger with Don as the pilot in Oxford 650. Later in the day, Joe logged thirty minutes of instrument time with Don as a passenger.

On 28 March Joe's logbook was stamped following the AFU course with a note that his "Proficiency as Pilot on Oxford" was "Above the Average."

Joe then went on to complete a course at 1518 Beam Approach School from 29 March until 3 April where he was again assessed as "Above the Average."

On 9 April Joe began a second advanced flying training course at 12 (P) AFU at nearby Grantham. More flights with Don were logged with the two young friends taking turns at the controls on 25 April, 6 May, and 14 May. Joe completed the No. 12 (P) AFU course on 18 May, the logbook stamp being accompanied by another "Above the Average" assessment.

Joe was now ready to train for operations at an Operational Training Unit (OTU).

No. 14 Operational Training Unit

On 19 May 1942 Joe and Don arrived at No. 14 OTU at Cottesmore in England's East Midlands. Here the training became much more serious and much more dangerous. The young airmen would now train as a member of a bomber crew and they would learn how to fly operationally on an actual warplane.

When Canada's Bomber Command Memorial was dedicated in Nanton, Alberta in 2005, the danger of training at an OTU became apparent when it was noted that of the 10,643 names on the Memorial Wall, exactly ten percent, 1064, had been killed while at an OTU. One of the reasons for this high loss rate was that the bombers that the trainees were given were generally old, 'clapped-out' aircraft from the operational squadrons.

Initially, Joe and Don did more flying in Ansons and Oxfords, again flying together during a night test on 27 June. Then on 1 July Joe made his first flight in an operational warplane.

The aircraft being used at 14 OTU was the Handley-Page Hampden. Like the Armstrong-Whitworth Whitley, Bristol Blenheim, and Vickers Wellington, the Hampden was a twin-engined bombers that had been operational at the outbreak of the war. These four aircraft carried the fight for Bomber Command until the much larger, four-engined Stirling, Halifax, and Lancaster became available.

Their crews ranged far over Europe during the early years of the war suffering great hardship from frostbite and enemy action. Forced to operate at night, navigation was by the stars and 'dead reckoning,' using compass, airspeed, and assumed wind directions. A Whitley pilot recalled,

"Rain used to come into the cockpit, and for three months my hands were frost-bitten. Everything was bare metal and sharp corners, and vital switches that were all too easy to brush against, especially when one's bulk was inflated by the multiple layers of clothing needed to keep out the freezing cold, plus a yellow 'Mae West' around the upper body for flotation. A leather flying helmet covered the head, bulging with the vital earphones. Except for the eyes, the face was covered by a carefully fitted mask that contained a microphone and supplied life-giving oxygen."[2]

Early successes included the destruction of many of the enemy barges assembled in French ports thus making an invasion on the British Isles less likely. During August 1940 Bomber Command played a pivotal rôle in the war when, after bombs were dropped on London, Prime Minister Churchill ordered Bomber Command to attack Berlin. Hitler was furious and retaliated in force against British cities rather than continuing to focus on the destruction of the RAF fighters and their airfields. This allowed Fighter Command to recover and eventually win the Battle of Britain. Following this historic defeat, Hitler was forced to abandon his plans to cross the English Channel and invade Britain.

Eight squadrons of Hampdens were operational at the beginning of the war and were in action immediately, raiding enemy naval installations and ships until the daylight formations encountered enemy fighters. Casualties became so heavy the aircraft was taken off operations, re-equipped with better armour and armament, and then used only at night.

As Joe was learning to fly the Hampden, it was nearing the end of its operational service with Bomber Command. The final bombing raid by Hampdens took place during mid-September 1942 when 408 Squadron RCAF were in action over the German naval port of Wilhelmshaven.

In mid-1942 virtually all the RCAF aircrew were simply thrown in with the other Commonwealth airmen, mostly British but with a considerable number of Australians, New Zealanders, and South Africans. It wasn't until January 1943 that 6 Group of Bomber Command, with almost all Canadian RCAF aircrew, began to operate. By the end of the war there were fourteen Canadian Squadrons operating under the control of 6 Group and another, 405, served as part of 8 Group, the Pathfinders.

The manner in which most bomber crews came together was quite informal. Murray Peden was a Canadian pilot who, like Joe, served with an RAF squadron. Of his 'crewing-up' at the OTU he was posted to, Murray wrote,

"The instructors and Admin officers, who wasted no time getting hold of us, organized the group into classes and laid out our syllabus. They dropped the word that within about ten days we would be teamed up in crews of five, each consisting of a pilot, bomb aimer, navigator, wireless operator, and air gunner. Equal numbers of each of these trades had been brought together to form our course, and we were told that if any five could agree amongst themselves that they wanted to form a crew and fly together, the Air Force would oblige and crew them up officially. But at the end of the ten-day period, all those who had not made their own arrangements would be crewed up arbitrarily by the staff and probably, we guessed, by purely random selection." [3]

Arthur Harris (left) was generally well liked and respected by Bomber Command aircrew.

Joe McCarthy and his Hampden.
The McCarthy Family

For the Hampden, Joe would only require a crew of three as well as himself and rather than following the general procedure by which crews were formed, for some reason Joe's crew changed for his various flights while at the OTU.

Air Marshal Arthur Harris had been appointed commanding officer of Bomber Command in February 1942. As Joe was training at 14 OTU, new tactics involving tightly grouped bomber streams calculated to swamp enemy defences were being implemented by Harris.

A study of the results of Bomber Command's early raids had indicated that they were not as accurate or successful as had been hoped. Harris knew that the future of Bomber Command was still in doubt and he approached both Prime Minister Winston Churchill and Charles Portal, Chief of the Air Staff, with the bold idea of assembling a force of 1000 bombers and sending them out in one massive raid. Harris wanted to persuade the doubters in the War Cabinet and catch the public's imagination.

Bomber Command did not have the capability to launch a 'Thousand Bomber Raid'without the participation of crews from the OTUs. With their assistance, the first raid was launched and was a turning point for Bomber Command as the new tactics were successful. There were losses due to mid-air collisions within the bomber steam but they were considered acceptable given the advantages of the narrow stream of aircraft. The time over the target would progressively be shortened until seven or eight hundred aircraft passed over their targets in less than twenty minutes.

Although not a 'Thousand Bomber Raid,' an attack on Düsseldorf scheduled for the night of 31 July/1 August required 630 aircraft and crews from 14 OTU were called on to participate. Even though they had not completed their training, both Joe and Don found themselves on the 'Battle Order.'

Don Curtin (left) and Joe McCarthy two days after Don received his Distinguished Flying Cross (note the ribbon below Don's wings).
The McCarthy Family

Joe's logbook shows that he flew Hampden 312 to Düsseldorf and carried four 500 pound bombs. His crew was made up of P/O Pellet, Sgt. Sommerville, and Sgt. Boyer. There were no comments in the log and although it must have been demanding in that it was the crew's first operation over enemy territory, it seems to have been a fairly straight-forward operation.

Don Curtin's was not. In fact Don's first combat operation led to his being awarded the Distinguished Flying Cross (DFC). Founded by King George V upon the formation of the Royal Air Force in 1918, the Distinguished Flying Cross is awarded for, "an act or acts of valour, courage, or devotion to duty performed whilst flying in active operations against the enemy." A citation describing the event or events for which the medal was presented accompanies each award. It was highly unusual and perhaps unheard of that an airman flying his first operation and not yet even part of an operational squadron should receive such an honour.

The citation that accompanied Don's DFC tells the story,

"This officer was captain of an aircraft (Hampden L4117 marked GL-N) detailed to attack a target in northwest Germany. When nearing the target area his aircraft was intercepted by an enemy fighter but Pilot Officer Curtin evaded it and flew on to the objective. Shortly after leaving the target area his aircraft was again intercepted by enemy fighters. In the ensuing engagement the rear gunner and wireless operator

were badly wounded. Pilot Officer Curtin was almost blinded by cordite from a bursting shell and the aircraft lost height by several thousand feet before the captain was able to clear his eyes and regain control. Later, when nearing the Dutch coast, the bomber was hit by fire from the ground defences. The navigator sustained wounds and the aircraft was damaged. Despite this, Pilot Officer Curtin flew on and eventually reached this country. In difficult circumstances he made a safe landing in a field (at Loddiswell in Devon). Afterwards he assisted his wounded crew from the aircraft and then went off for further help. In this, his first operational flight, Pilot Officer Curtin displayed great courage, determination and devotion to duty." [4]

Two of Don's wounded crewmembers recovered but sadly, P/O H.G. Clarke of the Royal Australian Air Force died as a result of his wounds.

4.6 percent of the 630 aircraft that participated in the raid were lost including a staggering five (10.5 percent) of the fifty-four Hampdens that were sent. Seven 14 OTU aircrew were killed, five became Prisoners of War, and three returned seriously injured. Clearly this was a sobering introduction to operational flying for Joe, Don, and the other young airmen at 14 OTU.

Joe flew no more operations while at the OTU and he and Don completed their training there. On 6 September 1942 they were posted to a Conversion Flight. This would be the final stage of their training, where they and their crews would learn to fly the aircraft that they would fly on operations, the four-engined Avro Lancaster.

Hampden bomber landing on grass.
Royal Canadian Air Force

No. 97 Squadron Conversion Flight

Avro Manchester of 207 Squadron.

The Lancaster evolved from Britain's concerns regarding the deteriorating international situation during the late 1930s. The Handley-Page Halifax, Short Stirling, and Avro Manchester were all in the planning stages as the war began in 1939. The prototype twin-engined Manchester flew in 1940 but was plagued by instability and insufficient power from its unreliable Rolls-Royce Vulture 24-cylinder engines. It entered service with No. 207 Squadron during November 1940 and flew its first operation on 24/25 February the following year. Eventually 209 Manchesters entered service before production was stopped in November 1941. The Manchester served with ten bomber squadrons and was also used by Coastal Command.

Roy Chadwick had designed the Manchester and he had faith in the aircraft's basic design. He determining that the solution was simply to use four of the proven Rolls-Royce Merlin engines rather than the two Vultures. The result was the Lancaster that made its maiden flight during January 1941. It began flying operationally in March 1942 and the aircraft was well received by their aircrew. The Lanc was regarded as 'a pilot's aeroplane' that inspired confidence. Evidence of this is the story of a Lancaster flight engineer who having feathered two engines and facing the prospect of flying over several hundred miles of cold, unfriendly ocean, turned to his pilot and said simply, "I suppose this means we shall be bloody late for breakfast!"

During World War II the Avro Lancaster was the most successful bomber used by the Royal Air Force and the Royal Canadian Air Force. The Lanc had speed, ceiling, and lifting power that no other aircraft could match. Generally flying under the cover of darkness, the Lancaster had virtually no defensive armour and carried only eight .303 calibre machine

Avro Lancaster.
Royal Canadian Air Force

guns for defence against enemy aircraft. Air gunners manned the rear and mid-upper gun turrets. A pilot, flight engineer, navigator, wireless operator, and bomb aimer/front gunner completed the crew of seven.

The Lancaster eventually proved to be the workhorse of Bomber Command, completing more than twice the raids of any other type and carrying 64 percent of the explosives to enemy targets. By war's end 7374 Lancasters had been built including 430 in Canada. A total of 3932 were lost in action.

When Joe began his training with 97 Conversion Flight at Coningsby in Lincolnshire on 6 September the Manchester era was coming to an end. However Joe did complete eight flights in Manchesters during the first six days of his conversion training. His first flight in a Lancaster was on 9 September.

Len Eaton.
Imperial War Museum

Somehow in all the busy-ness of a wartime air force Joe, either through good luck or some influential friends, was still able to arrange to go flying with his friend Don. On 13 September, they were together for two flights in a Manchester.

During this period the names of the nucleus of Joe's crew begin to appear in his logbook. A Manchester flight on 11 September included Sgt. Bill Radcliffe and Sgt. Ronald Batson, as did a number of Lancaster flights beginning the following day. Two days later the name of Sgt. Leonard Eaton is noted. The names of these three airmen would appear consistently in Joe's logbook throughout his operational flying with 97 Squadron and later with 617 Squadron. Sgt. Radcliffe was a flight engineer, Sgt. Batson an air gunner, and Sgt. Eaton a wireless operator.

Bill Radcliffe.
Dorothy Bailey

Four-engined aircraft such as the Lancaster required a flight engineer whereas the twin-engined bombers did not. The Flight Engineer sat beside the pilot on a seat that was hinged to permit crew access to the bomb-aimer's compartment in the nose of the aircraft. He assisted the pilot on take-off and landings by handling the throttles. In flight the engineer was constantly checking his gauges to monitor oil, fuel, and pressures and assess engine performance and fuel consumption from the Lancaster's six wing tanks. Although flight engineers were generally trained to fly the aircraft 'straight and level' they had no formal pilot training and hoped that they would never have to try to land the aircraft. Adding a flight engineer to Joe's crew would have been one of the first things to be done at the Conversion Unit.

Throughout the war Bomber Command's flight engineers were almost always British, even on the Canadian squadrons. But Joe somehow ended

Single-Engine Aircraft				Multi-Engine Aircraft						Pass-enger	Instr/C Flying cols. (1) t
Day		Night		Day			Night				
Dual	Pilot	Dual	Pilot	Dual	1st Pilot	2nd Pilot	Dual	1st Pilot	2nd Pilot		Dual
(1)	(2)	(3)	(4)	(5)	(6)	(7)	(8)	(9)	(10)	(11)	(12)

ATTACHED - 97 SQUADRON CONVERSION FLIGHT

SEPT 6 - 1942

TYPE - MANCHESTER

LANCASTER

A-QUEENIE SEPT 16 1942 "OVER CONINGSBY"

Opposite: This page of Joe's logbook corresponds to his posting to the Conversion Flight. He later flew the aircraft pictured on a mining operation to Gdynia and twice on bombing operations against Turin in Italy. Despite the fact that this aircraft was designated 'A' within the squadron. It was referred to as 'A-Queenie.' Lancaster R5548 was also referred to as 'Elizabeth' because she was named by the Queen herself during her visit to the AVRO factory on 20 March 1942.
The McCarthy Family

up with one who was Canadian. Bill Radcliffe would be at Joe's side throughout his operational flying.

As a young man of nineteen, Bill had left his home in New Westminster, British Columbia during March 1939 and travelled to England with his best friend Howard Godfrey to join the Royal Air Force. They knew that war was imminent and wanted to 'do their bit.' Bill originally trained as a 'flight mechanic' and was given a thorough, hands-on knowledge of aircraft engines. Joe knew this and this was one reason why he regarded him so highly. It wasn't until July 1942 that Bill was enrolled in a Flight Engineer course at St. Athan, Glamorganshire. As Joe's crew was being assembled, Bill flew his first operation, a raid on Dusseldorf with F/O E.E. Rodley. In a letter to his family written on September 10th, Bill wrote,

The McCarthy crew's mascot.
Dorothy Bailey

"I got in five or six hours in a Lancaster today but I hope that the next time I go over it'll be with our own crew. We got two air gunners yesterday so now all we got to get is a wireless operator, navigator, and bomb-aimer and a few more hours to get in and we'll be ready. We should be finished in a week." [5]

Another letter dated 22 September indicates that the crew had been established,

"We've got all our crew together now and they sure are a swell bunch. I'm getting quite good at flying the kite now too. Mac lets me take over quite a bit especially on the long trips." [6]

It was not unusual for Bomber Command aircrew to be somewhat superstitious. One of the more common rituals was to urinate on the tail wheel of one's aircraft before taking off.

Any crew that was able to survive the number of operations that Joe's did must have had a certain amount of luck. Some of Joe's crew's good fortune may very well have come from their mascot that was brought to the crew by Bill Radcliffe.

Dorothy Bailey, Bill's daughter wrote:

"I have a small Panda Bear about five inches high which my father had as a mascot, tucked into his boot during every flight. I have always understood that it was the mascot for the whole crew.

"All the wear on him must have happened whilst he was at war as he was never played with by me or my siblings. His right ear is quite worn down and his nose is threadbare! There are no tags to show who made him. I have a letter which an acquaintance of ours received from Joe McCarthy some time after 1994 in which Joe has written as a postscript, 'Enclosed is a picture of a panda bear, my crew's mascot on all our aircraft we flew. Bill Radcliffe returned with the panda which a young girl gave him on leave.'" [7]

As Joe neared completion of the Conversion Course, his crew 'got together' as he termed it. As well as Bill, his flight engineer, the crew was made up of Sgt. R. Muskett (rear gunner), Sgt. Ron Batson (mid-upper gunner), Sgt. Len Eaton (wireless operator), F/Sgt. W. Brayford (navigator), and Sgt. Westwell (bomb-aimer).

All Bomber Command aircrew were volunteers and their average age was only 22. Their lives were a unique mixture of danger and normality, at one moment on a terrifying bombing raid and then a few hours later safely home or at the pub. As well, bomber crews shared mutual trust, dependence, and experiences; both terrifying ones in the air and enjoyable ones while off duty. The bond between members of a bomber crew was very strong. F/Lt. Eddie Tickler wrote,

"You were seven men brought together by conflict and you came to know each other's every mood and reaction, ability, and humility, and likes and dislikes during your training and operational life together . . . Your crew were seven men who not only flew together but ate, drank, slept, and played together. . . You were 'one' and generally inseparable; rank meant little between you, yet you knew the dividing lines between respect, authority, and familiarity." [8]

On 29 September Joe's crew completed their final flight of the Conversion Course and was deemed ready for operations.

Both Joe and Don were slated to join 106 Squadron that was operating out of Coningsby but as Joe later wrote,

"A sister Squadron (97) was based at Woodhall Spa, just eight miles north of Coningsby. 97 had a bad night just as we were joining 106 Squadron at Coningsby and we were sent over to 97 Squadron as one of the replacements for the losses." [9]

Joe and Don's air force careers had proceeded 'lock-step' from the day they walked into the RCAF recruiting office in Ottawa until this day sixteen months later.

Don must have turned a few heads when he walked into the 106 Squadron's officers mess as a sprog pilot but with a DFC ribbon on his tunic. The commanding officer of the squadron was Wing Commander Guy Gibson.

Joe, Don, and the other Americans in the Royal Canadian Air Force wore this patch on the right shoulder of their uniforms.

Part Four

Operations with 97 Squadron

"Believe me I was relieved to find some of the other crews were scared as much as we were. Mac is a wizard at handling the machine. If it hadn't have been for him . . ."

No. 97 Squadron Royal Air Force

With its motto, 'Achieve Your Aim,' 97 Squadron had some history behind it when Joe McCarthy arrived at its base at Woodhall Spa. As part of the Royal Flying Corps, the squadron was formed at Waddington, Lincolnshire on 1 December 1917. The following summer it went to France equipped with Handley Page 0/400s to undertake night-bombing operations, not common during World War I. By the end of the war, 97 had flown 91 bombing sorties (the majority into Germany) and dropped 64 tons of bombs including three 1650 pounders. Following the war the squadron went to India where it operated on the Waziristan frontier and flew the first air mail services in India between Bombay and Karachi. 97 Squadron began operations in World War II flying Whitleys but in 1941 was re-equipped with Avro Manchesters. The squadron received its first Lancaster during January and flew its first Lancaster operation on 20 March 1942.

During the Second World War 97 Squadron flew a total of 4091 operational sorties and lost 130 aircraft.

97 Squadron at Woodhall Spa during the summer of 1942, just prior to Joe McCarthy's posting there.

The Pathfinders

The idea of using an elite corp of crews with high navigational ability evolved from the somewhat limited accuracy attained by bomber crews during the early years of the war together with the development of sophisticated and difficult to use electronic navigational aids. Although originally opposed by Arthur Harris, the hand-picked crews from operational squadrons were transferred to form the Pathfinder Force in August 1942.

The PFF was led by veteran Australian bomber pilot D.C.T. Bennett, who retained command throughout the war. It began operations within a few hours of its formation and continued its work of leading the main force against the enemy until the bomber offensive ceased shortly before V.E. Day.

Various techniques for marking targets with flares were utilized depending on cloud conditions. Often an initial marking of the target was improved upon or altered as the raid progressed. This was often co-ordinated by a "Master Bomber" who circled over the target.

As Joe began his operations with 97 Squadron, the Pathfinders were also beginning theirs.

Operations-Some Gardening but mostly to Italy

As was generally the case with a new crew on the squadron, the first operation that Joe flew with 97 was a 'Second Dickie Trip.' On these the pilot of the rookie crew went along as an observer with an experienced crew. It provided the 'sprog' pilot with an opportunity to experience a wartime operation and gain some experience without being responsible for an aircraft and a crew.

The trip was a short one, just four hours in length, to Krefeld on 2/3 October. F/O C.D. Keir was the pilot and their Lancaster was one of 188 aircraft on the raid. The Pathfinders encountered dense haze and their marking was late. As a result the attack was dispersed and little damage was done.

Joe's crew on his first operation included flight engineer, Bill Radcliffe, wireless operator Len Eaton and mid-upper gunner, Ron Batson, all of whom would still be flying with Joe on his last operation after having survived some 21 months of the most hazardous of wartime operations.

The rookie crew's first raid was on the night of 5/6 October. It was not very successful. The attack by 257 aircraft on Aachen, near Germany's boundaries with Belgium and the Netherlands, started badly when six Lancasters crashed in England likely due to thunderstorms that were present in areas where some of the squadrons took off. The Pathfinders had a difficult night again and most of their markers fell in a small Dutch town, seventeen miles away from Aachen. The bombing was widely scattered but some industrial buildings were damaged.

Eight of the attacking aircraft were from 97 Squadron. The crews experienced extremely bad weather conditions including electrical storms and icing conditions while outward bound. As well as the bad weather and icing, P/O McCarthy reported that his radio and instruments stopped working and that the aircraft's plexiglass blisters were broken by ice. He also reported that his bombs were dropped on the calculated ETA (Estimated Time of Arrival) over the target because of the lack of instruments.

This first night of operations left no doubt in the minds of those on Joe's crew that experience was no guarantee of making it back to base. One of the longest-serving crews on the squadron

A 97 Squadron Lancaster. The 'OF"' was common to all the squadron's aircraft. The single letter identified the individual aircraft within the squadron.

crashed near Limburg in Holland on its return from the target. F/O Briant and his crew were killed. Neville Briant was on his 34th operation and had been with the squadron since November 1941. His crewmembers were all experienced as well, including rear-gunner P/O Kenneth Harrison DFM who was on the nineteenth operation of his second combat tour.

Following their return, flight engineer Bill Radcliffe wrote a letter that provides a pretty complete picture of what must have been a terrifying introduction to operational flying with Bomber Command and makes it clear that the dangers weren't just the enemy's flak and fighters. The letter also indicates that, even though their flying time together had just begun, Bill had already developed a healthy respect for Joe's flying skills.

The letter was sent c/o 'Aunt Tan' but with the obvious expectation that it would be shared with all his family.

Dear Home:

You usually get a nice easy trip for the first time and we were told this one was going to be fairly easy. But it didn't turn out that way. After we took off and made a circuit we couldn't find the aerodrome it was so black. Anyway we set course and when we got up to 10,000 feet we ran into an electrical storm. It sure was pretty at first seeing sparks and flashes all over the windscreen and flashes all over the wings and fuselage and the tips of the props were glowing. But then it started to ice up and then the trouble started.

We climbed right up to 15 or 16 thousand and we were still in it. We'd pass through a cloud with a negative charge then hit one with a positive and the result was a big blinding flash that scared the daylight out of me. We weren't troubled very much by Jerry and we made the target O.K. and just managed to bomb through a gap in the clouds but couldn't see the results.

Coming back it got worse and we ran into a lot more ice. We must have dropped over 14,000 feet in less than nothing and the rapid change in temperature or the ice cracked the perspex windows on each side of the cabin and blew a two foot hole out of each side. Believe me then I was scared. I thought for sure we had been hit, my log and the navigator's log, pencil, and instruments etc just vanished outside. As soon as I realised what happened, I looked out and saw we were skimming the tree tops of France. You could see the roads and houses plainly and we passed over a large town that didn't seem to be blacked out at all.

We got everything under control again and made some height to cross the coast. When we got back to the aerodrome we couldn't get any answer from our radio and after over a half hour of circling we had to land by signals. When we got down we found the aerial inside the kite instead of outside. It must have broken off in the storm and come through the window. Believe me I was relieved to find some of the other crews were scared as much as we were. Mac is a wizard at handling the machine. If it hadn't of been for him . . . I think if I had to go through those storms on every trip I'd be grey before I'm 24.

Well I think I'll get cleaned up and get into Boston and see what's doing in town tonight.

Love & Kisses,

Bill [1]

During the latter half of October, Bomber Command began to focus on targets in Italy to support the Allied offensive in the Mediterranean and Field Marshal Montgomery's campaign in North Africa. Joe was on the Battle Order for six operations to Italy over a seven week period. As well, he was called upon to place mines and complete operations against German industrial centres.

The first of the Italian raids was against Genoa on the night of 22/23 October and was timed to coincide with the Eighth British Army's offensive at El Alamein. Genoa was a significant Italian port and a major centre of naval shipbuilding.

Led by the Pathfinders, 112 Lancasters flew over the Alps under clear moonlight and the Pathfinders' marking was said to be 'prompt and accurate' over the naval dockyards. Joe's was one of eleven 97 crews on the Battle Order. The raids to Italy were very long making them extra challenging to the crews. Joe's crew was airborne for over 8.5 hours that night.

One aircraft failed to take off and two others were forced to turn back because of engine problems and other equipment failures. Joe bombed visually in the bright moonlight from 16,500 feet. He reported, "Bombs dropped on large fire in vicinity of aiming point; Jetty protruding on west of docks was well alight."

Anti-shipping mine being dropped from a Bomber Command aircraft.

The crews returned to bad weather over their base and all were diverted. S/L Coton and crew had a difficult time, crash-landing after having run desperately short of fuel after being airborne for almost twelve hours.

Joe's next operation was another trip to Genoa on the night of 6/7 November. The squadron sent five of the 72 Lancasters. Two aircraft were lost but all of 97's returned safely to Woodhall Spa. Joe reported, "Town and docks clearly visible; Bombs not seen to burst; Incendiaries seen bursting in town to east of dock area; Port engine became u/s (unserviceable-It stopped running) roughly 600 miles from home on return journey."

Joe was then placed on the Battle Order for a 'gardening' or mine laying operation. The placing of mines in enemy shipping lanes was a lesser known aspect of Bomber Command's rôle. Over 18,000 gardening flights were made and some 47,000 mines were placed in enemy used waters, denying the Nazis the use of much of the Baltic Sea.

On 8/9 November, three 97 Squadron Lancasters flew a 6.5 hour sortie each carrying five mines. There were a total of seventy bombers gardening that night and mines were laid in numerous spots between Brest and the Frisian Islands. Two of the 97 Squadron bombers successfully laid their mines but Joe reported that their 'veg' was dropped but that they were unable to 'pin-point' owing to haze. They were able to see that the mines' parachutes opened.

The night of 13/14 November started off badly for the squadron when an aircraft was lost while returning from a training exercise. Lancaster R5569 was piloted by a Canadian, Sgt. Keith P. Mercer of Montreal, Quebec. It had been diverted to Scampton owing to limited visibility at Woodhall Spa. Sgt. Mercer misjudged his first approach and while attempting to go round again the Lancaster stalled and dived into the ground. All were killed except Sgt. Collings, who died from injuries the following day. A second RCAF airman, F/Sgt. Archie E. Shelson from Beausejour, Manitoba was part of the crew.

Although hundreds of Canadians were serving with Bomber Command in the Royal Air Force at the outbreak of war, the Canadian involvement was one that grew as the war progressed. Through the training of large numbers of aircrew in Canada by the British Commonwealth Air Training Plan, the number of Canadians serving in all aspects of the air war increased dramatically and members of the Royal Canadian Air Force played a major rôle. By the end of the war one third of all Bomber Command aircrew were Canadians.

Sgt. Mercer and F/Sgt. Shelson were two of 96 Canadian airmen who were killed while serving with 97 Squadron and whose names are listed on Canada's Bomber Command Memorial.

As this tragedy was unfolding near Scampton, Joe's crew was one of five squadron aircraft leaving Woodhall Spa for another trip to Genoa. Four of the Lancasters bombed the target.

F/O McCarthy's report in the squadron's Operations Record Book (ORB) tells of being attacked en route to the target, "Mission abandoned; Attacked by Ju 88 at 2122 hours at Lons-Le-Saulnier at 17,000 feet; Took violent evasive action and lost enemy aircraft in three minutes; Shortly afterwards port-outer engine caught fire; Bombs jettisoned." Lons-Le-Saulnier is located about 100 miles northeast of Lyon so Joe had not reached the Alps when the fighter attacked. All the squadron's aircraft returned safely although again, they were diverted to other aerodromes because of bad weather.

Luftwaffe Ju 88 fighter with radar equiptment mounted on the nose.

Guided by controllers on the ground and often equipped with on-board radar, night-fighters such as the twin-engined Junkers Ju 88 accounted for most of the bombers that were destroyed. They were armed with powerful 20 and 30 mm cannons. Some carried upward-pointing guns, making it easier for Luftwaffe pilots to attack the bombers from below where their defences were weakest.

The 'three minutes' of 'violent evasive action' Joe referred to would likely have been the corkscrew manouever, the standard action taken by a bomber pilot when threatened by a night fighter. This manouever involved abrupt dives and turns to one side and then to the other, flying through the air like a corkscrew with the hope that the bomber could shake off the attacker.

When an air gunner spotted a fighter on the left side, he would call "Corkscrew port!" The pilot would then begin a steep dive and turn to the left, toward the attacker, diving approximately 1000 feet, and then begin a climb. The bomber was still in a left turn, but after 500 feet and while still climbing, the pilot would change direction and makes a sharp turn to the right, which reduced speed and hopefully resulted in the fighter pilot flying past the bomber. If the fighter was still a threat when the pilot reached his original altitude, the corkscrew would be repeated. Three minutes of this, as Joe's crew experienced on the night of 13/14 November, would have been very frightening.

As a fairly inexperienced bomber pilot at the time, Joe likely learned something about avoiding fighters that night. Regarding the young bomber pilots he later related,

"A lot of these kids didn't know what to do. The message wasn't getting through to them or maybe the message was getting through but they didn't realise what the hell they were getting into. I made it a point that as soon as I got in the air to never stay in the same spot-back and forth, back and forth just keep rolling back and forth all the way out and all the way in. This gave the gunners a chance to see below and up and around me and gave me a chance to see what was going on.

"The only time I ever flew straight was over the Alps and I knew the fighters would not come over that way. If they lost a motor they were going to be up in the mountains. We could at least maybe have struggled back out. That was the only time too that we'd light a cigarette, have a smoke, and keep on going."

(Generally Joe would have been worried that light from a match or cigarette might have given away their position to fighters)." [2]

Joe and five other squadron aircraft were sent gardening on the night of 17/18 November but there were a number of problems. One aircraft did not take off due to mechanical problems and two returned early because of technical troubles. The remaining three successfully placed their mines. All of the aircraft were diverted to various aerodromes due to poor visibility at Woodhall Spa.

Joe's Lancaster's compass malfunctioned and he was one of the early returns although he was airborne for almost seven hours. Another letter written by Bill Radcliffe indicates that although not always documented in the crew's logbook or the squadron's ORB, there were some dangerous times on many of the crew's operations.

". . . something went haywire with one of our compasses and we were flying along over what we thought was peaceful country till hell broke loose. Boy did I sweat blood. We were only 1000 feet up and about a dozen searchlights couldn't help but pick us up. Our rear gunner didn't like

them either so he ups an knocks half of them out and the other half went out on their own so he concentrated on the guns then which were too damn close for comfort. It's no fun knowing you're the only kite all those guns are trying to hit, believe me. When we finally found out about the compass we were hopelessly lost so we set course for where we thought England would be and in less than nothing we climbed from zero feet to 20,000. It was really funny, one minute things were too hot and the next we were nearly frozen. I prefer to freeze." [3]

Being 'coned' by searchlights was terrifying. In his best-selling book, 'Boys, Bombs, and Brussels Sprouts,' 408 Squadron pilot J. Douglas Harvey wrote,

"I had just closed the bomb doors when I went blind. Absolutely blind. Terrified, I realised we had been coned. The world was a dazzling white, as though a giant flashlight was aimed directly into my eyes. I couldn't see my hands on the control column, couldn't see the instrument panel, couldn't see outside the cockpit. I was naked, totally exposed, helpless. We were a very bright and shiny target in the apex of fifty or more beams that were radar directed. They weren't going to let go easily." [4]

After diving for seven minutes at speeds reaching 350 mph, Doug was able to outdistance the lights and escape.

On the night of 22/23 November Joe's was one of 222 aircraft that attacked Stuttgart. A thin layer of cloud and haze obscured the ground and the Pathfinders were unable to identify the target area. Joe reported that they bombed the city and that large fires were seen in the western part. 4.5 percent of the bombers were lost.

Joe's aircraft was attacked by a fighter as a portion of one of Bill Radcliffe's letters describes:

"The next trip was to southern Germany and we had a pretty good trip. Our only real trouble was one night fighter and I think our gunners again turned the tables and it was the Hun full of holes and not us. If he wasn't full of holes he was too scared to come in for a second attack. Our two gunners really are beautiful, cool, and calm and no one's got more confidence in them than I have." [5]

Twelve 97 Squadron Lancasters took off for an attack on Turin, Italy on 28 November. Joe's port-outer engine overheated and his was one of two aircraft that developed engine problems prior to reaching the Alps. Both were forced to jettison their bomb load and return.

Joe received a promotion to Flying Officer prior to his next operation, a gardening trip on 4/5 December. Of the six squadron aircraft detailed, three successfully placed their mines, two jettisoned their mines and one brought theirs back to base.

Joe reported that the weather was, "very bad throughout the whole trip" which involved being airborne for 7.5 hours.

Adverse weather was again a factor during Joe's next operation when his was one of 272 bombers that attacked Mannheim. The target area was completely cloud-covered when the bombers arrived and most of the Pathfinders did not place their target marking flares. Joe, like most of the 220 crews that bombed, did so on a 'dead-reckoned,' estimated position. The bombing was widely scattered and little damage was done. 3.7 percent of the bomber force was lost.

Raids such as this were costly to Bomber Command and very frustrating as well as there was little to show for their efforts. However in less than two months, a long-awaited airborne ground-scanning radar system (H_2S) would become operational and allow the Pathfinders to see through the clouds and accurately mark targets.

After failing to reach the target on their two previous attempts to bomb Italian targets, Joe's crew was successful on a raid to Turin on 8/9 December. Although there was a slight haze, the Pathfinders illuminated the target well and the bombing was accurate. Joe reported, "Many fires seen and many incendiaries seen burning in town; One large flash, believed to be 8000 pound bomb, seen to burst in built up area." All ten of the No. 97 Squadron aircraft returned successfully. Other squadrons were not so fortunate as six percent of the 133 aircraft that took part in the raid were lost.

The following night Joe took off on another raid to Turin but had to turn back after losing his hydraulics. The undercarriage and flaps are hydraulically operated on a Lancaster so Joe returned to Woodhall Spa with his undercarriage down and was forced to make a high-speed, flaps-up landing.

There were two changes on the crew following this operation. Sgt. Westwell, the bomb-aimer, was a trained navigator and he took over the job from Sgt. Brayford and Sgt. George (Johnny) Johnson joined the crew as bomb aimer.

Operations-Berlin (The Big City) and other Industrial Centres

Bomber Command was now entering a new phase in its ability to successfully bomb enemy targets at night. Much of this was due to recently developed technology.

OBOE used two ground stations in Britain to determine the position of an aircraft over Germany and direct it to a release point. It could measure range very accurately so the aircraft, beginning from a known starting point, flew on a curved track and maintained a constant distance from the ground station. When the second ground station determined that the aircraft was at the appropriate distance from it, the crew in the aircraft was advised that it was over the release point. The Pathfinders made the most use of OBOE, installing it in the fast, twin-engined Mosquito aircraft that enemy fighters were not able to keep up with.

H_2S was a radar device that scanned the terrain that the aircraft was flying over. It was located in a perspex blister below the bomber's rear fuselage. The return from the ground would depend on the type of surface the aircraft was over. Water dispersed the signals so there was little return, farmland would return some of the signals but over a built-up area the buildings would reflect a lot of energy back to the receiver. The moving

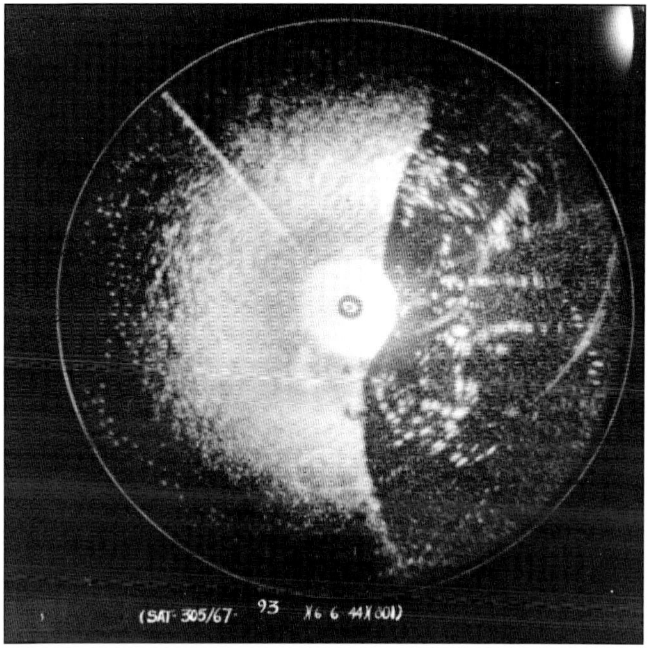

An H_2S display of the D-Day invasion fleet.

George 'Johnny' Johnson.
Imperial War Museum

image as seen on a cathode ray tube in the aircraft could then be interpreted. It worked best on coastal targets or those with a broad river or lake nearby. The Pathfinders received the first H2S sets and began using them during January 1943.

GEE was an on-board device that received synchronized radio signals transmitted from ground stations in different locations in England. Two signals gave the navigator a 'fix' so he could work out his aircraft's position on the route to the target at any time.

When flying near the ground stations over home territory, GEE's accuracy was very good. At increasing distances, the accuracy was reduced. However within a range of about 300 miles, GEE at least ensured that each bomber crew entered enemy territory with reasonable confidence as to their position. It was also very useful to navigators trying to find their base in bad weather following a raid.

Although H2S and OBOE were still in the experimental stage operationally, their development was rapid and led to an increased sense of optimism within Bomber Command.

A sortie to Munich in southeastern Germany on 21/22 December was the first for Joe's new bomb-aimer. George 'Johnny' Johnson would fly with Joe for the next sixteen months of operations.

Born in Lincolnshire to a farm manager, Johnny had imagined his future would be in farming but when war broke out he decided to join the air force. He failed to make the grade as a pilot but later decided to retrain as a bomb-aimer. "I did it because the training course was the shortest there was and I didn't want to waste any more time. I was just back from a bomb-aimer's course when I was selected to join the crew of a Flying Officer called Joe McCarthy." [6]

In a 2007 interview, Johnny's admiration for Joe McCarthy was clear as he recalled, "He was a big man; big in size, big in personality, and thank God, big in piloting ability. He was a superb pilot."

The raid on Munich was less than a complete success as Joe's and eight other 97 Squadron Lancasters were part of a force of 137 aircraft that was greatly hampered by what Joe referred to as, "terrible weather" including 10/10ths cloud cover.

A combat report was filed by his air gunners following debriefing describes Joe's aircraft being attacked by a fighter as they approached the target,

"Sighted an enemy aircraft at the range of 1000 yards. This aircraft was identified as a Ju 88. The enemy aircraft was first seen flying parallel with our aircraft, and it immediately turned in to the Lancaster's starboard. Our aircraft then turned in on top of the enemy who went underneath our aircraft's stern. The Lancaster once again turned into it. The enemy aircraft then turned into the port side of our Lancaster which turned on top of the enemy who again made a starboard approach and tracer from its guns was seen to pass beneath the nose of the Lancaster. The enemy aircraft then disappeared from view and was not seen again." [6]

The report illustrates the vital cooperation that was necessary between the air gunners, who would have been reporting the position and actions of the fighter, and their pilot who quite likely never saw the enemy fighter. It was generally the policy of the night-fighter pilots that once they had been seen and the crew of their targetted bomber was taking evasive action and aware of their position, it made sense to abandon the attack and find another bomber that was more susceptible to a surprise attack.

Following the attack Joe carried on to the target. The squadron record states that, "Most of the aircraft were forced to bomb through gaps in the cloud" but Joe reported the, "Built up area located by flares." The aircraft experienced engine problems as well with the starboard-outer engine failing completely and the the port-inner giving trouble as well. Joe was again forced to divert to an alternate aerodrome, this time to Bottesford in Lincolnshire.

A fellow 97 Squadron pilot, F/Sgt. West was fortunate to survive the raid. While returning from the target his Lancaster was attacked from below and astern by an unseen

Opposite: Joe's Lancaster ED430 with nose art featuring a panda bear carrying a large bomb. This photo was taken some time after Joe and his crew left 97 Squadron. The airmen are J. Saxton and his crew. [7]

enemy fighter. The fuselage was raked with cannon fire from nose to tail wounding both air gunners and the bomb-aimer. West dove into the clouds to escape only to find that his controls had been damaged. It took both West and his flight engineer pulling on the control yoke together to bring the aircraft out of the dive. (The Lancaster's rudders, elevators, and ailerons were all manually controlled with no hydraulic assistance). With great difficultly F/Sgt. West was then able to fly his aircraft to England where he managed a wheels-up crash landing.

The McCarthy crew was one of five squadron crews on the Battle Order for a raid on Duisburg on 8/9 January. Only 38 bombers were involved, three Mosquitos and 35 Lancasters. Joe reported that "PFF flares enabled us to locate target" although the weather over Duisburg was said to have been 10/10 cloud. It was a short trip of just under four hours.

This was Joe's sixteenth sortie and he had flown seven different Lancasters on operations. He flew Lancaster ED430 on the raid to Duisburg and for the remainder of his tour with 97 Squadron so this seems to have become 'his' aircraft. There were only four raids when he flew a different aircraft, likely because ED430 was not serviceable for those trips.

During World War II the personalization of an aircraft by giving it a name, painting an image on it, and in many cases doing both, began in the early months of the war, increased in frequency as the war progressed, and reached its peak in 1945. In the case of bombers a bomb tally was often added as well and this provided a powerful visual record of the success and longevity of the aircraft. In some cases, additional information such as whether an operation was a daylight raid or a night raid and the type of weapons carried was also indicated. The destruction of enemy fighters was sometimes shown and often other details such as awards received by aircrew while flying the aircraft.

If a bomber crew was assigned a particular aircraft, they were able to choose the name and artwork and this enabled a powerful bond to develop between the men and their machine. Most importantly, to quote RCAF pilot Jack MacIntosh, "The name and nose art made it feel she was 'our' aircraft and would always bring us home."

A. BRYER
F. BAKER
PILOT
ENGINEER

Bill Radcliffe's panda bear provided the idea for the nose art that Joe and his crew had placed on ED430. Above the panda bear is the aircraft's name, 'Uncle Chuck Chuck.' The reason for the choice of the name is not known. This nose art image and others featuring Bill's panda would be placed on other aircraft that Joe flew later in the war.

On 16/17 January Joe made his first trip to 'The Big City.'

Berlin was one of the most feared targets because of the long flight involved and the heavy defences.

Arthur Godfrey, an Australian pilot with 626 Squadron, described his vivid memories of being over Berlin which in many ways was similar to other heavily defended Bomber Command targets,

"Berlin was an angry, glaring, writhing enormity of a target. We rarely caught a glimpse of the city beneath the unbroken cloud cover, but there seemed to be thousands of searchlights. They did not move, they pointed upwards and illuminated the clouds. It was like flying across a vast, bubbling cauldron into which was poured the sky-markers and above which burst the 'scarecrow flares.' It was a target so bright that the spread of the bomber stream could be seen above, below, and around you. One was part of a vast armada of aircraft moving relentlessly across the target. Bomb doors could be seen opening. The black crosses on the fighters were clearly visible as they dived into the bomber stream, oblivious to the bursting flak, whose muffled crump could be heard above the roar of our engines." [8]

Regarding 'scarecrow flares,' many Bomber Command aircrew believed that they were deployed by the enemy to frighten and demoralize the bomber crews by deceiving them into believing they were bombers going down in flames. In fact, there were no such thing as 'scarecrow flares' and what the crews saw were bombers going down in flames.

Of the 201 aircraft that attacked the city on 16/17 January, eleven were from 97 Squadron. The commanding officer, W/C Jones, had placed himself on the battle order to lead the squadron. This was the first raid on Berlin in fourteen months and the first to utilize the Pathfinders' target marking techniques. It was a disappointment. OBOE and H2S were still not operational and with haze over the city, the bombing was scattered. But the defenders seemed to be taken by surprise and the city's defences had not reached the

Dave Rodger.
The Rodger Family

effectiveness that they soon would. Only a single Lancaster was lost.

Joe reported that his Lancaster could not climb above 14,000 feet so he bombed from that altitude (typically Lancasters bombed from about 20,000 feet).

This was Joe's last trip with rear gunner Sgt. Muskett. The rear turret on a Lancaster was the farthest point from the main wing and thus any motions of the aircraft would be accentuated at the turret. One can only imagine what it would be like to be in that position during the violent corkscrew and other evasive manouevers. Joe later wrote,

"Muskett was the oldest of the crew at about 36 years and could not stand the evading necessary to corkscrew the aircraft to evade searchlights, flak, and night fighters." [9]

Almost all the aircrew were young men like Joe, in their early twenties. Sgt. Muskett had traded positions with Ron Batson, the mid-upper gunner, for his last two operations likely in the hope that he would be able to handle the less violent movements at that position. Even they proved to be too much for him and Sgt. Muskett left the crew.

Muskett was replaced by Dave Rodger, a Canadian from Sault Ste. Marie, Ontario. The son of a Scottish carpenter, Dave had developed an interest in flying as a boy and was an avid collector of airplane magazines. After attending a local technical school, he worked for Algoma Steel while serving in the Canadian Militia. Dave was initially turned down by an RCAF recruiting officer for medical reasons. Following an operation on his nose, he was accepted in October 1941 and trained as an air gunner. After arriving at 97 Squadron in October 1942, Dave had a kneecap smashed in a crash and spent some time in hospital before joining Joe's crew. Dave would fly with Joe for his next eighteen months of operations.

The next night Bomber Command raided Berlin again, this time with 187 aircraft. The weather was better but again the Pathfinders were unable to mark the target area properly. For some reason the routes followed to and from Berlin were the same as those followed on the previous night and the German night-fighters were able to find the bomber stream and many were seen by 97 crews. Whereas only a single aircraft was lost on the first raid, 22 (a stunning 11.8 percent of the force) were lost on this one. No major damage within the city was reported.

Opposite: A Lancaster silhouetted over the burning city of Hamburg on 30 January 1943.

Eleven 97 Squadron Lancasters were part of the raid. One of them, Sgt. Rowson's aircraft, crashed into the North Sea near Holland while returning, killing all aboard.

Joe seemed unhappy with the Pathfinder's performance reporting, "No help from PFF who apparently failed to locate target." He seemed to have found the target though, writing in his logbook, "Primary target bombed; Own bombs seen to straddle marshalling yards; Fires observed over large area." Joe continued to be plagued with engine problems however, writing that he, "Completed return journey with three engines."

This was one of a number of times that Joe returned on three engines and there were other times when he had to abort a sortie because of engine problems. At some point during his time with 97 Squadron, he became very frustrated with engine failures and according to Joe Jr., his Dad told him that he,

"made an agreement with his engineer (Bill Radcliffe) that when they took an aircraft out for a test, if there was any question about the engine, I got the feeling that the engineer probably 'did something' right after that so that when they came back the engine had to be changed and after that he never lost an engine other than to enemy action. I got the idea he was a little touchy on engine failures. In the beginning you get airplanes that are a little worn out. The senior guys in the squadron get the pick of the new airplanes when they come in and the junior guys get what's left. It's always been that way." [10]

The night of 30/31 January saw 97 Squadron contributing thirteen Lancasters to a raid on Hamburg. Joe's was one of four that were forced to abandon the raid owing to technical problems, Joe's being an oxygen failure. F/O Moyle and crew were 'lost without a trace' after taking off. The six aircraft that were able to complete their bombing reported that they bombed "the red and green release flares and that two aircraft bombed the red markers."

This was the first H2S raid of the war and also the first recording in the 97 Squadron Operational Record Book of coloured PFF flares. The target indicators came in red,

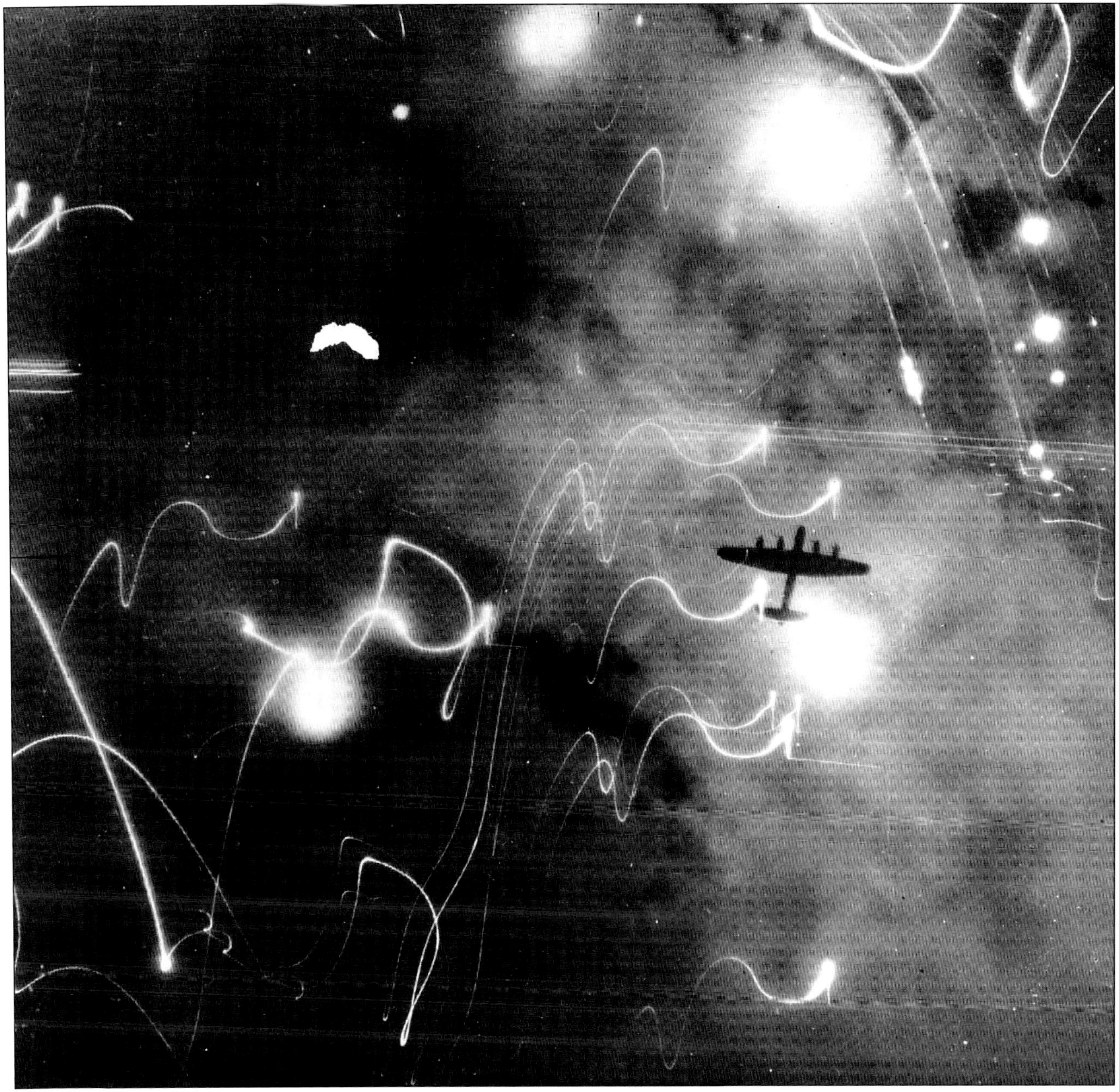

yellow, and green and were used for different purposes that were explained to the crews during their briefing or, on some raids, by radio over the target as the raid was progressing.

Joe and eight other 97 Squadron bombers attacked Cologne on the night of 2/3 February. All of the squadron aircraft successfully reached and bombed the target where bomb bursts and fires were seen. Joe reported that he, "Bombed on red marker flares" and that the PFF were, "On time."

Two nights later Joe's was one of five squadron aircraft to complete a long, eight hour trip over the Alps to bomb Turin. The 188 bombers were said to have caused serious and widespread damage. Joe bombed on the red marker flares, reporting that his bombs were seen to burst on a cluster of buildings and that there was one, "Large fire and lots of smaller fires seen in the centre of town."

Joe had now flown a total of 21 operations. His friend Don Curtin had been busy operating with 106 Squadron and had received a second decoration as well. On 10 February he was awarded a 'Bar to Distinguished Flying Cross,' essentially a second DFC. The citation read,

"Since the award of the Distinguished Flying Cross, this officer has participated in numerous operational sorties against heavily defended targets in the Ruhr and in north Italy. During a daylight raid on Milan in October, when attacked by enemy fighters, Flight Lieutenant Curtin skillfully evaded them and enabled his gunners to destroy one and drive off the other. On two consecutive nights in January 1943, he took part in attacks on Berlin, on the second occasion spending thirty minutes over the target to ensure accurate bombing. This officer has always displayed the greatest courage and devotion to duty." [11]

Clearly Don was making an impression on his commanding officer, W/C Guy Gibson.

The consecutive raids to Berlin during January were those that Joe was on as well. Both 106 and 97 Squadrons were part of 5 Group of Bomber Command and the Group coordinated and planned individual raids using their squadrons. So Joe and Don may very well been over many other targets together as well.

Since being posted to 97 Squadron and based at Woodhall Spa, Joe would have undoubtedly come to know the Officers Mess at the Petwood Hotel very well.

During the early twentieth century, an express train would bring wealthy Edwardians to the woodland setting of Woodhall Spa for 'treatments at the baths.' One of these frequent visitors was Baroness Von Eckhardstein. While going through a divorce, the Baroness was looking for a country retreat within easy reach of London and she decided to live at Woodhall Spa in her 'pet wood.' Soon she had a splendid home filled with maple furniture and, together with her new husband Sir Archibald Weigall, was ready to entertain on a lavish scale. Royalty, nobility, and stars of stage, screen and sport were all duly welcomed to Petwood over the years.

During World War I the home became a military hospital for convalescents and then in 1942 it was requisitioned by the Royal Air Force as the Officers Mess for 97 and 619 Squadrons, and later in the war for 617 Squadron. The officers were actually billeted in this elegant hotel while the NCOs were accommodated in huts nearby. For the wartime RAF Officers, the Petwood was fondly remembered as a 'splendid place,' remote from battle. Today the Petwood is a high-end hotel and the 'Squadron Bar' features a range of artwork, memorabilia and tributes to Guy Gibson VC, Leonard Cheshire VC, and other officers that frequented the mess.

Joe's bomb aimer, Johnny Johnson, recalled one incident that occurred there,

"We had a gunner on the squadron, Buckley, who said he reckoned he could drink Joe McCarthy under the table. He was five feet plus, Joe was well over six and built in the same sort of way, outwards as well as upwards. So, one non-operational session they had a competition. It started in the bar at lunchtime and after the bar had closed they had their little kip in the afternoon and came down for bar opening at six o'clock in the evening, and at half past seven Joe carried him to bed." [12]

The port of Wilhelmshaven is one of Germany's oldest and largest ports and during World War II it was an important naval facility. It is located along Germany's northwestern coast about sixty miles northeast of Holland. Wilhelmshaven was one of targets attacked by the RAF the day after war was declared.

Joe's was one of five 97 Lancasters that were part of a 177 aircraft raid on Wilhelmshaven on 11/12 February. When the Pathfinders arrived the area was completely covered by cloud and they

Joe McCarthy, with the Petwood Hotel beyond, during his 97 Squadron service.
The McCarthy Family

The main entrance to the Petwood Hotel in 2011

targetted their flares using H2S. The marking was carried out with great accuracy and the main force bombing was very effective. There was a huge explosion when the naval ammunition depot exploded and caused widespread damage to the naval dockyard and the town. This was the first clear success for the newly developed H2S device.

Joe reported that he, "Bombed on TI flares" and that he, "Saw a glow through the clouds" and a, "Much larger glow observed when aircraft was eighty miles away."

During the early days of the Pathfinders the target marking was quite primitive, makeshift flares being bomb cases filled with a mix of materials that burned fiercely but were relatively easy for the enemy to simulate. They would then set off false markers to distract the main force bombers. New markers of different colours had been introduced at the beginning of 1943 and as well, a 'sky-marking' technique known as 'Wanganui' had been developed to be used when the ground was totally obscured. This involved dropping parachute flares and having the main force bombers drop their bombs 'through' the flares to the target. Joe was obviously aware of this technique (although apparently not its correct spelling) and next to his logbook entry for this raid printed, 'Wangeroo.'

Joe's next operation was on 21/22 February, a trip to Bremen which Joe reported as "uneventful." He noted, "Bremen attacked from 18,000 feet; Cloud over target; Sky marker flares seen but bombed on TI markers; Markers in sights; Bomb flash seen; Glow of good fire seen through cloud."

During the night of 25/26 February nine 97 Squadron bombers were among 337 that were detailed to attack Nuremberg. Joe noted "PFF timing very late" but he, "Bombed green TI markers from 10,000 feet."

106 Squadron was part of this raid and Joe's best friend Don Curtin was over Nuremberg as well. His was one of nine aircraft that failed to return. Don's Lancaster crashed near Fürth, where he and his crew are buried. As well as F/Lt. Curtin, the crew included F/O R.J.F. Windsor, P/O A.F. Lear, Sub. Lt. P.M. McGrath, Sgt. V.E. Jack, Sgt. H. Rigby, and Sgt. K.O. Court.

This had been Joe's 24th operation and he was approaching the end of his 'tour' of thirty operational flights. When word reached 97 Squadron of Don's death, a decision was made not to tell Joe until he had completed his tour.

According to Joe Jr., "When Don was lost, they didn't tell Dad. Everybody kept it quiet. Dad still had a few missions to go." Later, in a letter to Alice, Joe said that it was a good thing that they had kept it from him. Joe Jr. went on to say, "I feel that he was strongly affected by Don's loss."

Joe and his crew were operating again the following night as 427 aircraft attacked the City of Cologne. All eleven Lancasters from 97 Squadron successfully reached and bombed the target in what was referred to as 'reasonably clear' weather. Joe reported that he "Bombed centre of green TI markers" and that his 4000 pound bomb was seen to burst in a built up area. According to Joe it was a "Good trip if PFF were accurate."

On 28 February/1March Bomber Command sent a force of 437 aircraft to attack the U-Boat base at the French port of St. Nazaire. Joe and nine other 97 Squadron pilots all reported that they had successfully bombed the target. One very large explosion was seen and there were many fires. From his point of view, Joe termed it a, "successful raid" and it apparently was as widespread destruction was reported.

Best Friends-Joe McCarthy and Don Curtin.
The McCarthy Family

Joe's third trip to Berlin was next on 1/2 March. The squadron records report nine of their aircraft successfully bombed the "target or target area" and that "the glow of many good fires was visible 150 to 200 miles away." The bombing was somewhat scattered as the Pathfinders had difficulty distinguishing the extensive built up area on their H_2S sets.

Sgt. Innis and crew failed to return to the squadron's base at Woodhall Spa.

Two nights later Joe went to Hamburg as part of a force of 417 bombers. The Pathfinders again had difficulty interpreting their H_2S returns and, although damage was done, most of the bombing was off of the intended target.

On 8/9 March, Joe was on another raid to Nuremberg where he, "Bombed cluster of green TIs in sights." The 335 aircraft destroyed more than 600 buildings and damaged 1400 more as factories and railway installations were hit.

The following night Joe was over Munich where much damage was done to the city including the BMW factory where aero engine production was put out of action for six weeks. When Joe arrived, "No TI markers were burning while we were over target so bombs were released on centre of fire area."

A raid to Stuttgart on 11/12 March was not successful, to some extent because of the use of dummy target indicators by the enemy and, although the Pathfinders claimed to have marked the target accurately, the main force bombers were reported to be late arriving.

The 'Battle of the Ruhr' was a five month focus by Bomber Command on Germany's Ruhr Valley area which had coke plants, steelworks, and ten synthetic oil plants. Despite inconsistencies, the new navigational aids, the Pathfinder force, the bomber stream tactics, and the increasing numbers of available bombers were all contributing to an improving level of success. The industrial haze and cloud cover that generally obscured the Ruhr Valley at night no longer offered protection.

Over the five months of operations against the Ruhr, known as 'Happy Valley' by the bomber crews, Bomber Command severely disrupted German steel and associated armament production. However the area was very heavily defended by radar-guided anti-aircraft guns and night-fighters and Bomber Command's loss rates rose significantly.

Joe's first raid during this phase of Bomber Command's efforts was on 12/13 March, a raid to Essen in the heart of the Ruhr Valley. Eleven 97 Lancasters were part of the 457 aircraft raid. The

Locomotive factory destroyed during the Battle of the Ruhr.

marking was by OBOE-equipped Mosquitos was very successful and the centre of the bombed area was right across the giant Krupps factory. Joe reported, "Essen bombed; 20,000 feet; Clear but hazy; Red TI markers in sights when we bombed; Very large explosion seen immediately after bombing; Target area well covered with fires; Other terrific explosions seen."

However five percent of the bombers were lost including a 97 Squadron Lancaster flown by a twenty year old Canadian, W/O Plaunt.

With this trip Joe's navigator, Sgt. Westwell, completed his tour of operations and was replaced on the crew by F/Sgt. Don MacLean. Originally from Toronto, Ontario, Don had become a teacher and taught in North Bay, Ontario prior to joining the RCAF.

F/Sgt. MacLean's first operation with the McCarthy crew on 22/23 March was its last with 97 Squadron. The target was the U-Boat pens at St. Nazaire and the squadron detailed a dozen crews for the raid. Accurate marking led to a concentrated attack by the 283 bombers. However Joe did not see the flares, reporting, "Bombed 11,500 feet; Scattered cloud with some ground haze; Aiming Point not seen; Position identified by river mouth; Fires and red glow seen in area of Aiming Point 'C' which we bombed; Uneventful trip."

Joe had now flown thirty-three sorties with the squadron. He was promoted to Flight Lieutenant and awarded the Distinguished Flying Cross, the citation reading,

"On many occasions this officer has attacked targets in Germany. As captain of aircraft he has participated in sorties to the heavily defended objectives in the Ruhr and took part in the successful raid on Essen on a night in March 1943. He has also attacked Berlin three times and Italian targets on five occasions. Throughout his whole career, his conduct has set an example of high courage and efficiency to other members of the squadron." [13]

Don MacLean.
Imperial War Museum

Joe McCarthy's tour with Bomber Command, although significant and something that he could be very proud of, was not unlike tens of thousands of others completed by Bomber Command aircrew. The fifteen months and 34 operations that followed would be very different from this first tour and much more challenging.

By now Joe would now have been told that Don Curtin had been killed. As well as having to suffer the tragic loss of his best friend, Joe would have had to reconsider his future. According to Joe Jr.,

"They planned on going back to the U.S. together. I don't know if they were planning on just taking a leave and returning or if they were thinking of joining the U.S. forces." [14]

With what must have been a painful suddenness, Joe no longer had Don to travel home with and do whatever it was that they had planned.

A telephone call from Guy Gibson may have helped him decide what to do next.

F/Lt. Joe McCarthy DFC. Note DFC ribbon below his wings.

Opposite: The McCarthy Crew. (l-r) Bill Radcliffe, Johnny Johnson, Ron Batson, Len Eaton, Don MacLean, and Joe McCarthy (missing is Dave Rodger).
The McCarthy Family

Part Five

The Dams Raid

"You didn't know what was coming . . . until it went by . . ."

Barnes Wallis' Idea

"I got the idea of attacking the dams by means of a special store (weapon) which could be placed accurately hard up against the face of the dam at any required depth below the surface. The whole success of the operation depended on inventing a weapon which would go hopping along the surface of the water until it struck the freeboard of the dam (the part projecting above the surface), sank, and gradually paddled itself, as it were, up against the dam face. As our experiments on the technical side went on I discovered that you can make a sphere run along the surface of water in a series of bounces if you impart to it, before it is released, a very high degree of what a tennis player would call backspin. The whole secret of the thing is in the backspin imparted to the bomb. Perhaps the original idea occurred to me from a practice adopted by naval gunners in Nelson's time. Occasionally if their target ship was out of range they would depress the gun until the shot struck the water and ricocheted thereby increasing its range." [1]

Barnes Wallis was a greying, 56 year old aircraft designer, the man who designed the famous Dirigible R-100 which made a return trip across the Atlantic in 1930. Wallis had also designed the Vickers Wellington, the most successful and widely used of the twin-engined bombers available to Bomber Command at the beginning of the war. The 'Wimpy' as it became known, pioneered the geodetic, or basket-weave form of aircraft construction.

The dams Wallis was referring to were the six main dams in the Ruhr Valley that were critical to the production of steel and the enemy's armament industry. If they could be breached, the torrents of water which would be released would sweep away bridges, roads, railways, and factories and significantly disrupt power and water supplies throughout the region.

Barnes Wallis knew that dropping a bomb directly on the top of a dam which would have required an unrealistic level of precision at that time, would not inflict permanent damage. But if the wall could be fractured at a considerable depth, then the

Barnes Wallis

AVM Ralph Cochrane.

massive weight of the water in the reservoir would push through and destroy the dam.

As the dams were protected by heavy steel netting, a torpedo-like weapon could not be used. So Wallis came up with the idea of a 'bouncing-bomb' with reverse spin that would skip over the nets, slow down as it approached the dam, and then strike the wall with sufficient spin so that it would claw its way down to the optimum depth of thirty feet and detonate against the wall, weakening it so that the water could push through. Thus a relatively small amount of explosive could cause massive damage.

Wallis built scale-models of the dams and tested his theory, determining that it would work. He also calculated that a weapon weighing 9500 pounds would be required and that the rate of backspin would need to be 500 rpm. He knew that the Lancaster would be capable of delivering it.

The idea was clearly revolutionary and required the diversion of valuable wartime resources to a project whose chances of success seemed to many, to be marginal at best.

The Chief of the Air Staff, Charles Portal, was in favour of at least considering the idea and a meeting in February was organized to discuss Wallis' proposal with Arthur Harris. His reaction was directed towards Wallis with, "My boys' lives are too precious to be thrown away by you!" He dismissed the theory that one could, "bounce a five ton bomb rotating at 500 rpm along a lake and break a gigantic structure like the Möhne Dam" as, "Tripe of the wildest description. The war will be over before it works-and it never will."

Another meeting was held in mid-March at which AVM Cochrane, the commanding officer of 5 Group, was present. Ralph Cochrane had served in the Royal Navy during World War I prior to transferring to the RAF in 1918. He served extensively in the Middle East during the early 1920s where he developed a close relationship with Arthur Harris. Cochrane had seen the experiments on film and was interested.

Guy Gibson's Lancaster with Upkeep fitted in the modified bomb bay. Note the belt driven system for imparting the required spin.

On 15 March 1943 and under pressure from Portal, Harris ordered Cochrane to form a special squadron to deliver the weapon. The last possible date to attack with a full moon and while the dams were full and could provide maximum pressure was 26 May, just nine weeks away. Somehow, the Upkeep weapon had to be perfected and manufactured, Lancasters had to be modified to deliver it, and a special squadron formed and its airmen trained to deliver it.

Code-named as 'Upkeep,' the bouncing bomb was not a bomb at all. The final design was a cylinder-shaped, aerial mine with a total weight of 9250 pounds. It was made of metal, 3/8 inches thick and had a width of sixty inches and a diameter of fifty inches. It contained 6600 pounds of Torpex explosive. Hydrostatic pistols detonated the explosive at a depth of thirty feet.

The Lancasters that would carry Upkeep were modified by removing their mid-upper gun turrets and bomb doors. Two arms were placed below the wing to hold the weapon.

Each arm was fitted with a disk. A hydraulic motor generated the energy required to spin the disks at the required 500 rpm as the dam was approached.

Delivery of the weapon was critical of course, with an exact altitude, speed, and release distance from the dam being required. As well the weapon had to be delivered at night. The crews would have to be the best and their training rigorous. When the delivery parameters were finalized, it was determined that Upkeep must be dropped from an altitude of sixty feet while travelling at a speed of 230 mph, 1350 feet from the dam. There was also the matter of getting to the dams and returning to base at low-level in darkness to avoid detection by radar and fighters.

The Leader and the Crews

On 17 March the new squadron was officially formed and designated initially as Squadron X. It was to be made up of crews from AVM Cochrane's 5 Group of Bomber Command and Arthur Harris stipulated that it was to be commanded by the highly regarded, 24 year old Wing Commander Guy Gibson DSO and Bar DFC and Bar. During his time as the commanding officer of 106 Squadron, W/C Gibson had developed it into what was thought to be the best squadron in 5 Group. Joe's friend Don Curtin had been one of his pilots.

According to Fred Sutherland, who served as an air gunner on the new squadron,

"Gibson was a born leader. He was a short, cocky, very confident person. He was the leader and he let you know it. There was no monkey business. It was wartime and when he said, 'I want this done.' you did it and that was that." [2]

Joe McCarthy held Guy Gibson in high regard as well,

"Guy I found a very, very friendly and congenial man. He was one of the lads, he was friendly with all the crews and he made sure that they got whatever equipment that was available for them throughout the raid. His favourite sport was shooting which we did quite a bit of in the local area and the second was visiting the pubs located in that part of England.

"Guy was one of the finest gentlemen I met in the war. As far as operations went, well, he was the King." [3]

Guy Gibson.

Harry Humphries was 617's adjutant so he spent a lot of time with W/C Gibson looking after the management side of operating the squadron. He recalled,

"Gibson was a bit of a hard nut; some people called it arrogance. He was hard and had a very short fuse; and he wasn't a particularly feeling sort of personality. I never saw him show much in the way of sentiment . . . The first thing he said to me after I'd been installed as adjutant of 617 Squadron was that this squadron would either make history or be wiped out." [4]

Johnny Johnson, Joe's bomb aimer, recalled his impression of W/C Gibson,

"Guy Gibson was a little man; with quite a big opinion of himself; but after all, he had done an awful lot more than any of the rest of us. I'd say he had the right to be a bit self-important." [5]

W/C Gibson had recently returned from a raid to Stuttgart on three engines to complete his third tour, two on bombers and one flying night-fighters where he had shot down at least four enemy aircraft. It was his 71st operation on bombers. He had plans for a holiday in Cornwall with his wife Eve.

A few days later AVM Cochrane met with Gibson and asked, "How would you like to do one more trip?" Gibson agreed.

Cochrane was not able to be specific at this point and it was some time before Gibson was told what the target was. Initially he was only told that low-level flying would be involved, that he would be based at Scampton, that only experienced crews would be involved, and that he would be flying in four days.

The aircrew had to be quickly assembled for the new squadron; 21 pilots and crews, 147 men in all. Les Munro recalled how he ended up on the new squadron,

Ken Brown

"On reading the circular from 5 Group calling for volunteers I discussed the request with my crew with the result that I should volunteer, which I did." [6]

It is thought that Gibson personally approached the three crews from his former squadron, F/Lt. Hopgood, F/Sgt. Burpee, and F/Lt. Shannon. He undoubtedly made the request to some of the others who he knew personally or by reputation.

Others, like RCAF pilot Ken Brown, were simply 'posted' to the new squadron by 5 Group Headquarters. Upon returning from a raid to Berlin, Ken was ordered to report to the 44 Squadron's C/Os office and, as he recalled, was told,

"'You are transferred to a new squadron.' I wasn't too happy about that. I said, "Sir, I'd rather stay here and finish my tour with 44.' He explained in his very curt manner that, 'This was impossible. It was a name transfer and he could do nothing about it.'" [7]

Joe had first met Guy Gibson while with the Conversion Flight at Coningsby during September 1942. Gibson later wrote that,

'He (McCarthy) had tried to get in my squadron once before, but despite all the strings we tried to pull between us it did not work." [8]

It appears that Joe would have preferred to have flown his operations on the same squadron as Don Curtin.

Joe McCarthy was one of those that got a telephone call directly from Gibson. Had Don Curtin not been killed, it seems almost certain that he would have been asked to volunteer as well. Gibson must have held Don in high regard as he would have had authorized the recommendation for the Bar to Don's DFC. It's interesting to speculate knowing that in the past, Joe and Don made decisions together. Would they have chosen to both join Gibson's new squadron or would they have returned together, at least temporarily, to their home in the United States?

Joe and the Canadians in his Dams Raid crew (l-r) Dave Rodger, Don MacLean, Joe, Bill Radcliffe.
The McCarthy Family

Joe recalled,

"Gibby gave me a call at Woodhall Spa in March 1943. He asked me if I'd like to join a special squadron for one mission. He also asked if I could bring my own crew along knowing that I'd just finished my first tour with 97 Squadron. He couldn't tell me what we were going to do, where we were going to go, or anything but he emphasized that he needed a crew if my crew would come which I couldn't promise. I had three Englishmen and three Canadians in my crew and I had to go and ask them if they wanted to go along. He said, 'Well at least try to bring some. If you can't bring the whole crew take as many as you can. We'll probably find some for you, but we would prefer your crew.'

"I explained it to my crew and I got a lot of flak back, quick, 'Why? What are we going to do?' Some things I asked and I just had to tell them I didn't know but it was just going to be one trip. I don't know whether I, at that moment, had any decision from them that they would accompany me. But in two days I

arrived at the Officers Mess and I was looking around and I found my crew there all with a brief, but proud little grin, and they were all ready and waiting to go again. So I had the original crew all the way through.

"The next thing we knew we were at Scampton. Gibby didn't fool around." [9]

Bomb aimer Johnny Johnson recalled,

"Joe McCarthy was known to Guy Gibson. We were at the end of our first tour and supposed to be going on end-of-tour leave. Then Guy Gibson personally asked Joe if he would join and Joe said he would and asked us what we thought. We said we would go with him. We thought it was for one special trip, then that would be it. I don't know what the connection was but Gibson was very fond of Joe, perhaps because he respected his ability as a pilot." [10]

Dave Rodger remembered what it was like arriving at Scampton,

"The first night at Scampton the squadron reminded me of an All-Star NHL team; lots of medals, tons of operational experience and ability, but no real squadron spirit. Everyone more or less backing up the squadron from which they'd just come." [11]

Like Bomber Command itself, the squadron was made up of airmen from the Commonwealth and the Canadians were well-represented. There were five RCAF pilots, three from the Royal Australian Air Force, one from the Royal New Zealand Air force and twelve from the RAF. As Joe recalled,

"When we arrived a lot of the skippers were in and I knew about 85 percent of them. There were Australians, New Zealanders, English, some of the Scottish people, and of course me being the one Yank." [12]

Joe's experience on the Dams Raid would closely parallel that of fellow RCAF pilot, Ken Brown. A native of Moose Jaw, Saskatchewan, Ken had flown just seven operations prior to his posting to 617 and wore no decorations. There must have had a good reports about his flying ability but Ken immediately wondered why he had been chosen,

No. 617 Squadron was formed in this hangar at RAF Scampton.

"The Wing Commander (of his former squadron) wished me well and said, 'Do you realise Brown, you're going to be the backbone of this new squadron.'

"Well, we arrived over at Scampton and we started to look around as to who was there. There were an awful lot of DFCs, not so many DFMs. We realised that perhaps we weren't really all that we were set up to be.

"My wireless Operator sauntered up to me and said, 'Skip, if we're the backbone of this squadron. We must be damn close to the ass end.' I began to wonder how I'd got there." [13]

As he later wrote in 'Enemy Coast Ahead,' W/C Gibson welcomed the members of his new squadron with these words,

"You're here to do a special job, you're here as a crack squadron, you're here to carry out a raid on Germany which, I am told, will have startling results. Some say it may even cut short the duration of the war. What the target is I can't tell you. Nor can I tell you where it is. All I can tell you is that you will have to practice low flying all day and all night until you know how to do it with your eyes shut. If I tell you to fly to a tree in the middle of England, then I will want you to bomb that tree. If I tell you to fly through a hangar, then you will have to go through that hangar even though your wing tips might hit either side. Discipline is absolutely essential." [14]

LOW LEVEL-Training for the Dams Raid

The airmen were at Scampton but of course there were lots of equipment needs. As Joe recalled,

"All the commanding officers of other stations were instructed to supply either vehicles, personnel, equipment, parachutes and aircraft and parts to the new squadron to get it started. I think the major problem, of course, was that the equipment anybody had that was not worthwhile or unserviceable was sent to us. This included our aircraft which came without parachutes and for four days we flew without parachutes.

"I think one of the most interesting highlights were the unserviceable personnel that arrived. We had six WAAFs sent to us and I think the other C/Os thought it was a good idea. Three of them had to be sent back because they were pregnant when they arrived at our station.

"Some of the lads that came to us were not interested in staying with the squadron. They didn't know what the aim or the operation was going to be and so they asked for a release to return to their old squadron. All in all it's difficult to operate and form a new squadron, especially when you get second-hand equipment.

"The first few days it was hectic. We didn't have any equipment, we had no aircraft. It was just a matter of searching around even to find places to put your gear. We had no lockers, no space in the hangar, we didn't know where to go. But finally it got organized. Quickly, aircraft were flown in from various places. However in the case of the aircraft, they were only temporary until our own squadron aircraft were built by A.V. Roe and they came along in about seven weeks time and we had brand new aircraft to fly." [15]

Low-level flying has always been dangerous and exhilarating. It was not part of training within the BCATP or in Britain but most pilots, when the opportunity presented itself, were unable to resist the temptation.

For the next eight weeks low-level flying was all the crews of 617 Squadron would be doing. The crews, and as the training began not even W/C Gibson, had no idea what the target was. All they knew was that it would be attacked at low-level and at night. As Joe recalled,

617 Squadron Lancaster at low-level.
The McCarthy Family

"None of us had been trained in low-level flying. We were given the task of learning how to fly low-level, both in daylight and at night." [16]

Although it was the pilots that had to perfect the art of low-level flying, it definitely affected the way the navigators with the help of the bomb-aimers did their work. Joe's navigator, Don MacLean, recalled,

"Many of the aids that we'd depended on in the past were useless. Our main aid was visual pin-pointing. Some of the bomb-aimers and navigators dreamed up a system whereby they put their map on two rollers and turned this as they moved along the route but this was a dangerous business in that if they got too far off track then these roller maps became useless. We used the straight maps." [17]

Johnny Johnson, Joe's bomb aimer, recalled,

"I had been used to being at 12,000 feet and only seeing the target at the last moment. Now we were at 100 feet or even lower and I could see everything. It was amazing. Nobody else was able to fly low so it felt very special." [18]

"McCarthy was six foot plus, and almost as broad as he was tall with hands like hams, and they really held that airplane wherever he wanted it to go. At Sutton Bridge there are some electric cables which went across the canal then over the bridge, and we used to fly underneath them. We weren't supposed to of course, but it was an added buzz and it was a bit of daredevil stuff. We were young and stupid at the time and nobody got hurt doing it; so we just went on doing it. On one occasion we ended up on the bombing range to do a practice run, and we were flying at thirty feet, and someone flew underneath us." [19]

The crews flew a lot and the exercises were demanding as Joe describes,

"It was an ordinary Lanc that we first started flying and the only policy that was said was that we were going to fly low-level and that we'd start flying at 300 feet and we'd do a certain amount each day for a given period of time, maybe thirty or sixty days, both day and night . . . I averaged about two trips a day, sometimes three; low level starting at 300 feet, we gradually worked that down to 200 and then eventually we were flying at about 100 feet.

"Now, we only flew the 100 feet at night when there was a bright, moonlit condition but as far as daylight was concerned we would fly at one hundred feet above ground level. They started using a blue covering over our windows to give us the feeling that it was night so that we could get some experience anyhow or some practice in before the time ran out on us.

"Now we did not know at this point what the targets were nor did we even know what weapon we were using. We were just flying an ordinary Lanc, doing what we were told to do, low-level cross-country with precision." [20]

Although the Upkeep weapon was designed to be released at low-level, these skills were also vital to reach the target and then return to Scampton. The entire flight was planned to be below radar to avoid fighters being directed towards the bombers and to maintain the element of surprise.

Somehow Joe's crew was able to arrange for a brief respite from the intense training regime. The squadron was shrouded in secrecy and all leaves had been cancelled. This was a bitter blow to Johnny Johnson who was due to get married on 3 April.

617 Squadron Lancaster at low-level.
The McCarthy Family

"I was getting married on my post-tour leave. Then I phoned my fiancee saying we were just going to do this one trip. She told me, 'If you don't turn up on 3 April don't bother turning up again.'" [21]

Joe used the excuse of a shortage of aircraft to request a leave for his crew and Johnny did make it to his wedding on a Saturday but all were back flying again on Monday.

Ken Brown described some of the low-level night runs they did at the Scampton Aerodrome,

"They put a great sheet across the runway at one end and so many yards down another sheet. You had to start at the beginning of the runway at 1500 feet and dive, crossing the first sheet at seventy feet, cross the second sheet at seventy feet, and at the end of the runway be at 1500 feet. It was quite tricky." [22]

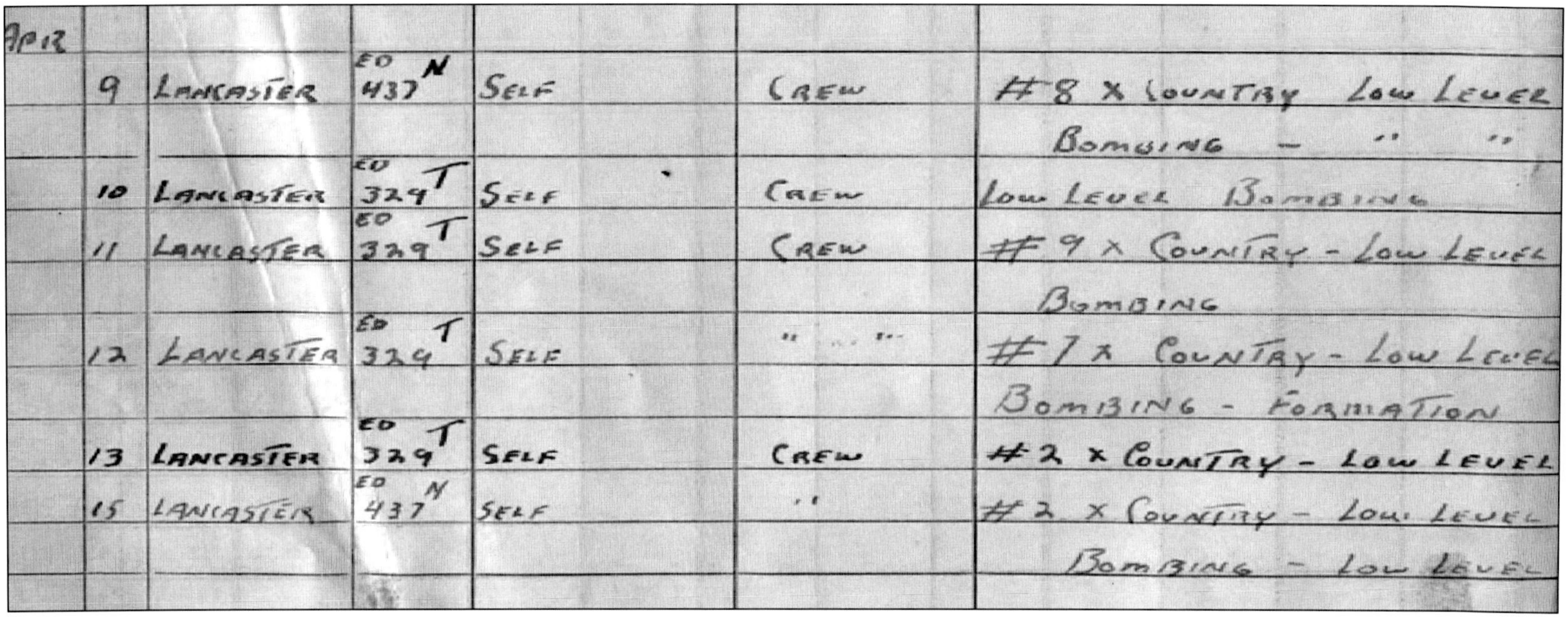

APR						
	9	LANCASTER	ED 437 N	SELF	CREW	#8 X COUNTRY LOW LEVEL
						BOMBING – " "
	10	LANCASTER	ED 329 T	SELF	CREW	LOW LEVEL BOMBING
	11	LANCASTER	ED 329 T	SELF	CREW	#9 X COUNTRY – LOW LEVEL
						BOMBING
	12	LANCASTER	ED 329 T	SELF	" "	#7 X COUNTRY – LOW LEVEL
						BOMBING – FORMATION
	13	LANCASTER	ED 329 T	SELF	CREW	#2 X COUNTRY – LOW LEVEL
	15	LANCASTER	ED 437 N	SELF	"	#2 X COUNTRY – LOW LEVEL
						BOMBING – LOW LEVEL

Logbook entries for some of Joe's low-level training.
The McCarthy Family

As the low-level training progressed, those stationed at other aerodromes knew nothing about this new squadron and their training for a secret operation. Joe describes one incident,

"Seems we were flying all the bloody time. Sometimes we'd lay on a triangular cross-country exercise whereby two aircraft would take off from Scampton and arrange to meet at a designated spot half-way around. This was to improve navigation, map reading, and the ability to maintain constant air speed all the way around. We'd picked an aerodrome for the passing point one day and managed to put up a real 'Black' (a black mark against their name).

"The c/o of this station was holding a full-dress parade inspection for some visiting VIPs. We didn't know this of course so as a result when I came barrelling along at about 230 knots and one hundred feet off the ground they all hit the deck. They'd just gotten to their feet with the c/o hollering for my number when my buddy came screaming in from the opposite direction and flattened them again. I heard Gibby was kept pretty busy for a while sorting that one out." [23]

Ken Brown had a similar experience,

'We started our low-flying cross-countrys over England at about 200 feet. That lasted about three days. Then we were down to 150 feet.

'I did a cross-country one day and I came across a new aerodrome that was being built with an awful lot of people around it. There I was headed straight for the hangar and I thought, 'Well, I'd better pull-up. There's no point in trying to go through it.' So I pulled up and over the hangar.

'Let me explain that the Royal Observer Corps kept track of us all the time so Guy got our altitudes no matter where we were and had a report on them the next morning. So at briefing the next day he said, 'Brown, what were you doing going over the hangar?'

'I said, 'I thought it was a good idea.' And he said, '200 feet! Hardly, you'll do that one again.' It wasn't a bad cross-country anyhow so I did it the next day.

'When I came to the hangar; same thing, all these men were working on top of the hangar and the side of it and so forth. So I put it (the aircraft) down on grass level and then came over the top of the hanger and there were people sliding off it and running in all directions. So next day at briefing, he (Gibson) looked in my direction and said, 'Brown, I said low, but not that low.'" [24]

Some of the aircrew like Johnny Johnson seemed to enjoy watching ground features whip by only feet away as he lay in the nose of the Lanc looking through the bomb aimer's perspex,

"I found the low flying exhilarating. We'd been so used to the high-level stuff and it was great. The Lancaster at low-level gave us no problems." [25]

Others, such as Grant McDonald, Ken Brown's rear gunner weren't so sure,

"Low level flying was a bit worrying and quite a bit different from what we were used to. At that time Bomber Command had been attacking targets from higher and higher. We had all been stacked up to 20,000 feet and above. Suddenly it was all low-level and quite alarming in the rear turret watching the ground go by so quickly. You heard a lot about people flying under high tension wires and so on. Some aircraft suffered some damage by going through the tops of trees –Henry Maudslay, for one, came back with branches stuck in his tail wheel." [26]

617 Squadron Lancaster at low-level. Note the shadow below the aircraft.
The McCarthy Family

Dave Rodger, Joe's rear gunner, described the low-level training succinctly,

"You didn't know what was coming . . . until it went by." [27]

The operation they were training for was to be done at night. Pilot Dave Shannon described how their training was adapted for this aspect,

"To counteract the shortage of moonlight we practiced at dawn and dusk, but even so we needed more realistic moonlight conditions. This was achieved by lining the Lancaster cockpits with blue Perspex and the crews wearing yellow-tinted goggles. The effect was very eerie –one had a strong desire to tear the goggles off and see what the hell was going on, but on overcoming that urge, one realised it offered a pretty fair comparison with moonlight flying and was certainly better than dawn and dusk flying." [28]

As the training progressed testing of the Upkeep weapon continued. It was found that dropping from 150 feet, as was originally envisioned, caused the outer case to shatter. Barnes Wallis determined that the weapon needed to be released from an altitude of sixty feet while flying at 220 mph. Flying at sixty feet over a lake at night was much different from flying at 150 feet. The problem was solved, as recalled by Dave Shannon, by placing two spotlights on the bottom of the fuselage such that they converged at an altitude of sixty feet,

"The problem was getting down to sixty feet. This was done by the navigator looking through the side blister in the cockpit and calling to the pilot through the intercom, 'down, down, down' until the spots converged. It worked but was fairly dicey. At first we thought the chap calling 'down, down, down' would never stop." [29]

As the training progressed, it became necessary to practice over water and the Derwent Dam was chosen because of its similarity to the German dams. It was located in a rural area about twenty miles east of Manchester. There were many complaints by the rural residents nearby about a number of things including loss of roof tiles, drops in milk and egg production, and the aircrew out joy-riding at a time of serious fuel shortages.

The new, specially modified aircraft with the arms for carrying the weapon arrived at Scampton about the beginning of May as Harold Roddis, a member of the 617 ground crew recalled,

"I was out on dispersal when I saw for the first time the new aircraft arriving. They looked as though a great chunk had been taken from the underside and someone suggested that it looked like a Lancaster that had had an abortion and thereafter they became known to the ground crews as 'abortions.' They looked even worse on the ground. The neat lines of the Lancaster were completely destroyed. It could not, however, have affected the performance as training went on continuously." [30]

Johnny Johnson had some concerns when he first saw them as well,

"When the new special aircraft arrived the first reaction was, 'God, do these things fly?' . . . They had lost the mid-upper turret and the bomb bay, and in place of that they had this cutaway underneath the belly with a couple of arms sticking down, one on either side." [31]

Now the aircrew knew that they weren't going to be dropping conventional bombs and the speculation as to the target intensified. Joe recalled,

"Our assumption at this time was anything from the (Battleship) Tirpitz to the submarine pens, to any of the capital navy ships that were in the harbours along Bourdeaux or up in Norway. None of us had any idea it was the dams. Not a person I know even said, 'I'd thought of that.'" [32]

DQS

Opposite: Lancaster PA474 of the Battle of Britain Memorial Flight over Derwent Dam.

Fred Sutherland had no idea what the target would be either but he was certain of one thing,

"The only thing we were sure of was that it was going to be tough. We'd all had quite a bit of experience and after a while you got a feeling for a tough target. We had a feeling; I know I did; that this was going to be real tough." [33]

On 11 May Barnes Wallis made a decision that would affect Joe and his crew as well as Ken Brown and his. Wallis advised that he had decided that the proposed method of attack would not be appropriate for the Sorpe Dam which was very different in construction compared to the two other primary targets, the Möhne Dam and the Eder Dam. As well, the Sorpe didn't have towers on either side which the bomb aimers required to determine their distance and thus the point at which to release the weapon.

The Sorpe was to be attacked by flying along the 1965 foot wall of the dam (rather than perpendicular to it as all the crews had been training to do) and that the bomb not be spun, but simply dropped just short of the centre and some twenty feet from the edge of the water. The Lancasters were to attack "from the lowest practicable height" at an indicated airspeed of 180 mph.

Joe remembered that they finally got to see the weapon when some of the pilots were given concrete-filled Upkeeps to test,

"We tried that out about five days before the raid. We had a little bit of a problem there because the initial drop was to be a little bit higher and we dropped them from that height but the splash from that height was so great that it actually damaged the ailerons on the Lancaster, coming right through the fabric. So they gave us a bit of a change, they asked us to drop a little bit lower, down to sixty feet and with the forward speed increased. This eliminated the problem of the splash getting us after you'd dropped your weapon." [34]

On 14 May, the day after a live Upkeep was dropped in training, the final decision was made to proceed with the attack on the night of 16/17 May.

57 Squadron was based at Scampton as well. They were aware of the training and all the secrecy related to 617 Squadron. But they were also aware that

During testing F/Lt Les Munro has just released an Upkeep from his 617 Squadron Lancaster at the Reculver Bombing Range, east of Herne Bay in Kent.
Imperial War Museum

Parts of some fuselage panels fall from Les Munro's Lancaster after being damaged by the plume of water thrown after the weapon's first bounce during the tests in Kent.
Imperial War Museum

while their squadron was regularly going out on wartime operations, 617 was just training. Joe recalled one incident,

"The sister squadron on the base used to call to us and say, 'When are you boys going to go to war?' and all this sort of business. It didn't bother us but things got a little hectic. So two nights before the actual raid there was a little binge going on in the mess and the 617 boys got a little browned off with the other squadron's officers and they really had a go at it. They ended up taking the pants off the boys in the other squadron and throwing them out the window and they were running around in their shorts. All of a sudden Gibson came in and that was the end of it. We were told to all go to bed. That was just a pre-warning. He wanted to make sure we'd be in good shape." [35]

The following day, the pilots and navigators were briefed and the target revealed. Joe continues,

"I didn't know about it (the target) until the afternoon of the fifteenth. The pilots and navigators were called together for a briefing and the security was very high. They revealed that the targets were the dams and there were models of the dams. They also provided the route. We reviewed the routes in and the routes out to see if we could find any flak spots or any danger areas that we would encounter that were not covered in the operational plan originally. We studied both the routes in and out and the models of the dams themselves. I could see that I was going to have a little problem with mine but I didn't really figure that it was going to give me as much problem as it eventually did. Of course the security was imposed on us and we were told that we were not to tell anybody else until the final briefing that would be the following day.

"Next morning at 9:00 am all the crews reported in and again the security was very high. We had everybody down there. They had Bomber Harris, the Air Vice Marshal, they had Barnes Wallis, the gentleman who designed it and of course all the intelligence factors and weather conditions and when the target was revealed there were a lot people who said, 'Why are we going for the dams?' Barnes Wallis revealed the history behind the dams and what they could do. He was a lovely gentleman, very mild and meek. When he was finished we were briefed by the intelligence people, we were briefed by the squadron commander and we were told we'd be departing that night." [36]

This detailed model of the Sorpe Dam was used to brief the five crews of Joe's wave and others in the reserve wave that might be sent to the Sorpe. Note the small village of Langscheid to the left of the dam. Joe would use the steeple of its church as a marker as he flew over the village prior to making the steep descent to the level of the reservoir to release his weapon.
Imperial War Museum

George 'Johnny' Johnson recalled that day and the briefing,

"I don't know of any particular concerns about the possible danger at the briefing. I don't think any of our crew had any particular thoughts about anyone getting the chop. Nobody on our crew mentioned it. We just thought of it as a job to be done and if it wasn't going to be successful we wouldn't be asked to do it.

"We had no practice of our type of attack (flying along the crest of the dam) on the Sorpe at all. We didn't know in fact what kind of attack it was going to be until the briefing. That gave us the style of the attack but the actual geography of it we didn't know until we got to the Sorpe. All our practicing had been with the bouncing-bomb method at right angles to the objective. None of it had been running along the line of a dam wall. I'm certain I heard Barnes Wallis say at briefing it would take at least six of the special bombs to crack the Sorpe and the weight of the water would do the rest. In fact six crews were briefed for that particular dam." [37]

The Dams Raid

The Ruhr Dams are located southeast of Essen, about 330 miles east-southeast of Scampton. After crossing the North Sea the attacking force would pass over Holland before entering Germany. They would not, of course, travel in a direct line to their targets but would attempt to avoid areas that were known to have anti-aircraft guns in place.

The nineteen 617 Squadron Lancasters would be made up of three waves. The first wave, led by W/C Gibson, was made up of nine aircraft and would attack the Möhne Dam. If successful they would then proceed to the Eder Dam. The second wave of five aircraft would be led by Joe McCarthy. It would follow a quite different and more northerly route to the Sorpe Dam. The third was a reserve wave of five aircraft and would follow the same route as W/C Gibson's first wave, but about two and a half hours later.

The aircraft would all be flying low-level at all times and Joe agreed that this was critical,

"The hundred feet to me was essential because even if you ran into flak positions or you ran into searchlight positions as long as you could go right directly over them it was pretty hard for them to pivot the guns and pivot the searchlights to get after you. Only if they were on your side, they may be able to get you

Guy Gibson and his crew board their Lancaster ED932 on the evening of the Dams Raid.

as you were coming by. So the one hundred feet was the secret. You could actually get behind trees and in bright moonlight conditions some of us did drop down behind trees after we had the flak and searchlights coming after us." [38]

Joe would be the first of the squadron to take off as his wave was flying a longer, more northerly route in order to confuse the enemy and keep them guessing as to what the targets were. He would lead his wave into the air at 9:30 pm. W/C Gibson's wave would take off next, about five minutes later. The reserve wave would take off at midnight.

Harry Humphries was selected by W/C Gibson to be the squadron adjutant. Of all the authors who have written about the Dams Raid after the war, only Gibson and Harry Humphries were actually there, working on a daily basis with the bomber crews. In his book, "Living with Heroes," Humphries recalls Gibson saying to the crews,

"Well chaps, my watch says time to go,' and there then being a general exodus as the buses began to fill and the airmen were taken to the waiting Lancasters dispersed around the perimeter track. Soon there were only a few ground staff left as well as a few WAAFs, waiting to watch their favourite pilot take-off." [39]

One of the 617 Squadron Lancasters taking off from Scampton for the Dams Raid

When the airmen reached their Lancaster there were pre-flight checks to do and then more waiting. F/Lt John Hopgood was part off the second wave and his bomb-aimer was a young Canadian, John Fraser. John recalled the waiting until it was time to board their aircraft,

"Before takeoff we were hanging around and I would say perhaps a little tense. Our navigator was a fellow called Ken Earnshaw from Bashaw, Alberta. I'd been with him on my first tour at 50 Squadron at Skellingthorpe. He was kind of a psychic fellow. He used to say things like, 'I don't think that crew has much longer to go, maybe one or two more trips,' and as we stood there I said, 'Ken, what do you think of tonight?' Well, he says, 'I think perhaps we might lose eight tonight and you know, I think we might go ourselves.' I think he was pretty right." [40]

At 9:10 pm Gibson's wireless operator fired a red flare into the cloudless, evening sky signalling that all aircraft in the first and second waves should start their engines.

Ken Brown was part of the third wave. His rear gunner, Grant MacDonald, recalled the departure,

"I watched the first four (aircraft) take off independently (Joe's wave) followed by three flights of three aircraft (W/C Gibson's wave) each take off in formation. I had never seen Lancasters take off in formation. It was quite a sight. We still had two hours to wait being in the reserve wave and didn't leave until shortly after midnight." [41]

But there were five aircraft in the second wave and Grant only watched four take off. Joe was having problems,

"My own aircraft that I had spent a lot of loving care on and worked with the ground crew to have in excellent shape for that night turned sour on me. That was the old 'Q for Queenie' that I had and I used to call it 'Queenie Chuck Chuck.'" Unfortunately, just as we started up we had a coolant leak on the 4 engine, the starboard-outboard engine. It was necessary for me to change aircraft to the replacement aircraft that was called 'T-Tare.'" [42]

According to Joe's bomb-aimer Johnny Johnson,

"Typically, Joe's reaction was, 'For Christ's sake get into the other aircraft quick before some other bugger gets it and we don't get a chance to go." [43]

Joe continues,

"In the hurry to get out, and knowing that we only had one spare aircraft and to make sure that I did get that spare aircraft before somebody else's aircraft went u/s and tried to claim it, we started throwing all our equipment out the window. Unfortunately my flight engineer caught somebody's (Joe's) parachute on the window hook as it came out and it blossomed all over me on the ground. We got all the equipment into the truck which was standing by and beat it for the 'T-Tare' aircraft, the spare one." [44]

At this point Joe was preparing to depart without a parachute but he was convinced to wait for few minutes while a replacement was obtained. Then there was another problem,

"It (T-Tare) had just arrived at noon that day from the factory. Nobody tested it except the ground crew ran it up and checked a few things. They also put a weapon on it and then they swung the compasses. Normally you do compass swings before you put weapons on and then you swing with weapons on after so that you have a deviation factor from the magnetic field set up by the steel." [45]

Harry Humphries described what happened next, perhaps with some embellishment,

"The silence was disturbed by a roar resembling a clap of thunder and we suddenly saw Mac (Joe McCarthy) emerging and charging towards the flight offices like a runaway tank. Flight Sergeant Powell, ever alert, met him before he could reach us.

T-Tare (Lancaster ED825) This was the aircraft Joe flew on the Dams Raid.

'What's the matter sir?'

'McCarthy spluttered. 'My bloody aircraft is u/s, I've got to take the spare. There's no compass deviation card. Where are those lazy, idle, incompetent compass adjusters?' We calmed him while many willing people searched for the missing compass card. The excitement and exertion had really disturbed his equanimity. His shirt was wringing wet and he gulped in great breaths of air. His huge hands were clenching and unclenching spasmodically.

"'Calm down old boy,' I said. 'You'll make it.'

"Flight Sergeant Powell came running towards us with the all-important card in his hand. 'Here you are Sir,' he said as the sound of engines warming up could be heard." [46]

Joe was clearly unhappy with this turn of events and his crewmembers were as well as rear gunner Dave Rodger recalled,

'We had done all our training in old 'Q-Queenie' and I had the rear turret to my liking. We'd removed the sliding panel of perspex in front of the gun-sight so as to give unrestricted vision.

It was very disconcerting to get a turret you weren't sure of. Some helpful ground crew tore out the perspex panel for me which was a big help. But everybody, including Big Joe, was in a real flap. The ground crew told me later they never expected us back. We were twenty minutes late taking off and we were supposed to lead this section." [47]

Radcliffe was able to make up much of that time as Joe later wrote,

"Bill Radcliffe's experience as an aeromechanic on Spitfires and Hurricanes made him a valuable crew member and one who you could trust. I often tried to have him increase the power of our engines on operational trips to no avail. He was conserving the engines and gas so we had sufficient fuel to return if anything went wrong was his answer. However on the Dams Raid we were delayed on takeoff and had to make up thirty minutes. Sixteen minutes were made up over the North Sea and we were only nine minutes late on the target-the Sorpe Dam." [48]

Shortly after take off, Len Eaton (Joe's wireless operator) advised that he had lost communications with 5 Group Operations Headquarters at Grantham. Joe was not going to let this stop him from going on the raid. He described his reaction,

"The order was that if you lost radio contact and you couldn't receive anything then you had to go home. We lost it in the first twenty minutes. I told the wireless operator, 'You didn't tell me until later on in your logbook.'" [49]

As Joe was making up time across the North Sea and approaching the Dutch coast, two of the Lancasters in his wave were in serious trouble. One hadalready been shot down and its crew were dead. Joe later thought that part of the reason for the enemy gunners' success was that it wasn't completely dark as they reached the Dutch coast,

"I was with the first group to take off because it was our job to go into the northern part of Germany and attract any night-fighters into the air. It turned out even though all the plans that we made were perfect in my mind, we missed one little detail. The daylight sun was just disappearing on the horizon and (one) of the aircraft of the original four (in my group) was destroyed shortly after getting inland and (another) so seriously damaged that it was useless for them to go on and they had to return home to base." [50]

As F/O Geoff Rice reached the Dutch Coast near the Island of Vlieland. He was flying so low that his aircraft grazed the surface of the sea, ripping off his Upkeep weapon and leaving a large hole in the Lancaster's fuselage opposite the crew door. With seawater in the fuselage and no longer having a weapon, Rice aborted the sortie and was fortunate to be able to reach Scampton and land safely. Joe described what happened,

"While dodging the flak and the searchlights, he bounced off the sea and smothered one motor, the starboard-outer, and he lost the weapon off the rack. Now he was in water to do that. He finally got it airborne again, I don't know how and neither does anybody else. As a matter of fact he bent the tail wheel of the aircraft up and it jammed the turret with the rear gunner facing backwards. By this time, the gunner was sitting in water. It drained eventually as they went back to England but they couldn't get him out. I think they cut the glass out and pulled him through that way." [51]

P/O Vernon Byer's aircraft was struck by flak at about 11:00 pm just off the southern tip of the Island of Texel as he attempted to enter the Zuider Zee. His aircraft crashed into the sea in flames and all aboard were killed.

Close-up of the Upkeep mounted underneath Guy Gibson's aircraft.

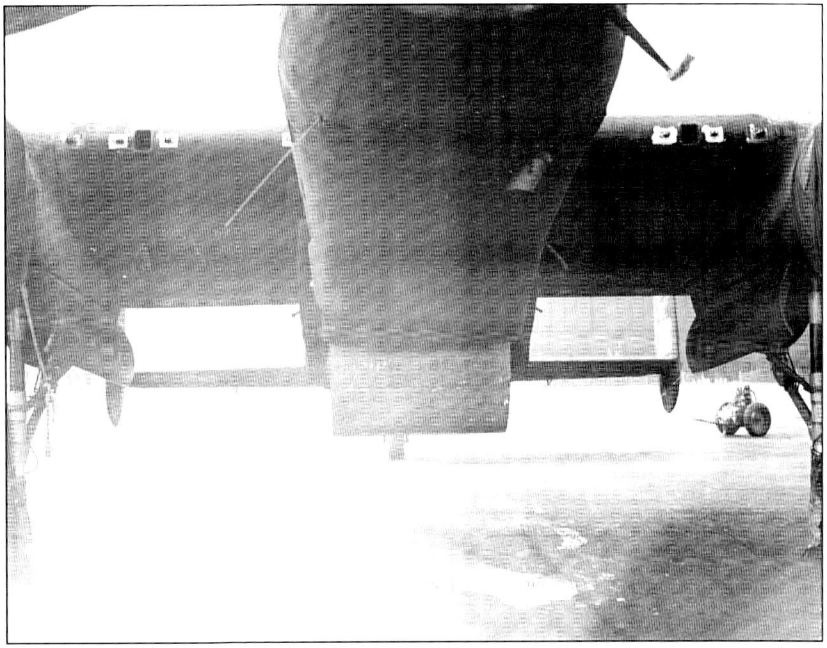

As Les Munro, who had flown with Joe on 97 Squadron, crossed over the Island of Texel he was struck by light flak and forced to abort the operation. He later wrote,

"I can well remember seeing the breakers ahead of us and the sand dunes rising behind them. I actually had to gain height to clear the dunes and was losing height on the Waddenzee side when we were hit amidships by a light flak shell from, judging by the tracer, a single gun. The shell blew a hole approximately thirty

inches in diameter midway along the fuselage severing all communications and electrical wiring systems, but without injuring any crew members." [52]

F/Lt. Barlow had made it across the series of coastal islands along the Dutch coast. The enemy gunners were alert now as Joe was about to cross them and enter the Zuider Zee,

"I was about twenty minutes behind them and even at that I got a very hot reception from the natives when I crossed the coastline. They knew the track that we were coming in on so their guns were pretty much trained when they heard my motors but thank God there were two large sand dunes right on the coast. I snuck in between them and was able to get into the Zuider Zee area before any damage was done. Although it sounds silly to say it now and I know that some people have scoffed at it, we actually used trees and hills to escape from searchlights and the 'ack-ack' which was firing at us. With the moonlight conditions which we had this was very easily done. In many cases if we couldn't get away from a searchlight, we'd run right over it with our guns firing downwards and just blow it up as we went by. The method of the low-level and the moonlight really baffled the night-fighters because quite frequently we could see them floating along at a thousand feet above us but we were down at one hundred feet and they never even saw us at all. We'd go directly underneath or they'd be going the opposite way over us going to wherever they thought we were. I don't think they expected us down there at all.

"I turned down the Zuider Zee and there were fires on the side, one on the coast to my right and the other one straight ahead of me at the end of the Zuider Zee. But I thought they were just house fires or farm fires or something because they didn't look like aircraft and I proceeded on down to the Sorpe Dam. I had lost contact with Bomber Command because one of the things that went wrong with the aircraft I took as a substitute was that the radio had failed about thirty minutes out. It just wouldn't receive anything. The second thing that went wrong was my GEE navigation box. It stopped operating about the time we got to the Zuider Zee and then the third thing that happened was that was the light came on in the nose compartment and I could see these fighters above me. I was down at about one hundred feet and I could see fighters above me at about a thousand to fifteen hundred feet and with the light on I figured, 'Boy we're going to be a good target.' We couldn't find out how the light came on so my engineer (Bill Radcliffe) broke it with a crash axe." [53]

At about midnight, Joe had flown south-southeast along the length of the Zuider Zee and was crossing Holland. It was at about this time that F/Lt Barlow's Lancaster had just entered Germany. His was the only other aircraft of Joe's wave still heading towards the target. Shortly after doing so, the aircraft struck the top of an electricity pylon along the Rhine River near Rees and crashed in flames near Haldern. There were no survivors. Joe didn't know it of course, but now his was the only aircraft of the second wave still flying towards the Sorpe Dam.

Despite all that had already happened to Joe's second wave, the third wave was still waiting for their take-off time. Ken Brown, who at that time didn't know that his would be the second aircraft to attack the Sorpe Dam, recalled,

"We were perched out on the grass. It was a beautiful night, clear sky, no cloud, waiting for the buses to take us out to the aircraft. John Burpee came over to me and thrust out his hand and said, 'Goodbye, Ken.'

"I said, 'Goodbye, John.' I didn't expect he'd come back. You see some people feel that way.

"Then we got on board the bus. There were three crews to one bus. The bus stopped to let the first crew off. Then the second crew got off and as the bus moved on my tail gunner (F/Sgt. Grant MacDonald) was very quiet. Then it stopped for us, and we moved over towards the aircraft. My gunner stood there, where he'd got off the bus.

"I said, 'Come on Mac. Let's go.'

"He said, 'Skip, you know those guys aren't coming back, don't you?'

"I said, 'Yeah, I know.'

"So he said, 'Well, damn it!'" [54]

Meanwhile, Joe and his crew were very busy, concentrating on their individual assignments as they flew across Holland and eastern Germany at low-level. Bomb aimer Johnny Johnson recalled,

"Don (Don MacLean, the navigator) and I had an arrangement whereby we both had maps with the track marked on. I would pick out various pinpoints not necessarily on track and report back to him and he would use the information to keep our course. (Don would have been at his desk, behind a curtain in the fuselage that kept his light from being seen). We didn't use the roller map method. Don was of the opinion

that should the situation arise where you got badly off track you would have no map to refer to because the roller kept you to a certain width of track. The ordinary maps took up that much more space, but they were so much better, we felt, for us." [55]

Joe's gunners were busy as well as Dave Rodger recalled,

"Going over Holland I was looking for flak guns. Well inland I took a whack at a battery that started shooting at us." [56]

At midnight as the third wave was taking off and Joe was approaching the Sorpe Dam, W/C Gibson's wave was roaring across Germany at tree-top height towards the Möhne Dam. At 12:15 am, F/Lt. Astell struck an electricity pylon and crashed in a ball of flames killing all aboard. Avoiding searchlights and flak as best they could, the remainder of the first wave aircraft arrived at the Möhne Dam. Gibson later wrote that,

"As we came over the hill, we saw the Möhne Lake. Then we saw the dam itself. In that light it looked squat and heavy and unconquerable." [57]

W/C Gibson made the first run at about 12:30 am. With navigator Harlo 'Terry' Taerum watching the converging spotlights and calling out the altitude, his flight engineer, John Pulford, ensuring that the required speed of 230 mph was reached, wireless operator F/Lt. Bob Hutchinson ensuring that the weapon was rotating at the required 500 rpm, and bomb aimer P/O Fred Spafford using his device that utilized the towers on the sides of the dam to determine when to drop the Upkeep, Gibson flashed above the calm waters of the Möhne Reservoir towards the dam. Spafford released the Upkeep and it began skipping across the water towards the dam. From the rear turret, F/Lt. Dick Trevor-Roper watched and as the aircraft turned in the moonlight, a huge column of white water was thrown hundreds of feet into the air. However the Upkeep had not quite reached the dam and it did not break.

Following Gibson's attack the enemy gunners were ready and waiting. F/Lt. John Hopgood was shot down as he made the second run over the dam. His Upkeep bounced

(l-r) Harlo Taerum (W/C Gibson's navigator), Dave Rodger, Joe McCarthy.
The McCarthy Family

over the dam and destroyed the power station. Then F/Lt. Mickey Martin attacked. Just as he was reaching the release point the aircraft was hit in the wing by flak, blowing a large hole in an empty fuel tank and tilting the Lancaster. His weapon veered off to the left and ended up on the western shore of the reservoir.

The fourth attacker, S/L Melvin 'Dinghy' Young, placed his Upkeep perfectly. The fifth aircraft to attack was being flown by F/Lt. David Maltby. As he approached the dam and just prior to releasing his weapon, Maltby realised that, "The crown of the wall was already crumbling" and that there was, "a breach in the centre of the dam."

Young had been successful. Maltby recorded,

"Our load sent up water and mud to a height of a thousand feet. The spout of water was silhouetted against the moon. It rose with tremendous speed and then gently fell back. You could see the shock wave at the base of the jet." [58]

The effect of Maltby's weapon is not known but Wallis' theory had been vindicated. The first accurately placed Upkeep (Dinghy Young's) had breached the dam. With the weight of millions of tons of water against it, the initial fracture burst into a gaping breach almost 300 feet across and a raging torrent of foaming water headed down the valley.

When the coded report was received at 5 Group Headquarters at Grantham, Barnes Wallis leapt to his feet in triumph and waved his hands in the air triumphantly. Those who knew him said that it was the first time they had ever seen him show such emotion. Harris declared, "Wallis, I didn't believe a word you said when you came to see me, but now you could sell me a pink elephant."

W/C Gibson ordered the aircraft that had attacked to return to Scampton. Then, together with Dinghy Young as Deputy Leader, he led the remaining three aircraft still carrying Upkeeps to the Eder Dam.

At about 12:40 am Joe was approaching the Sorpe Dam and saw that thick mist had formed over the area during the coolness of the night. But although there was mist in the area, there was none over the dam itself and he was able to see the target from a distance of about five miles. Unlike the Möhne, the Sorpe was undefended although as

The Möhne Dam following the raid.

Dave Rodger recalled,

"As we were reaching the Sorpe we flew past a battery of five 20 mm flak guns on the side of a hill. They had a crack at us, but didn't hit us." [59]

What most surprised Joe and his crew was that although they were late, none of the other four second wave Lancasters were there. They had expected to see them circling in the surrounding hills or attacking. It wasn't until they returned to Scampton that they heard what had happened to the others in their wave.

As Joe was positioning his aircraft to attack the Sorpe Dam, Len Eaton heard Gibson's wireless operator transmit 'Nigger' over the radio-the code word to signal that the Möhne Dam had been breached. Joe described the dam he was focussing on and what he would have to do,

"The Sorpe, because of it's earthen construction, had no vertical wall to stop the skipping mine and hence had to be attacked along the water side of the dam, running parallel to the dam and not at right angles to it as with the Möhne and Eder. This necessitated coming over the top of the hill and closely following the slope down to the dam, using flaps to keep speed under control, dropping the mine, and then climbing out quickly as the hill rose on the other end of the dam." [60]

Joe's initial reaction was said to have been, "Jeez! How do we get down there!" The flying was going to be challenging because of the short distances involved (the dam was only about 2000 feet across and the Upkeep was to be released at the mid point of the dam). Joe described what happened,

"I had to come over a little hill in the town (Langscheid) which was on the edge of the dam and I found that it was very difficult to get my aircraft down to the level that I required in the distance that was available. I had a quarter of a mile to get down from about 250 feet and drop my weapon.

"Eventually I used the steeple of the church in the small town and I found out that by flying over that high enough I got the line up from there into the dam site and by using this as a judge in coming around it again I was able to line up and I think it was the ninth time we dropped or the tenth." [61]

Joe Jr., who visited the Sorpe with his father, recalled being told that,

"Although the steeple was useful as a marker, it was definitely in the way as he attempted to line-up on the dam. At one point he considered having his air gunners set it on fire to make it even more helpful as a marker and less of an obstacle. He decided against this, possibly because of his Catholic upbringing and the likelihood that it would attract enemy fighters." [62]

Joe continues,

"The crew was getting upset because we were there so long. There was no flak or searchlights immediately in the area, but there was some to the north of us. So I had a real easy target there but I couldn't get it down low enough to let the weapon go. The crew was getting upset and the bomb aimer was being cursed for not letting the damn thing go anyhow. But he was going to put it right where he wanted to and later pictures showed he put it right in the centre.

'I pulled up and climbed away and as I was climbing I turned back and there was a spout of water from the explosion. I was about 300 feet at that time and it was still about two or three hundred feet above me and it was going up as I was turning." [63]

Rear gunner Dave Rodger, at the tail of the fuselage, was really hanging on as the attack proceeded. According to bomb-aimer Johnny Johnson,

"He got the worst of the dummy runs because coming down very steeply, then flying a short distance straight and level, then climbing like hell to get out he was getting a lot of G-force." [64]

"We made ten runs on the Sorpe and dropped the weapon on the final run. I found out that night how easy it was to become the most unpopular member of the crew very quickly. Nine times I called dummy run. It didn't do the morale of the crew much good, but I knew that if we had to do it, we had to do it properly.

'We didn't have the spotlights, of course. But I think we dropped from thirty feet. It had to be a bit of a 'by guess and by God' attack. The idea was that the lower you got, the forward travel of the bomb was reduced that much more. We lined up the port engine with the dam wall, so that when we dropped the bomb it went down the water side of the dam and rolled down to the prescribed depth before it exploded allowing us time to get away-pretty essential.

'When it finally went, I shouted: 'The bomb's gone!' and a voice from the rear turret muttered 'Thank God'." [65]

"American Dambuster"
A painting by Mark Postlethwaite depicting Joe McCarthy's Lancaster over the Sorpe.

Dave recalled,

"The last run, as we ran across, didn't seem any different to me at all but I could feel the jar when the bomb went and then we banked off to our starboard, I believe it was, and cut around back and I could see the bomb go off and a terrific plume of water went up about 1200 feet in the air." [66]

Joe described what he saw after the Upkeep was released,

"After we dropped it I pulled up and went out and started to climb. I was at about 300 feet coming around when it went up as I finished my turn. I could watch it. The explosion was right against the face of the dam and it went up and up and up and up and I'll bet the spout was around 700 feet in the air. I could see it when I swung back over it; the water was coming down and we were running through rain. The dam had a road across it, asphalt and walks, and on the whole side where the bomb was dropped, it lifted that concrete, the bricks and the mortar; big concrete blocks. It just turned them upside down on the top of the dam." [67]

Johnny Johnson recalled his view as the Lancaster completed its turn after releasing the weapon,

"When the mine exploded it was a terrific sight. We were nose up at that stage and turning. The explosion was between our aircraft and the moon and Dave Rodger in the rear turret had a clear view. He said, 'God almighty,' then as we turned I saw it. By then it was starting to fall back, but it was still a fair amount of water." [68]

When Joe arrived at the Sorpe and began his runs over the dam, he woke up Josef Kesting, a machinist who was over-nighting at the power station below the dam,

"I had no idea what was going on. I went outside . . . A plane flew towards the dam from Langscheid. I saw it fly way below the crest of the dam and over the roadway that runs along the middle. It was less than 100 metres from me. I recognized the English emblems-the rings. Shortly after this another plane (actually the same aircraft) appeared, flying parallel to the dam. It dropped an instrument like a huge septic tank over the crest and down onto the water side. A few seconds later a column of water thundered a hundred metres up and tipped over onto the air side of the dam. . . The column of water cascaded down the dam. I thought the attack was aimed at the power station." [69]

As Joe was completing his turn over the dam and examining the damage,

"My rear-gunner was really upset. He called me up and said, 'For God's sake get down. You're too high. The fighters are up here.' We were only at 300 feet. We got down and we went from there to the Möhne Dam . . . I knew that the Möhne had been destroyed and I went up there to take a look. I figured I'd be the last one through from my group and I'd be able to find out and tell intelligence when we got back." [70]

Johnny Johnson described what he saw when they reached the Möhne Dam,

"It was tremendous to see; an amazing sight I'll always remember. It was just like an inland sea. There was water everywhere in the moonlight, where before it had been a pretty reasonable valley. We could see the hole in the dam and the water shooting out. The level was well down. There was a great sense of satisfaction to see that the job had been done." [71]

Following the visit to the Möhne, Joe headed back to Scampton,

"We left the Möhne and we were going to go east of Hamm. My route back was to follow the route that Gibson and his group came in and were going out on, picking our way through all these defences. As we were going along there was a train. It was a beautiful moonlit night and my gunner asked if he could shoot it up and I said, 'Well, okay, go ahead.'" [72]

Johnny Johnson described the surprise when the gunners opened up,

"It was an armoured train and fired back. If we'd known it was armoured we perhaps wouldn't have been quite so keen. The train's response to our .303s was a little heavier. We knew we'd been hit, but it didn't impair the aircraft so we could still press on. But the damage from the train would cause problems later." [73]

Dave Rodger described the attack as he saw it from his position in the rear turret,

"I started pumping away at it and he was pumping back at me and we were pumping at each other I guess for about two miles. As soon as I stopped, he stopped. I wished I had stopped a heck of a lot sooner. I couldn't tell if I'd hit him or not. We were bouncing up and down over hedges at that time trying to get down as low as we could. We pretty near scraped the belly on the ground though." [74]

As the attack on the train proceeded, Joe could see trouble ahead,

"The heavens opened up right in front of us; searchlights, flak was coming up and I could see a railroad yard and a city in front of me and then something coned over the city and being fired on by flak. I didn't find out till later on that it was one of our third wave, a boy called Ottley. He'd gotten himself up to 300 feet. You don't get that high with all the flak around. They coned him and shot him down.

"I quickly made a 180 degree turn to figure out why I was over here when I should have been east of Hamm. Between the navigator and I, we got a rough idea that we were eighteen or nineteen degrees west of our course. We made alterations for that. In the meantime I'd made two or three circuits.

"During this period I'd felt a thud in the aircraft and I asked several of the crew if anybody had been hit, did they feel anything, see anything, smell anything, or was there anything on fire. Nobody said anything.

"I realised that my compasses weren't that reliable and that I could pick my way through the defences on the route going out. They (the 5 Group personnel who planned the raid) didn't want me to come back on the route we came in simply because by about that time the moon was going to be in such a position that if we came up the Zieder Zee over the surface of the water and with the moon's reflection we'd be perfect targets for fighters from above; they'd be able to see us. Coming in they couldn't see us because of where the moon was situated but as the night progressed the moon was moving and I would be picked out over the surface of the water even though I was down at 100 feet.

"I figured it was the better of the two evils. I thought I could compete with the fighters down at that level but I couldn't compete with the defences that I was going to go out through because there were numerous ones on both sides of the track.

Joe's gunners: Dave Rodger (left) and Ron Batson.
The McCarthy Family

"So we decided that we'd map-read through the Zieder Zee and go home the way we came in. We scooted up the Zieder Zee. My engineer (Bill Radcliffe) had flown with me on many, many trips. He and I always used to argue about speed. I'd be asking for more speed and he'd say, 'No we've got to save gas, we've got to save gas.' He'd never give me my speed. But this night, coming out I was saying, 'Cut those motors back, you're going to burn them out.' He had them set right up to the max and we were really tooting along. He had it all set like that until we got out into the middle of the North Sea." [75]

Dave Rodger recalled the discussion as well,

"When we were over the Zuider Zee it was beginning to get light. Bill Radcliffe, our flight engineer from Vancouver who usually babied our engines, had them flat-out doing about 260 mph. Big Joe noticed this and said something like, 'Hadn't you better cut them back a little?' Bill replied, 'Don't you go worrying about those Merlins. They're doing real fine. Just you get us to hell out of here before sun-up.' We sure ribbed him about that later on-but not at the time." [76]

As Joe was making his way across Holland, W/C Gibson was overseeing the attack on the Eder Dam. Upon reaching it, some of the pilots were having difficulty finding the dam as fog had formed over the low-lying areas. Situated in a deep valley, the Eder was a more difficult target than the Möhne had been.

At 1:30 am W/C Gibson had reached the Eder. He fired a red flare and soon the three remaining Lancasters of the first wave that still carried Upkeeps were circling and preparing to attack. There had been heavy flak throughout the attack on the Möhne and F/Lt. Hopgood had been hit and shot down, but the pilots knew there were no enemy defences at the Eder.

Fred Sutherland, an RCAF air gunner, was in the nose turret of P/O Les Knight's Lancaster, one of the three who would attack,

"We were in the third group of three and Maudsley was our leader. We got across the coast and something happened to Maudsley; I think he hit a tree. The guy on our starboard, he got across the Rhine River then he got hit and blown up. I thought he was a little bit off course but he got shot down right there.

"We went to the Möhne Dam. They were bombing then and Hopgood was just being shot down. Once the Möhne was broken we went to the Eder." [77]

Fred spoke of his admiration for the Dams Raid pilots, including his own,

"It was really very difficult for the pilots. Remember old Les (22 year old Les Knight) had been flying our Lanc for more than four hours when we got to the Eder and just about all that flying had been tough, very tough. Low-level, high-speed, lots of jinking around; nerve-wracking stuff. Sure, we all had our job to do when the time came to do it, but the pilot was working all the time." [78]

S/L Maudsley and F/Lt. Shannon both struggled to manouever into position to release their weapons, making numerous attempts. Eventually Shannon's was released. It was seen to strike the dam and explode with a towering column of water that reached 1000 feet into the air. But the dam held. Maudsley's bomb aimer released too late and the Upkeep struck the dam's parapet and exploded on contact.

The next aircraft and the last of the three that had Upkeeps was Les Knight's and as Fred Sutherland recalled,

"On the second run Grayston (Sgt. Raymond Grayston), our engineer, had the speed right down and everything was right. Johnny (F/O Edward Johnson) let the bomb go at the right time. The airspeed, height and everything was perfect and we let the bomb go. Then we had to climb over the hill, Les pushed them through the gate and we climbed over the hill." [79]

Following the release both Knight and Grayston were pulling on the Lancaster's control yoke as hard as they could to clear the high ground beyond the dam (The elevators were controlled manually, with no hydraulics to assist).

The delivery of the Upkeep had been perfect. The breach was narrower than that at the Möhne but deeper and this allowed a higher flood wave to develop and wreake havoc below.

Fred described what he saw,

"It was a bit scary but it sure broke. I didn't see it break but after, when we were going up, you could see the results. The water just came out, a wall of water on the bridges and houses and everything." [80]

F/Lt Len Sumpter was Dave Shannon's bomb aimer. He recalled,

"The water came through just like a big wall . . . and it didn't have time to spread like it did at the Möhne . . . I think the wave was about forty or fifty feet high." [81]

Meanwhile, Joe was following his outgoing track back to base. He described what happened after crossing the Zuider Zee,

"From there on it was safe coming in and we stayed at 100 feet. The only one big error was the convoy that appeared on the horizon. Since we weren't planning on coming back that way nobody had briefed us for that convoy being at that position. Since I came back the way we went out, I didn't know that convoy was there. So I stayed low-level. I wasn't going to climb. The gunners on those navy ships were real trigger-happy and we just picked our way through the formation and got home.

"It wasn't until I landed that I found out that the thud I'd felt was a shell that had gone through the engine nacelle and through my tire on the starboard side. It came out through the top of the wing, through

The Eder Dam following the raid.

the fuselage and the shell hit the astro-navigation equipment over the navigator's head and it fell down on his desk. He just thought it was a part of the aircraft that fell off." [82]

Dave Rodger recalled,

"The starboard tire had been flattened, unknown to us. As we came in to land though, Joe did a wonderful job. He managed to hold that wheel up by applying aileron until we were just about stopped. We just spun around once. Then when we got out we had a welcome cup of tea. We were relieved to be home." [83]

But the Dams Raid wasn't over and ten minutes prior to Joe's landing at Scampton, F/Sgt. Brown, who had received the order to attack the Sorpe Dam once the operations room at 5 Group Headquarters was notified that the Eder had been breached, was beginning his attack.

Ken described his flight to the Sorpe and his attack during a speech at the Bomber Command Museum of Canada in 1993. The reserve wave had followed the route flown by W/C Gibson's wave,

"As we came onto the Dutch Coast, immediately we were in the area of Glize-Reijen which was a fighter-drome. We all knew that the Luftwaffe night-fighters were there at the time. P/O Burpee was about a mile and a half off the north coast and they opened up on him and he blew up on the airport. So I knew we had one less.

"We went on towards Hamm and I just couldn't help it. There was a train moving along a gentle slope and I said, 'Okay gunners. Here's where you can get your exercise now and your target practice.'

"So we took on the train as we flew right along side it.

"We were having trouble, as was everyone else, with high-tension wires. They were our greatest danger at any time. If the wires in the moonlight were to flutter up here (motions above his head), we knew we'd have to go under them. If they were to flutter down there (motions below his head) we knew we'd go over them. It was that quick. We lost two aircraft to those wires. They merely slapped into them. Deadly stuff.

"As we came along to Hamm they were really waiting for us. The other two waves had passed that way. So they poured it (flak) down. As a matter of fact, they were firing down at us. They were on a little bit

of a lip as we went through the valley. P/O Ottley was on my starboard side at about one o'clock and they hit him. He immediately blew up. His tanks went first and then his store (his Upkeep).

"The whole valley was just one orange ball. Then there was a road off the port side. Everything was trees but this road. I couldn't see because of the fire from his aircraft. So I dove and went along the road. Then much to my consternation that damn road led right into a castle, and I'll never forget that castle door. We had to dip and the left wing went between two turrets as we went through the castle.

"We arrived at the Möhne Dam. It had been breached by that time. The gunners were still fairly active. We thought we'd leave them alone and we went over to the Sorpe Dam.

"The only problem was the whole damn valley was full of fog when we arrived there. They told us that there would be a church up on top of the village. We found that all right; but just the spire of the church.

So I tried to position myself from the spire. I didn't do too well. I got behind the dam on the first run. I found myself at ground level, behind the dam . . . It didn't do my nerves any good at all. Because I was on top of the trees, I had to do a flat turn. I couldn't move the wing down to get around. I had to stand on the rudder to get around and then we were down in the valley again.

Well we did quite a number of runs on the dam before we were able to clear enough of the fog away and with the propellers constantly going through, we did. And I must say, according to the historians today, it was a near perfect drop. And I didn't even write them about it. However, we were pleased with it and as far as the explosion was concerned, the waterspout went up to about a thousand feet and so did we." [84]

Like Joe, F/Sgt. Brown visited the Möhne on his return, exchanging fire with the gunners who were still manning their positions despite the fact that the reservoir had been drained. But as Ken described, the worst was yet to come,

"It was then daylight or just breaking. We had to go across and up the Zuider Zee. There was no horizon; the mud from the Zuider Zee and the sky were all one. So I started across, strictly on my altimeter with my head below the cockpit top at fifty feet and I hung onto it. I'd been told by a famous Wing Commander in the RAF, 'Never, ever pull up. If you're low, never pull up.'"

"So I hoped he was right because all hell broke loose within a matter of fifteen minutes.

"Searchlights, even though it was light, caught us from the starboard side and straight on. There was a lot of light flak immediately in front of us. The cannon shells started to go through the canopy and the side

Ken Brown returning from the Sorpe Dam.
This painting by John Rutherford was commissioned by Ken Brown.

of the aircraft was pretty well blown out. There was only one thing to do and that was to go lower, so I put her down ten feet. Their gun positions were on the sea wall so they were firing slightly down at us and I guess they couldn't believe we were lower than they could fire. So in this turmoil with the front gunner blazing away at them, I just got a glance, for a moment, and I could see the gunners either falling off because they were hit from our guns or rather they were jumping off to save their skins.

'I pulled up over the top of them and we all gave a great sigh of relief. We figured we had it made at this stage of the game.

'I called each of the crewmembers and I was really surprised to find that no one had been hit. There was a great deal of damage.

'My wireless operator said, 'Hey Skip. Come on back and crawl in and out of the holes.'

'I did go back. I wondered how badly and what damage had been done to our landing gear." [85]

Ken landed safely at Scampton at 5:30 am. Of the five aircraft in the third (reserve) wave, Ken's was the only one that attacked the Sorpe. Two had crashed en-route, another flown by F/S Anderson had been forced to return early, and P/O Townsend made an unsuccessful attack on a fourth dam, the Ennepe. He released his Upkeep on the fourth run but it failed to breach the dam.

Ken recalled his thoughts after landing,

"We didn't really know of the losses however until we'd landed. Even then we were kind of naive because when we went into my dispersal point where ten aircraft should be and there was one. We thought, 'I wonder where the other fellows landed.' We couldn't quite believe that there were so many missing. When we got out of the aircraft, the ground crews of all the aircraft were standing around long-faced, tears running down their cheeks. We were the only ones that were sort of elated in saying, 'Well, we made it back.'" [86]

Upon landing Joe recalled,

"After I made my reports in the briefing room we retired to the mess. Although this was the early hours of the morning, there was already a large collection of beer cases on the floor which gradually grew in quantity as the morning went on and each crew returned. The few WAAF officers that were sleeping were immediately wakened up and they joined the party. Our sister squadron were sleeping that night. When they came down to breakfast they were amazed to find this big party going on and unknown to them we had just completed the Dams Raid." [87]

Dave Rodger recalled,

"I guess we were feeling no pain, but we were kind of feeling bad about all the boys who just didn't make it that time. There were such a lot of experienced crews lost, including a fellow that I had known very intimately and I thought it was kind of a washout but I think it was a great success actually given the damage that was done." [88]

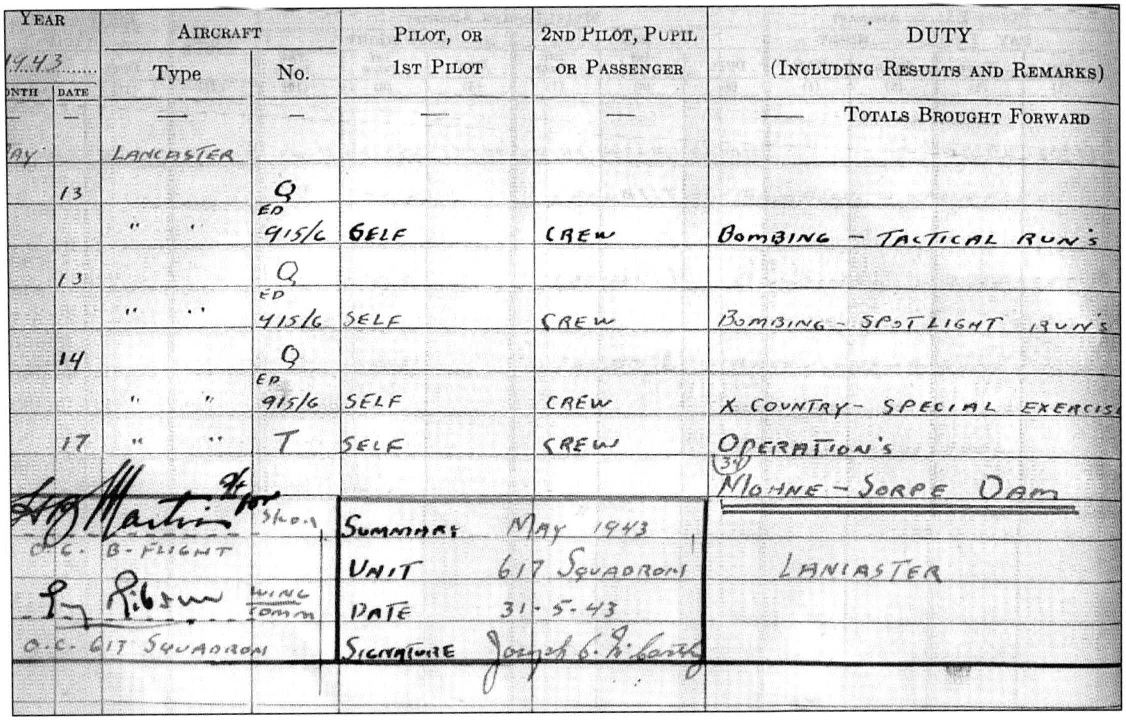

YEAR 1943 MONTH	DATE	AIRCRAFT Type	No.	PILOT, OR 1ST PILOT	2ND PILOT, PUPIL OR PASSENGER	DUTY (INCLUDING RESULTS AND REMARKS)
—	—	—	—	—	—	— TOTALS BROUGHT FORWARD
MAY		LANCASTER				
	13		Q			
		" "	ED 915/6	SELF	CREW	BOMBING – TACTICAL RUN'S
	13		Q			
		" "	ED 915/6	SELF	CREW	BOMBING – SPOTLIGHT RUN'S
	14		Q			
		" "	ED 915/6	SELF	CREW	X COUNTRY – SPECIAL EXERCIS
	17	" "	T	SELF	CREW	OPERATION'S (34) MOHNE – SORPE DAM

O.C. B-FLIGHT

O.C. 617 SQUADRON

SUMMARY MAY 1943
UNIT 617 SQUADRON
DATE 31-5-43
SIGNATURE

LANCASTER

Joe's logbook entry for the Dams Raid.
The McCarthy Family

The Aftermath and the Celebration

The breaching of the Möhne and Eder Dams were major achievements and the raid is considered to be amongst the most outstanding tactical operations of World War II. The Möhne reservoir contained nearly 140 million tons of water and was the major source of supply for the industrial Ruhr Valley, twenty miles away. The water released caused widespread flooding and disruption of rail, road, and canal communications and of the supply of electricity and water. The water-supply network was particularly affected by the silting up of pumping stations by the flood water.

The Eder was even larger than the Möhne, containing 210 million tons of water, but it was sixty miles from the Ruhr. The city of Kassel, 25 miles away, and the inland waterway system in the Kassel area, were more affected by the attack on the Eder than was the Ruhr area.

The downstream side of the Sorpe Dam after the raid.
The McCarthy Family

The Sorpe was of a different type of construction altogether. It was an earthen dam with a solid core and earth on either side. Barnes Wallis had said that six Upkeeps would be necessary. He believed that the Sorpe could be destroyed by placing the weapons on the upstream slope of the dam. His thinking was that the shock wave would crack the thick concrete core. Then seeping water would damage the earth bank on the downstream side and then the concrete core would collapse when the support was gone.

However, only two Upkeeps were dropped. Through impressive airmanship, the skills of the crewmembers (particularly the bomb aimers), and perseverance the weapons were placed precisely against the dam. A 400 foot stretch of the paving above the dam's concrete core was damaged. The clay around the core was loosened over a distance of eighty feet and at this level a slight leakage of water occurred through the expansion joints of the drainage system.

According to a German Intelligence Branch Report, "considerable damage" was caused including "deep fissures which had undermined the stone work to such an extent as to make its removal (and replacement) imperative."

Albert Speer, Hitler's Minister of Armaments and War Production, wrote,

"Fortunately the bomb hole was slightly higher than the water level. Just a few inches lower and a small brook would have been transformed into a raging river which would have swept away the stone and earthen dam." [89]

The Sorpe Dam after the raid. Note the damage in two separate spots along the crest of the dam-one by Joe's Upkeep and the other by Ken Brown's.

Had four more been dropped, perhaps the Sorpe would have been breached as Barnes Wallis thought it could be.

Following the raid, the Nazis protected more than two dozen dams in areas they occupied by installing anti-aircraft guns, smoke-screens, torpedo nets, anti-bouncing bomb deflectors and camouflage.

Joe's personal evaluation of the raid was that,

"It was quite successful when you realise the damage that was completed right in the Ruhr Valley itself with the coal industries, the airfields that were completely covered with just the tails of aircraft sitting up above the water, some seventy-five or eighty bridges were destroyed and a few others badly damaged. It accomplished the aim of the operation which was to destroy their water facilities which produced steel to produce guns, weapons, tanks, and airplane parts." [90]

Regarding the losses, Joe recalled,

"We knew it was going to be tough and it was. Thirty Canadians went to the Dams that night; sixteen survived." [91]

Of the nineteen aircraft that took off, eight failed to return. It is thought that four were shot down by light flak, one crashed after being damaged by the

Royal Canadian Air Force aircrew who returned from the Dams Raid Back Row: Steve Oancia, Fred Sutherland, Harry O'Brien, Ken Brown, Harvey Weeks, John Thrasher, George Deering, Bill Radcliffe, Don MacLean, Joe McCarthy, Grant MacDonald
Front Row: Percy Pigeon, Harlo Taerum, Revie Walker, Chester Gowrie, Dave Rodger.

explosion of its own Upkeep, two crashed after hitting electricity cables and one after striking a tree when its pilot was dazzled by a searchlight. Of the 56 crew members in these planes, 53 were killed and three became prisoners of war, two of them being badly injured.

One of those taken POW was F/Lt. Hopgood's Canadian bomb aimer, John Fraser who had parachuted from Hopgood's Lancaster shortly after it crossed the Möhne Dam and only seconds before it crashed.

Barnes Wallis, who had paced nervously during the night and held his head in his hands as the reports came in of Upkeeps delivered but the Möhne still standing, is said to have jumped for joy and thrown his hands in the air when word came in of the success. Later in the night however, he was heard to say that if he'd known so many aircrew would be lost he would not have embarked on the project.

According to Johnny Johnson,

"Barnes Wallis actually cried because he felt he was responsible for the loss of all those young men's lives. He wasn't of course; but that was the way he felt it. And it was pretty shattering to think we'd lost so many, and then to realise how lucky we had been to survive." [92]

In spite of his initial reaction to Wallis' idea, Arthur Harris was quick to congratulate him. In a telegram to Wallis, Harris wrote,

"But for your knowledge, skill and persistence, often in the face of discouragement and disappointment, in the design, production, and servicing of the equipment used in the destruction of the dams the efforts of our gallant crews would have been in vain. We in Bomber Command in particular and in the United Nations as a whole owe everything to you in the first place for the outstanding success achieved." [93]

The day after the raid Joseph Goebbels, Hitler's Minister of Propoganda, wrote in his diary,

"The war in the air dealt us heavy blows last night. The attack on the dams met with great success. Der Führer is completely broken up over the faulty defence installations and is very impatient." [94]

The eventual outcome of the war was very much in doubt during May 1943 and for a war-weary nation and Commonwealth, this daring strike by Bomber Command deep into the Nazi heartland was welcomed and celebrated. The impact of the Dams Raid on the morale of the Allied side was enormous. During a very trying time the daring exploits of Gibson and his crews fueled the imagination of those in Bomber Command and the public at large. The raid's audacity and innovativeness were widely celebrated.

Harris telephoned Chief of the Air Staff Portal and Prime Minister Churchill who were at a conference in Washington.

On 19 May, Churchill made the most of the success during an address delivered to the United States Congress and relayed live to the British Broadcasting Corporation saying,

"You have just read of the destruction of the great dams which feed the canals and provide power to the enemy's munition works. That was a gallant operation costing eight out of the nineteen Lancaster bombers employed but it will play a far-reaching part in reducing German military output." [95]

Whether Churchill or any of his audience in the Congress realised that one of the pilots on the raid was an American is not known.

On 24 May a number of decorations to be presented to 617 Squadron aircrew were announced. The Victoria Cross would be awarded to W/C Guy Gibson and 32 other decorations to members of his squadron. Joe would receive the Distinguished Service Order (DSO) to go with his DFC. Whereas the DFC is awarded only to air force officers, the DSO may be awarded for meritorious or distinguished service by officers in any of the armed forces during wartime, typically in actual combat.

His bomb aimer 'Johnny' Johnson and his navigator, Don MacLean, would both be awarded the Distinguished Flying Medal (DFM) as would Ken Brown's bomb aimer, Canadian Steve Oancia. Ken Brown would be awarded the Conspicuous Gallantry Medal (CGM).

During the King and Queen's visit to Scampton on 27 May, W/C Gibson presented his suggestion for the 617 Squadron crest which was eventually approved.

The following day's newspaper.

The Queen and Joe McCarthy. On 27 May King George and Queen Elizabeth visited Scampton to congratulate the crews.

617 Squadron aircrew line up for a photo shortly after the Dams Raid.

Part Six

617-A Special Duty Squadron

"There was a ladder that the crew's name went on and once you stayed in that group (at the top of the ladder) you could drop the heaviest bombs we had. So it was always a fight to stay on it. I never came off it."

Quiet Times and Changes

Although saddened by the losses, Arthur Harris was delighted with the success of the Dams Raid. He ordered that 617 be retained as a 'Special Duty Squadron' within 5 Group and that it continue to be manned by experienced crews and deliver sophisticated, specialized ordinance. The squadron flew no operations during the remainder of May nor in June although training flights continued.

On 2 June 1943 W/C Gibson went on leave and S/L David Maltby took temporary command of the squadron. Gibson was now a celebrated war-hero and both Harris and Cochrane decided he had done enough. They felt that they could not allow him to continue to lead the squadron and quite possibly be killed or what might be worse, be taken prisoner. Although Gibson remained in command at Scampton he never flew with 617 Squadron again.

Joe's notoriety as a member of the Dambusters may have attracted the attention of the United States Army Air Force. The squadron records show that on 4 June he travelled to London to meet with them. Perhaps the USAAF hoped that he might be convinced to join the American air force.

The squadron continued low-level training flights and during one of these on 9 June, Joe sighted a dinghy in the North Sea.

The occupants were a Beaufighter pilot and his navigator. Joe's navigator noted the

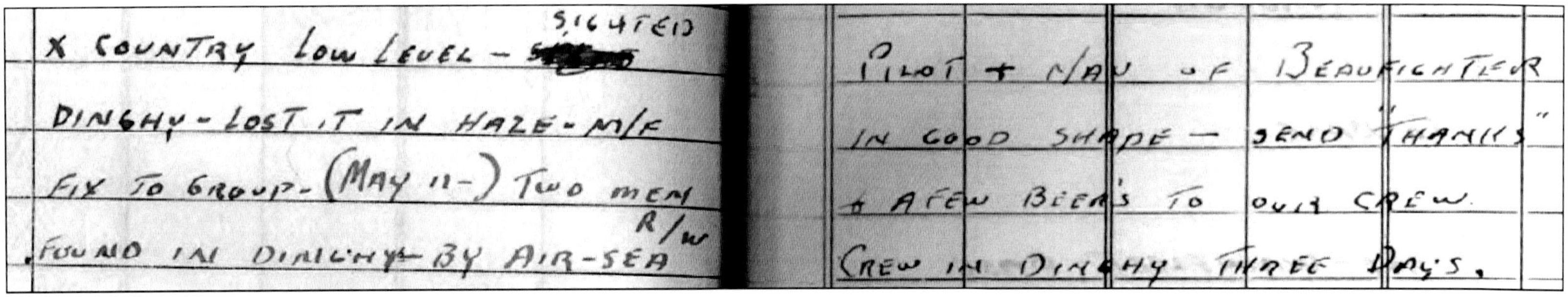
X COUNTRY LOW LEVEL - SIGHTED [redacted]
DINGHY - LOST IT IN HAZE - M/F
FIX TO GROUP - (MAY 11-) TWO MEN
FOUND IN DINGHY BY AIR-SEA R/W

PILOT + NAV OF BEAUFIGHTER
IN GOOD SHAPE - SEND "THANKS"
+ A FEW BEER'S TO OUR CREW.
CREW IN DINGHY THREE DAYS.

The references to the 9 June dinghy sighting and subsequent rescue from Joe's logbook.
The McCarthy Family

position and the following day the two were rescued after spending three days in the dinghy. 617 Squadron received a telephone call from the airmen, thanking Joe for his assistance.

On 21 June the 33 members of the squadron who were to be decorated for their rôles on the Dams Raid travelled to London. Much to everyone's surprise, it was the Queen who presented the medals at the investiture at Buckingham Palace the following day. Not normally shy by any means, Joe was said to have been somewhat overwhelmed when presented with his DSO. When the Queen took his massive hand in hers and asked about his home life in New York, it has been said that he could only mutter a few syllables in response.

Following the investiture, a party was hosted by A.V. Roe, the company that designed the Avro Lancaster. In addition to 617 Squadron members, Roy Chadwick, the designer of the Lancaster, and Barnes Wallis were present.

This period of time with no operations wasn't necessarily appreciated or enjoyed by the members of the squadron as Adjutant Humphries wrote,

"The boys didn't like it very much. Other squadrons were working night after night . . . The ground crews were beginning to be affected. They were fed-up with the inactivity, and finding it hard to face the jibes of their counterparts of the other squadrons. The 'One-op Squadron' gag was no longer funny." [1]

In early July S/L George W. Holden DSO DFC and Bar arrived at Scampton as C/O Designate of 617 Squadron. However W/C Gibson did not leave immediately as expected. Rather he spent a couple of weeks working with the new c/o and made arrangements for

Guy Gibson with RCAF airmen following the Investiture (l-r) Joe McCarthy, Revie Walker, Ken Brown, Guy Gibson, Steve Oancia, George Deering, Don MacLean, Harlo Taerum.

The post-Investiture party hosted by A.V. Roe Joe is near the front holding a glass of beer immediately above W/C Gibson's head.

W/C George W. Holden.
Imperial War Museum

his (Gibson's) crew to become W/C Holden's crew.

W/C Holden was an experienced bomber pilot having completed 45 operations. His operational career began as a Whitley pilot with 78 Squadron in September 1940. He went on to fly Halifaxes with 35 Squadron prior to becoming the commanding officer of 102 Squadron.

During this time new crews were arriving at Scampton to replace those lost during the Dams Raid. One was Bunny Clayton's crew. Bill 'Jock' Hume was Bunny's rear gunner. Bill was a Scotsman. He had trained at Carnarvon in Wales for six weeks and then, by-passing the normal training at an OTU, was posted directly to a squadron. "We're short of gunners," Bill was told. "You're going right to a squadron." Bill was well along in his tour when,

"After the Dams Raid 617 needed fresh crews so they picked them out and Bunny was one of them. So he said, 'I'll go on one condition; that I can take my crew with me.' They said, 'That's no problem.' So that day, boy, we were cleaned out of that station. We didn't even have to check out." [2]

When asked, "Did you want to go, even though they'd just lost all those crews?" Bill's immediate reply was, "Yeah. We never even queried it. We just said, 'Let's go.'"

Like the original Dams Raid crews, the new crews had to do low-level training. Bill recalled,

"We used to go over Lincolnshire at low-level, practicing. If there were low-level aircraft people used to report them-get their number. We were the only squadron that could go low-level and there were no questions. I used to like it. We'd be out there and there'd be someone out in their hay field with their horse and hay rake and they couldn't hear us coming. When you went over them the bloody horse was gone!" [3]

Sgt. Hume, who was a rookie on the squadron, remembered F/Lt. Joe McCarthy,

"Big Joe,-He was always talkative. He was a good guy. He'd always talk to you if you were in the crew room." [4]

To Italy and North Africa

During July 1943 the war in Italy was reaching a crucial phase. The Nazis were directing reinforcements and equipment to the south to try to hold off the invading Allied armies that were now in Sicily and poised to move north. Power supplies and the electric railway network were targeted by Bomber Command.

Rather than fly to the Italian targets and return to base as Joe had done with 97 Squadron, this time the Lancasters would fly southwest after bombing and land at Blida, twenty miles southwest of Algiers, in North Africa. Joe's first post-Dams Raid operation was set for 15 July.

The Battle Order for the operation showed W/C Gibson as 'Officer in Charge of Night Flying.' S/L Maltby and S/L Holden would be leading the squadron. Gibson was not pleased with this and according to Adjutant Humphries,

"He gave all the boys a cheery goodbye prior to take off, but shortly afterwards said, 'If there's anything I hate Adj. it's watching other people go to war. I like the idea of going to America, but I'd sooner bloody well fly with my own squadron.'" [5]

Gibson was going to the United States and Canada with none other than the Prime Minister who would be meeting with Stalin and Roosevelt at Quebec City to make plans for the invasion of Europe. Churchill had earlier referred to Gibson as his 'Dam Buster,' thus coining the term.

Following the conference Gibson went on a gruelling, four month tour that saw him visit the United States and make speeches at BCATP schools all across Canada.

Arthur Harris wrote that upon his return, Gibson was,

". . . put on his Group's staff. A few days later he was found in his office with; literally; tears in his eyes at being separated from his beloved crews and unable to go on operations. It was in fact breaking his heart. He always had direct access to me, and upon further pressure from him and his AOC I quite wrongly allowed him to return to operations. He appointed himself 'Master Bomber' on his last operation, which was of course a complete success. He was heard to give his crews a pat on the back over the radio and then started homeward. He never returned." [6]

Joe and eleven other 617 Squadron Lancasters and twelve from other squadrons took off late in the evening of 15 July and flew across France and over the Alps to attack two electric power plants just north of Milan. Joe and five of the 617 Squadron aircraft led by S/L Maltby bombed the transformer station at San Polo D'Enza at 3:30 am, dropping 6000 pounds of high explosive and 360 pounds of incendiaries from just 800 feet. Although Joe noted that "Hazy conditions made accurate bombing impossible," blue flames were seen as Joe's bombs exploded. He also reported that, "Nose of aircraft hit by shrapnel from one of our own bombs."

Although the operation was considered a moderate success, it was the opinion of the pilots was that flares should have been carried. As Joe put it, "If we'd had some flares with us we might have been able to see what we were doing."

The aircraft continued on to Blida, Joe landing at 7:45 am after being airborne for over nine hours and twenty minutes. He made two more similar trips that month and he and the crews were able to enjoy the benefits of the somewhat exotic nature of Blida, including dinner that evening at a French restaurant. Fruits, vegetables, and wine that were unheard of in wartime Britain were readily available along the Mediterranean coast.

The RAF members stationed at Blida were assisting in the planning of the Italian operations. Although there were some benefits to their posting, they were somewhat deprived as well and pleased that the Lancasters had been loaded with kegs of beer as well as bombs prior to leaving Scampton.

Lancasters in the North African desert.

This was Bunny Clayton's first operation with 617 Squadron and rear gunner Bill Hume recalled an experience he had in Blida,

"We had a ball. Coming back we were loaded with groceries, bringing stuff back from the guys that were there. When we were there the skipper came up and said, 'Bill, you've got to go to the Medical Officer.' I said, 'Now what have I done?' He said, 'Oh you'll find out.' I went into the Medical Officer and it was Jim Trainor, the doctor from my home town in Kelso, southeast of Edinburgh. He says, 'Will you do me a favour Bill? Take this home to the wife.' It was three or four pairs of silk stockings." [7]

As Joe Jr. relates there weren't just groceries in Joe's Lancaster when it returned to Scampton,

"On one of Dad's trips to Blida, a Canadian soldier came up to him. The soldier had found out that the pilot of one of the bombers was a Canadian and he asked Dad if he could fly back to England with him. Dad told him that they couldn't do that; for one reason they would be doing a bombing trip on the way back and taking passengers along on a combat flight likely wasn't permitted. The soldier really wanted to get back to England. He had a month's leave but if he'd gone by a shipping convoy that would have likely taken two weeks and then he'd just have to turn around and come back again. Dad tried to talk him out of it but then finally relented.

They scrounged up a parachute and some warm flying clothes and the guy came back to England with him. The soldier thanked Dad very much after they landed. Somehow, Dad snuck him off of the base and told him to keep his mouth shut. Dad, of course, made no logbook entry regarding his passenger.

Soon after the war, Dad was in Detroit visiting my Mom's family. While there, the family loaded up their car with various things that a recently married couple with a new baby would need, some of which were not readily available in post-war Canada.

When they reached the border, the Canadian Customs agent took a look at the packed car and directed Dad, 'Over there' for a thorough inspection. As the agents were going through the trunk, one noticed Dad's air force cap and asked if he was in the air force. Dad said, 'Yes'

and the agent asked to see his leave papers. So Dad dug out his leave papers. The agent looked at the leave papers and looked at Dad. Then he asked to see his I.D. card.

All of a sudden the agent stopped, looked at Dad and asked, 'Where were you?' In England, with Bomber Command,' Dad replied. 'Did you ever go to North Africa? the agent asked. Dad said, 'Yeah, we had a couple of trips through there.'

"Well, it turns out this was the soldier that Dad brought back. So Dad and the agent sat down and talked for about twenty minutes. The agent finally asked, 'What are you doing with all this stuff?' Joe explained about setting up a home in Canada and having a new son. Then the agent stood up and said, 'I'll tell you what. Just get in the car and go but don't tell anybody!' So Dad hopped in the car and off we went." [8]

The twelve 617 Lancasters didn't leave Blida until 24 July after spending eight days on the Mediterranean coast. During the return flight S/L Holden led the squadron as they attacked the dock and harbour installations at Leghorn, about 180 miles northwest of Rome. Despite heavy cloud and haze, Joe reported, "Identified built-up area by light of flares; Bombs seen to burst oil storage dump north of town; Large clouds of black smoke given off."

Adjutant Humphries recalled the squadron's aircrafts' return to Scampton,

"I met the machines at their dispersal points. I found it hard to believe my eyes. Piled against each Lancaster there were many items we had not seen for a long time; oranges, onions, and dates were abundant. Heated discussions were in progress as to ownership." [9]

The ground crews back at Scampton weren't forgotten either as Harold Roddis recalled,

"We were given one crate of oranges to share between us. My share was about fifteen or twenty oranges. I hadn't seen an orange since before the war and I ate the lot in about two days. This I found was an extremely stupid thing to do as they worked as an efficient laxative, so I was never without 'The Daily Mirror' and it wasn't for the news it contained." [10]

There was a second trip to Africa planned for 29 July and according to Adjutant Humphries,

"There was plenty of competition amongst the crews to appear on the Battle Order. Those who had already visited Africa wanted to go again, and those who had not yet been, were curious to see the country." [11]

This was to be a 'nickel' raid. These involved the dropping of propaganda leaflets and generally were not the crews' favourites. At this point in the war the Italians were close to revolting against Mussolini and the pamphlets were designed to encourage them to end their country's rôle in the war as an ally to the Nazis. Joe apparently did not see the benefit to the dropping of leaflets and referred to this operation as, "Like selling god-damned newspapers."

Joe was to deliver his leaflets to Bologna as seven other squadron aircraft dropped theirs over Milan, Genoa, and Turin. With no moon finding the targets was difficult but all were successful except for Joe who was unable to locate Bologna and spread his over Milan instead. The Lancasters again landed at Blida. Joe's aircraft required servicing and he didn't return to Scampton until 5 August; but with a load of fresh fruit and wine.

During August the squadron moved to a different base. Scampton was simply a grass field and it was thought that this was not sufficient for what was being planned for 617 Squadron. Nearby Coningsby had recently been upgraded with concrete runways and other improvements and it was decided that the squadron should move there and share the base with 619 Squadron. The move was completed on 30 August.

The Dortmund Ems Canal

Soon after their arrival at Coningsby it became apparent that 617 Squadron was being readied for another special operation. W/C Holden was seen holding meetings with civilians and service personnel who were not known to those on the squadron. Then heavy trucks were seen arriving at the bomb dump laden with huge, ominous looking shapes covered by tarpaulins. As well, a flight of Mosquito aircraft from a night fighter squadron arrived on the airfield. Training involved low-flying Lancasters accompanied by Mosquitos roaring across the Lincolnshire countryside.

A 12,000 pound high-explosive bomb as used on the Dortmund Ems Canal raids.

This operation was to be an attack on the Dortmund Ems Canal with the newly designed 12,000 pound high-capacity bombs that were simply three 4000 pound 'cookies' bolted together. This thin-case weapon was not a Barnes Wallis design and was to explode on the surface. The Lancaster, with its single, 22 foot long bomb bay, was the only aircraft capable of carrying the weapon.

The Dortmund Ems Canal was a critical part of Germany's system of inland waterways and part of the only shipping link between the Ruhr industrial area in western Germany and the Baltic and North Seas. Although only 12.5 feet deep and 100 feet wide, it carried hundreds of millions of tons of freight to and from the Ruhr factories including iron ore from Sweden.

The operation required careful planning as the enemy realised the importance of the canal and the vulnerable sections of it were heavily defended.

Bomber Command's plan was for the canal to be breached by placing these huge bombs at regular intervals in the relatively soft material that formed the side of the canal at a point where it was elevated. After delayed action fuses exploded the bombs, the breaches made by the detonations would join together forming a gaping hole in the side of the waterway which would then drain into the lower level adjacent countryside. The weapons had to be placed within forty feet of the canal. The success of the low-level attack depended on this level of accuracy. Good visibility (moonlight) was required. The attack would take place on 14 September near Greven where the canal divided into two branches.

The force of eight Lancasters was divided into two groups of four, each with three Mosquitos as escorts to deal with flak and searchlights.

Joe was not on the Battle Order.

While the force was crossing the English Channel at low level, a weather reconnaissance Mosquito flying ahead of the main force reported fog over the target and the force was recalled. While turning at low-level S/L Maltby's wing tip is thought to have touched the water and he spun into the sea.

Fred Sutherland, Les Knight's front gunner, was on the raid. He remembered,

"We all thought that he'd (Maltby) gotten into somebody's slipstream and when you're flying that low you don't have any hope at all. Dave Shannon circled around until the air-sea rescue guys came but they only found Maltby's body. We had to carry the bomb back so we had to land with all this weight." [12]

The following night eight Lancasters were again sent to attack the Dortmund Ems Canal. It would be the blackest day in the history of 617 Squadron. Adjutant Humphries wrote,

Adjutant Harry Humphries in 1943

"After take off, I watched the eight Lancasters take up position and fly across the airfield in tight formation. They were rather difficult to see for the night was dark, but with lights on their wings and tails it was just possible to discern the silhouettes against the night sky. 'I watched the lights disappear out of sight and then decided to go back to my office and work for a while. When I entered the door I saw I had two visitors, Big Joe McCarthy and Les Munro. They both looked as miserable as sin.

"'What the devil is the matter with you two?' I asked.

"Munro merely grunted. Joe was more exciteable. 'Just to think I have to sit around and twiddle my God-damn thumbs while the boys are out. It sure burns me up.'

"Les and Joe were both 'ace' pilots (but neither were on the Battle Order that night). Joe was in charge of night flying.

"Joe heaved his huge bulk out of my chair. 'I'm going to sit over in the watch office,' he said. 'Are either of you two coming?' 'I hadn't intended to leave the office for some time but I felt like company and I knew I should get first hand information if I joined forces with these two. So off we went." [13]

Fred Sutherland.
Rob Taerum

It is said that Joe hated bureaucracy and anything from ground staff that smacked of a lack of appreciation of the risks that the aircrew took every night they went out. Prior to the aircraft departing that day Joe had heard a WAAF officer comment, "My God, I hope they get there tonight. The trouble the AOC's gone to over this."

Joe silenced her with a snarl, "The hell with you and all the AOCs. What about the seven lives in every kite!" and stormed off.

Fred Sutherland was on both trips to the Dortmund Ems Canal. He described what happened during the second,

"The next night we were back again. We had this new guy, S/L Holden. He just came off high-level. He had never flown low-level. So the first thing we did was we crossed into Germany and went over a small town. Instead of staying down and going around the church steeple, he went up to about a thousand feet. The story is that Martin and everybody else stayed down low but that's not true. When Holden went up, we all went up. Holden was in front of us and he got hit and he made a flamer. He went in front of us. We were on the port side and a guy called Wilson was behind us and Martin was on our starboard side. There were four in the formation. When they shot Holden down he just went like a torch. He went right in front of us (Fred was in the front turret so he had

Dortmund
Ems Canal
(Ladbergen)
KS. 1578

Opposite: A wartime photo of the Dortmund Ems Canal.

an excellent view). You could see the flames coming up between the ailerons. Then Wilson got shot down shortly after that. He went down in flames. The rear gunner said, 'There goes Jimmy Wilson.' So there were two of us left, Martin and Knight." [14]

The visibility was very poor with low cloud over the target as the airmen attempted to spot the stretch of canal that was targetted and the road bridge they had as their marker. They had to fly at about 150 feet to have any chance of seeing it and then when they did, they were right on top of it so there was no chance of a proper run. There were light flak emplacements guarding the canal as well. F/O Harold Hobday, the navigator, describes what happened to Les Knight's Lancaster,

Les Knight.
Fred Sutherland

"Unfortunately our pilot was looking to see if he could see the target. Suddenly Johnny (F/O Edward Johnson), who was the bomb-aimer in the front of our aircraft, said, 'Pull-up.' Les Knight pulled up because we were aiming straight for some trees on a little hill. Well we brushed the trees and two of the engines were damaged and the tail." [15]

Fred continues,

"There was a heavy ground fog in the target area and we could not see the ground or the canal. The next thing we saw were about three coniferous trees sticking out of the mist. Too late to climb, we knocked the radiators off the two port engines and damaged the air frame which made the a/c very hard to control.

"Les asked Mickey Martin, 'Can I drop this bomb safe?' Martin said, 'Oh yes, go ahead Les.' We were staggering back but the airframe was twisted. As well, we'd lost the coolant out of two motors so they had to feather those. Then the starboard motors started to heat up too. Harry O'Brien, the rear gunner, was asked to come forward and help pull on the rudder pedals from the bomb aimer's compartment. O'Brien was the largest and strongest person on the crew. I was asked to go the rear and help the mid-upper gunner throw guns and ammunition down the flare chute. We were just kind of staggering through the sky. It was really scary.

"We got back to Holland near a little place called Den Ham. I was throwing stuff down the chute and it looked like we were over the water so I said, 'Les, are we going to ditch?' He said, 'Yeah, get ready.' So I pulled out the black-out curtain and I looked down and we were over land so I asked, 'Are we bailing out or what?' He says, 'Yeah, jump.' So that's how close it was. I went out the rear door. There's not much room because you have to go out low or you hit the tailplane. I skinned my knees on the door. I was so scared. I was going to get out. I wasn't going to hit the tailplane. We were at about a thousand feet.

Les could not leave the controls or it would have gone straight in. So he held it steady so the rest of his crew could jump. He tried to land in a pasture and was doing fine when he hit a ditch and his neck was broken." [16]

Les Knight, like many other heroic Bomber Command pilots, had kept the aircraft flying and under control long enough for his crew to escape.

Upon landing, Fred and the five other survivors from his aircraft,

. . . met up with some Dutchmen right away. They were really tremendous, lots of courage because if they got caught with us they were dead. They kept us in barns for about a month." [17]

Two were captured but Fred and four others were assisted by the Dutch and later the French Resistance. Two and a half months later, after travelling across occupied France, over the Pyrenees, and through Spain, Fred reached Gibraltar.

But that wasn't the end of it for 617 Squadron that night. As F/Lt. Wilson flew low over the target his Lancaster was hit by flak. He made a belly landing but all eight airmen were killed. F/Lt. Allsebrook dropped his bomb and then directed two others to the target. Then he was shot down and all aboard were killed.

The aircraft piloted by Mickey Martin and Dave Shannon were both able to locate and bomb the target, but Martin spent ninety minutes trying. On the thirteenth circuit over the target he released his bomb. It missed by just a few feet and landed in the canal, throwing up a huge water spout.

Dave Shannon spent seventy minutes attempting to bomb. He too was just a few feet off target and the bomb exploded on the canal's tow-path. Neither Martin nor Shannon caused significant damage to the canal.

P/O Rice spent over an hour in the area but could not identify the target. After being badly damaged by flak he jettisoned his bomb safely.

Back at Coningsby Adj. Humphries was on the balcony of the tower as Joe was receiving reports from the aircraft,

"An hour or two must have passed when McCarthy came rushing out onto the balcony.

"'We've lost George Holden, Adj.,' he panted. 'Shot down just over the German frontier, a place called Nordhorn.'

"I just said, 'Good God,' and added 'that takes care of most of Gibby's crew, Mac.'

"'Yeah, I know,' said the big American, 'Poor old Spam (P/O Fred Spafford had been Gibson's bomb aimer on the Dams Raid). He said 'Poor old Spam,' because in all instances like this, one thought of one's personal friends first."

"Joe continued, 'I reckon we are going to take a beating tonight. Les Knight signalled back that he was in trouble; lost two engines. He is going to try and return to base on the other two. I haven't much hope somehow. It's a damn long way on four, never mind about two.'

"Eventually Mac left me and went in search of further information in his capacity as Officer-in-Charge of Night Flying." [18]

The raid had been a total disaster. After losing Maltby and his crew the previous night, the squadron had lost five of eight aircraft, including its Commanding Officer's. 41 aircrew had been killed, two became Prisoners of War and five, including Fred Sutherland, successfully evaded. Martin, Shannon, and Rice made it back, but their Lancasters were all heavily damaged.

With the exception of the flight engineer, W/C Holden's crew had been the airmen that flew on the Dams Raid with Guy Gibson. It must have been devastating for Joe to lose so many of his friends over the two nights, particularly when he was not flying with them.

617 Squadron had now lost fourteen of the 21 crews originally on strength when the squadron was formed just four months earlier.

AVM Cochrane immediately promoted Mickey Martin to the rank of Squadron Leader and acting commanding officer of the squadron.

The Antheor Viaduct today.
Ian Leech

The Antheor Viaduct

Despite the losses 617 Squadron went to war the following night (16 September) and this time Joe McCarthy's name was on the Battle Order. The target was the Antheor Railway Viaduct on the south coast of France near Cannes. 540 feet long and 185 feet high, it is built on a curve and made up of nine arches. The structure carried a double-tracked railway that moved an estimated 14,400 tons of military supplies to Italy and directly to the Italian front each day.

619 Squadron shared the Coningsby station with 617 Squadron and as the latter was so depleted, six 619 Squadron aircraft joined Joe and five others from his squadron to attack the viaduct. The raid was led by W/C Abercromby, the officer commanding 619 Squadron. Conventional 1000 pound bombs were to be used.

Visibility was excellent and the target was located easily. Bunny Clayton had icing problems and had to jettison his bombs and return early, but the other aircraft all bombed the target and opposition was negligible.

Joe reported making one dummy run and then dropping his bombs from 300 feet on his second pass over the viaduct.

However, only minor damage was caused and the railway was said to have been repaired within 24 hours. One of the 619 Squadron Lancasters was struck by flak and ditched in the Atlantic Ocean off of Porto, Portugal. The crew was very fortunate as they were rescued by fishermen. It is not known why the aircraft was so far off course.

However the main force did not go directly back to Scampton as Joe recalled,

"I went back across southern France and over Bordeaux, over the Atlantic, and up to Land's End. What had happened was the winds were completely reversed. We were coming back short of fuel and they (the pilots returning from the raid) were screaming all over the country (on the radio) that they had no more fuel and wanted to land." [19]

Joe landed at Predannack in Cornwall after being airborne for ten hours.

The heavy losses that the squadron had sustained on the Dams Raid and the Dortmund Ems operation combined with the lack of success on both the Dortmund Ems and Antheor Viaduct attacks led to a reconsideration of 617 Squadron's rôle and tactics.

Arthur Harris and others concluded that low-level attacks with heavy bombers, even when away from heavily defended areas, were too risky and these types of operations were suspended. The squadron now began training as a special high altitude bombing unit and the developing technology in this area would hopefully lead to more successful results.

617 Squadron was to be rejuvenated with new crews, new tactics, and a new commanding officer, Leonard Cheshire. It would be over three months before Joe would fly another operation.

Joe and "Uncle Chuck-Chuck" nose art at Coningsby in September 1943. "U for Uncle" was Lancaster DV246 and was brand new when Joe first flew it on 6 September 1943.
The McCarthy Family

uncle chuck chuck

Opposite: The nose art on DV246 depicted Joe's British/American connection. Note the American flag on the panda's hat, the Union Jack on his shirt, the Churchill cigar, and the Roosevelt cigarette holder.
Nose art replica painting by Clarence Simonsen

The SABS

The Stabilizing Automatic Bomb Sight (SABS) was a precision instrument that had been under development for some time. It was designed to provide greater accuracy from high altitude than the Mk. XIV/T-1 bomb sight that was being used by the bomb aimers during this period of the war.

In conjuction with this more advanced bomb sight, Barnes Wallis was designing new bombs that would require very accurate placement. The new bomb sight was now ready to be introduced into operational service and the new bombs would be ready within a few months.

A Stabilizing Automatic Bomb Sight in the bomb aimer's perspex dome of a 617 Squadron Lancaster.
Imperial War Museum

The SABS was stabilized by a gyroscope and incorporated a complex mechanical computer that was able to calculate its own wind corrections which the Mk. XIV/T-1 could not. After generating automatic aiming instructions for the bomb aimer, the SABS was then able to automatically release the bomb. These were qualities it shared with the American designed Norden bomb sight.

A number of factors had to be precisely measured prior to being utilized within the bombsight to attain the accuracy required. The aircraft's groundspeed, airspeed, and altitude had to be determined and, as well, the outside air temperature at the point of release was critical. This indirectly indicated air density and an error of one degree celsius would result in a bombing error of 21 feet. It was found that obtaining this measurement was not a simple matter as air passing over a thermometer creates heat by friction. However a system was devised to determine an accurate temperature.

As the target was approached the pilot had to hold his exact course for about ten miles while the flight engineer manipulated the throttles to maintain a constant speed. This need to fly straight and level ruled out any evasive action leaving the aircraft vulnerable to radar-predicted flak and fighter attacks during the bomb run.

As soon as the bomb aimer had the sight's cross hairs on the target he clicked a switch and the SABS used its gyroscopes to assist in the tracking the target. It was found that considerable practice was required by the bomb aimers to maintain accuracy.

Johnny Johnson, Joe's bomb aimer, described using the SABS as follows,

"You set on height and groundspeed and you then manipulated the target light with a couple of handles so that you got it in line with the target and as the target came into the light these two points on the bombsight came together and the bomb was released." [20]

Joe described the instrument that he used in the cockpit so that he could fly the aircraft to the release point that was determined by the SABS,

"There was a little thing in front of my eyes with a zero, and then there was 1, 2, 3, and 5 on the left and 1, 2, 3, and 5 on the right and this needle would go back and forth. Now wherever that needle was, it meant that I had to bring that needle back (to zero)." [21]

The SABS was a much more complex sight to use and to maintain than the Mk. XIV/T1 and required many more man-hours to manufacture. Its success was said to have been largely due to S/L Don Richardson who joined 617 Squadron during August 1943 in order to train the crews to use the new device.

S/L Richardson became known as, 'Talking Bomb.' It was said that he spoke of nothing else but the SABS from dawn until dusk. He flew on eight raids in order to watch his bomb sights in operation. For all the other squadrons in Bomber Command, the Mk. XIV/T1 was quite adequate for their operations.

The accuracy that 617 Squadron was able to attain with the SABS was truly remarkable. Their bombs were generally dropped from 18,000 feet while flying at a speed of 200 mph and several miles back from the target. From that height and distance even the white square on the bombing range looked like the size of a pin-head.

Although it was claimed during the war that an American bombardier using the Norden

Bomb Sight could drop a bomb into a 'pickle barrel' from six miles up, this was of course a myth. USAAF bombardiers were never able to match the accuracy developed by 617 Squadron's bomb aimers using the SABS.

In fact, as Joe recalled,

"Now the Americans with the Norden sight said that they could put a bomb in a pickle barrel but this was crazy. They came to visit us when they started bombing, Eaker and another two (Lt. General Ira Eaker was the Commanding Officer of the United States Eighth Air Force which was the American's bomber force based in Britain). They visited us and watched what we were doing and watched us bomb. They were amazed at the consistency; 75 yards or less from 20,000 feet.

"Somebody made a caustic remark about this pickle barrel bombing and I think it was Cheshire who said, 'Well, let's have a competition. We'll put up three crews and you put up three crews and we'll see who comes out the best.' They wouldn't do it." [22]

The SABS provided a focus for Joe and the other airmen as the squadron was being rebuilt during this difficult time. At the same time Barnes Wallis was working on the special weapons that 617 would use with great success in conjunction with the new bomb sight.

Leonard Cheshire takes Command

At 25 years of age, Leonard Cheshire had become the youngest Group Captain in the Royal Air Force and had been given command of RAF Station Marston Moor. He had completed two tours of operations and been awarded a DSO and Bar and a DFC. He also had an honours degree in law and was married to an American film star. Cheshire was well on his way to becoming a legend as one of the greatest pilots and leaders in Bomber Command history.

The job at Marston Moore was not to his liking. Like many others in similar situations, he longed to return to operational flying and when the opportunity came to take command of 617 Squadron he was more than willing to have his rank reduced to Wing Commander in order that he could take the position.

Leonard Cheshire.

617 Squadron Adjutant Humphries recalled his impression of Cheshire,

"You couldn't help but like this pleasant, slim ex-Varsity man. He always will remain in my mind as the perfect RAF officer. He knew how to get the very best out of everyone with the least possible effort. His manner of obtaining this maximum efficiency with minimum effort was by setting a perfect example himself, both in the air and on the ground. A born leader, I suppose." [23]

For two days after his arrival on the squadron the C/Os driver, a young lady of the Women's Auxiliary Air Force (WAAF), became upset after having watched W/C Cheshire walk by when she was parked outside his office with nothing to do. Finally she knocked on his office door and introduced herself. She was shocked when he confessed that he didn't know he had a car at his disposal. It was said to have been typical of him, never taking for granted what lesser men demanded.

Others have referred to Cheshire as quiet with an irrepressible, bubbling sense of humour and a ruthless determination to go to war.

Cheshire took command of the squadron on 10 November 1943 and it is said he brought direction and purpose and set it on a path towards operational success.

Joe recalled Cheshire's arrival and the squadron's focus at that time,

"Cheshire took over the squadron after Gibson. He got very enthusiastic and tried to get us going. We were at the stage of training on this high-level bomb sight which was a pain in the ass. We'd rather have been fighting the war than fighting the battle of small practice bombs. So we used to do a lot of things like hitch-hike across to the coast and back again.

"We had exercises where they'd drop us off and they wouldn't tell us where they had taken us. You couldn't see out of the bus. It was all blacked out and you had to try to sneak back home to base. They'd alerted the home guard and army units to look out for us. I was with Shannon, my buddy. When they dropped us off, we knew what direction they had taken us so we had an idea. There was enough daylight for us to see.

We took off in a hurry cutting across country and wound up in this town that we were heading for. "There was a fellow there that Dave knew. He was a country farmer but he was a doctor or something of that nature but he was a gentleman farmer. He had a big spread. We snuck into town just at dusk so the local police wouldn't see us and there he was. We sneaked in and we told him the story.

"So we hung out with him. We were drinking all the time. We had damn good whiskey, good food, and everything else. Finally he drove us back. Everybody else had been back for two days and they were waiting for us. We never did tell them what had happened, but Cheshire knew damn well." [24]

All the training was paying off however and it soon became obvious that the SABS bomb sight would improve bombing accuracy dramatically and it did. Joe recalled,

"We had an average error of 75 yards or less from 20,000 feet. There was a ladder that the crew's name went on and once you stayed in that group (at the top of the ladder) you could drop the heaviest bombs we had. So it was always a fight to stay on it. I never came off it. Those were the things that were very important to us. The crews coming in just couldn't figure out how we could do it." [25]

12,000 Pounders from High-Level

The new SABS bomb sight was used for the first time on the night of 11/12 November when 617 made a second attack on the railway viaduct at Antheor. The crews were at less risk because with the new bomb sight the attack could be made from higher altitude, out of range of the small calibre flak guns that had extracted such a heavy toll during the previous raid two months earlier.

This was also the first time that 12,000 pound high-capacity (thin-walled) 'cookies' were dropped from high altitude. S/L Mickey Martin led ten Lancasters to the viaduct but from the bombing altitude of 7000 to 8000 feet most of the crews could not distinguish the target. Four bombed but the closest bomb struck 180 feet away and caused no serious damage. Four new searchlights and a half a dozen additional anti-aircraft guns had been deployed in the Antheor Viaduct area but despite this, all the Lancasters that attacked the viaduct landed safely at Blida in North Africa.

The crews that were unable to see the viaduct bombed a railway bridge embankment near Cannes but, frustratingly, there were only near-misses. Sadly, a week later F/Lt. Youseman and crew were lost

A 617 Squadron Lancaster about to be loaded with a 12,000 pound high-explosive bomb as used on high-level raids.

without a trace while flying over the sea while returning from North Africa.

This raid began to make it clear that it would be necessary to have accurate target marking to hit this type of small, specialized target.

Leonard Cheshire led his first raid as the new c/o of the squadron on 16 December. The target was a bit of a mystery at the time; a series of structures that looked like ski-jumps. They were all menacingly pointed towards London. Aerial reconnaissance and the network of informants that had been established throughout occupied Europe were suggesting the existence of secret weapons with which Hitler intended to make devastating attacks on the cities of southern England.

This would be the first Bomber Command operation against targets related to the V-1 Flying Bomb. The first of three un-manned 'vengeance' weapons developed by the Nazis, the V-1 was launched from a firing tube built onto an inclined 160 foot long ramp. Once airborne it navigated

V-1 Flying Bomb shortly after launch.

A portion of a V-1 launch ramp preserved at Watten, France.
Clare Bennett

its way to the target by means of a pre-set guidance system. Some 35,000 were built of which 9000 were successfully launched against Britain. Each delivered almost 2000 pounds of explosive and the weapon had a maximum range of 160 miles.

Nine Lancasters attacked the site near Flixecourt with 12,000 pound bombs that were released from 12,000 to 14,000 feet. The target area measured 900 feet by 750 feet and consequently demanded a very high level of accuracy. Target markers were placed by an OBOE equipped Pathfinder Mosquito but they were 1050 feet from the target. The bombs were accurately delivered with an average bombing error of only 280 feet and two bombs hitting within ninety feet of the mis-placed marker. Unfortunately, the target was left untouched.

Following this raid, and others where the 617 pilots felt that the target marking was not accurate enough, Cheshire and Mickey Martin began advocating that the only way to take advantage of the SABS and their squadron's precise bombing capability was to have the squadron mark its own targets from low-level rather than having the Pathfinders do it for them from high-level.

The Tempsford Detachment

Adjutant Humphries received a telephone call from W/C Cheshire in early December,

"'Special call from Tempsford, Adj. Four Crews. They will be McCarthy, Clayton, Weedon, and Bull. Detachment will last for approximately a week. Will you make all the arrangements?'

'I said, 'Yes Sir,' and as if in answer to my unspoken question he said, 'I don't know much more than that myself, I'll tell Joe McCarthy. He'll be O/C (Officer Commanding) for the detachment.'" [26]

RAF Tempsford in Bedfordshire, was perhaps the most secret Royal Air Force airfield during World War II. Its rôle was unique in that it specialized, not in dropping bombs, but rather in dropping off and supporting secret agents and the resistance forces in occupied Europe.

During March 1942, 138 Squadron began operations from Tempsford flying Whitleys, Halifaxes, and Lysanders. The following month they were joined by 161 Squadron with Whitleys and Lysanders. It appears that these squadrons were committed to other operations and 617 was to help out because of their experience with low-level operations.

Joe and the three other 617 crews flew to Tempsford on 9 December. Sixteen ground crew were detailed as well

Bill Hume was F/Lt. Clayton's rear-gunner and referred to Tempsford as, "a 'hush-hush' place. There were military police all over the place."

The Lancasters took off from Tempsford the following night to drop ammunition, arms, and other supplies near the village of Doullens, 24 miles north of Amiens. The trip was predicted to be relatively easy because enemy fighters or flak guns were not expected to be in the area. However what is now thought to have been in the area was a mobile enemy anti-aircraft battery mounted on a railway car. The operation went very badly as Adj. Humphries wrote,

"The first intimation I had that something had in fact happened was when Joe McCarthy landed back at base a few days later. He came into my office quietly, and dumped a couple of kit bags on the floor.

'Weeden's and Bull's kit,' he said. 'They've had it.'

Control Tower at RAF Tempsford.

"'Had it, Joe? When?'

"'Last night. We operated on a special low-level attack. Dropping arms and ammunition. They must have hit trouble. . .'

"Just as he said this, Sergeant Heveron came in from the orderly room, and handed me a couple of signals. He began to say 'Weeden . . .' I nodded.

"'Alright Sergeant, I know." On seeing McCarthy the sergeant realised my source of information.

"'Should I carry out the usual procedure sir?'

"'Yes please,' I nodded.

'Joe carried on where he had left off. 'I have got to go back to Tempsford,' he said. 'The remaining two of us may have to finish the job.'" [27]

This plaque honouring those such as Joe and the other 617 aircrew who flew from Tempsford has been placed on a brick barn that still stands on the former airfield.

W/O R. Cummings.

Of the three Lancasters on the operation, two did not return. W/O Bull was struck by flak as he flew at low-level over the dropping point. With one wing on fire he succeeded in reaching an altitude of about 800 feet to give his crew a chance to bale out, albeit at extremely low level. Five of the crew survived but the wireless operator and rear gunner failed to get out in time and were killed in the crash.

F/O Weeden, an RCAF pilot, and his crew were not as fortunate. They were also struck by flak at low-level and all were killed including two RCAF crewmembers. WO2 Robert Cummings was, like Joe, an American serving with the RCAF. The aircraft they were flying was Lancaster ED825, the aircraft Joe McCarthy flew on the Dams Raid.

Bill Hume was aboard F/Lt. Clayton's Lancaster. His recollections describe their fortunate escape,

'It was low-level, we dropped from fifty feet. We didn't see them (the two other aircraft) get hit but I saw the fire coming up from the ground. We were going low and I was looking out and I could see and hear

the guns, 'th, th, th.' We were at about fifty to 100 feet. That bloody train or whatever it was in the right place at the right time. I could see them running around." [28]

W/O R. Bull and his crew.

The German gunners were either very lucky or they must have known that the planes would be flying over Doullens that night. One of the Resistance fighters waiting for the arms drop was Jean Tillwait who recalled,

"My job was to try to support the arms for the Resistance cells; rifles, revolvers, and grenades. There were traitors everywhere. It is possible that a traitor warned the Germans about the arms drop that night and they were waiting to shoot the planes down." [29]

It appears that for some reason Joe didn't fly on this operation. Of the three that did, two were shot down. Adj. Humphries wrote what Joe knew as well,

"The loss of Weeden and Bull on this particular job made me think more than ever how a bomber crew's life depended on the flip of a coin." [30]

On 12 December, F/Lt. Ken Brown, who had attacked the Sorpe Dam with Joe, and P/O N.R. Ross flew from Coningsby to join the Detachment at Tempsford. Together with Joe and F/Lt. Clayton, a second sortie was flown to France on 20 December although it is not known whether it was to the Doullens area again. As with the first one, the target could not be located. The operation was abandoned and the crews returned to Tempsford with the badly needed supplies.

The Tempsford Detachment returned to Coningsby the following day.

Attacking the "Ski-sites" and the Low-Level Marking Idea

Joe's next operation, his fortieth, was on 22 December and it was his first flying Lancaster ME559. This would become 'his' aircraft and Joe and his crew would fly it on a total of thirteen operations.

The target was a V-1 site in France between Abbeville and Amiens. A conventional bomb load of fourteen 1000 pound bombs was taken. Cloud obscured the target and prevented the raid from proceeding. Joe reported that the 'PFF failed' and the squadron returned to Coningsby with their bombs still on board, Joe on three engines. Geoff Rice, one of the founding pilots of 617 Squadron, was struck by flak at 14,000 feet during his return. F/Lt. Rice was the only survivor and evaded for four months before being captured after he was reported to the Germans while at Antwerp.

Joe's logbook entries for operations were made in red ink. Interestingly, following his "PFF failed" note and in blue ink is written, "Ha! Ha!" perhaps suggesting that he and likely others on the squadron were poking fun at the Pathfinders for not being up to the standards required by their squadron.

This nose art image features a Canadian Maple Leaf.
It was on Joe's Lancaster ME-559-"Q-Queenie."
Dorothy Bailey

On 30 December Joe was bombing V-1 sites again but this time he dropped his first 12,000 pound bomb. Six Pathfinder Mosquitos placed markers for the ten 617 Lancasters but again, they were not accurate enough and fell 600 feet from the target.

Again the squadron's bombs were well grouped around the markers and the target was left undamaged. Joe had his own problems as the bomb did not release during his run over the target. A second run was made over the target and the big bomb remained 'hung-up.' Joe would have made the most gentle landing possible upon his return to Coningsby.

Joe, his aircrew, and presumably members of his ground crew in front of Lancaster ME559 'Q-Queenie'.
Back Row: (l-r) Dave Rodger, Don Maclean, unknown, Bill Radcliffe .
Middle Row: (l-r) unknown, unknown, Johnny Johnson, Len Eaton, Joe McCarthy, Ron Batson.
Front Row: All unknown.
The McCarthy Family

Mickey Martin

As 1944 began Cheshire and Martin were becoming more and more frustrated with the lack of accurate marking. In fact on 4 January, they both 'quite unofficially' dropped markers themselves over a V-1 site from 400 feet. However the shallow nature of their approach caused the markers to skid before burning and the raid was not as successful as was hoped.

On 9 January the squadron was on the move again, this time a short hop to Woodhall Spa just 2.5 miles north of Coningsby. It was felt that 617 Squadron should operate as the only unit on the station, given its rôle as a Special Duties Squadron.

For Joe and his crew this was like going home as this was the station where they had completed their tour with 97 Squadron. As well, they would again be able to enjoy the Officers Mess in the Petwood Hotel. Joe's next operation was on 21 January and was the first for the squadron while operating from Woodhall Spa. Twelve aircraft attacked a V-1 Flying Bomb site and Mickey Martin 'unofficially' tried out a new target marking technique. He had noted that he could bomb targets as small as clumps of seaweed in the sea by using his Lancaster as a dive-bomber provided he dove low enough. So he marked the target by accurately dropping markers from 400 feet while in a high-angle dive.

The remainder of the force then dropped their bombs with great accuracy and inflicted a massive amount of damage to the site. Joe utilized the markers and reported bombing with good visibility from 11,000 feet. He referred to them as, "red spot fires." This raid was a turning point as henceforth the squadron was permitted to continue with this new technique that Mickey Martin had developed.

Following the war, Leonard Cheshire wrote of Mickey Martin,

"The backbone of the squadron were Martin, Munro, McCarthy, and Shannon and of these by far the greatest was Martin. He was not a man to worry about administration but as an operational pilot I consider him greater than Gibson and indeed the greatest that the air force has produced. I have seen him do things that I, for one, would never have looked at." [31]

On 25/26 January Joe completed his forty-third operation, to another "ski-site" as they were now referred to. W/C Cheshire marked the target with green and red target indicators but reported, "Marking above cloud not possible; Marking below cloud difficult because the speed flares (the ones used to illuminate the target) drifted across target." Conventional 1000 and 500 pound bombs were used on this operation.

Joe and the other pilots felt that the raid was successful, Joe reporting, "As red spot fires were given as being to N.W. of target, own bomb believed to have undershot by 200 yards; Many sticks seen to be in target area before own bombing; Blue sparks seen in target area lasting for about one minute."

Prior to going on leave, Joe and S/L Martin travelled to the A.V. Roe facilities at Woodford where they were presented with a cheque for the RAF Benevolent Fund by the employees of the plant. Given 617's notoriety it was not unusual for squadron personnel to make morale-building appearances at various functions.

Limoges and the Antheor Viaduct Again

Joe was on leave when the accuracy of the new low-level marking technique was combined with the accuracy of high level bombing with the SABS in a most dramatic way. On 8/9 February W/C Cheshire led an attack by twelve 617 Squadron Lancasters on the Gnome-Rhône Aero Factory at Limoges, 200 miles southwest of Paris.

This plant specialized in aircraft engines and was clearly a worthwhile target. However 300 French citizens, most of them women, were employed in the plant which operated through the night. As well, the factory was surrounded by their homes. Concerned about the likelihood that large numbers of these French civilians would be killed, the target had previously been struck from Bomber Command's list.

Leonard Cheshire signed and presented this photo to 'Mac.' It's one of the most remarkable pictures taken of a Bomber Command operation. W/C Cheshire's markers and incendiaries are exploding on the roofs of the Gnome-Rhône aero-engine factory. The tail-wheel of his Lancaster may be seen at the top of the photo.
The McCarthy Family

Cheshire had been given official permission to mark the target at low level and a full moon would enable it to be easily identified. Arriving over the factory prior to the other aircraft, he made three low-level passes in order to warn the factory workers to escape. On his fourth run he dropped a load of incendiaries and target markers from 200 feet. Cheshire reported that the markers were dropped in the centre of the target.

The Lancasters then dropped their 12,000 pound bombs from between 8000 and 12,000 feet with great accuracy, ten of them hitting the factory and one landing in the river alongside. The factory was severly damaged and production almost completely ceased. There were few, if any, casualties among the French people and the twelve aircraft returned safely to Woodhall Spa.

Cheshire took a cameraman from the RAF photo unit with him on the attack and the striking photos that were taken of the target marking were widely publicised in the press, reminding all of the capabilities of the squadron.

The Gnome-Rhône aero-engine factory prior to and after the precision attack by 617 Squadron.
Imperial War Museum

It has been written that a message reached England from Limoges that read, "The girls of the Gnome-Rhone factory wish to thank the RAF for their considerate warning and would be pleased to welcome the people concerned after the war."

Obviously a complete success for the squadron, the tactical importance of this raid was that it proved the squadron's new method of marking targets was effective although concerns remained that it might be prohibitively costly against defended targets.

On 12/13 February while Joe was still on leave, ten Lancasters led by W/C Cheshire again attempted to bomb the Antheor Viaduct. Again they were unsuccessful despite low-level runs by both Cheshire and S/L Martin. The sides of the valley were very steep and the target was defended by guns which damaged both of their aircraft. F/Lt. Hay, the bomb aimer in Martin's aircraft and the squadron's bombing leader since 617's formation was killed.

W/C Cheshire had flown Joe's 'Q-Queenie' for this raid as his regular aircraft was not available and Joe was on leave. Upon landing following the Antheor operation 150 holes were found in the aircraft and the port wing had to be replaced. When Joe returned from leave, he commented to others, with tongue-in-cheek and Cheshire within ear-shot, that,

"It's a remarkable coincidence that the Wingco has been flying his own aircraft for three months without getting a spot on it and then sends me on leave and takes mine and does this to it." [32]

Nine Op's in March

Joe flew no operations during February 1944 but he was certainly busy during March flying a total of nine between the second and the twenty-fifth of that month. In fact the entire squadron was busy, completing a total of 149 operational sorties and accumulating almost 1000 hours of operational flying time, remarkably, without the loss of a single aircraft.

These raids were characterized by achieving, in most cases, bombing that was exceptionally accurate and effective utilizing their newly developed technique.

Joe was part of a force of fifteen 617 Squadron Lancasters that attacked an

Armourers at Woodhall Spa demonstrate the various sizes of bombs. At the rear, is a 12,000 pound HC 'Blockbuster'. Note the six-finned ballistic tail.
Imperial War Museum

aircraft engine factory at Albert in France during the night of 2/3 March. It was led by W/C Cheshire and this was his 75th operational flight. Formerly a machine tool factory, the facility had been taken over by the Nazis and was being used to build engines for the Focke-Wulf 190 fighters that were regularly shooting down Bomber Command aircraft.

Following an attack during May 1943, the facility had been camouflaged, the main building being covered with netting that had been painted to resemble roads and small buildings.

F/Lt. Hubert 'Nick' Knilans was another American now flying with 617. Like Joe, he had joined the RCAF prior to the United States entering the war and trained in Canada. He and Joe became best of friends. Nick described what he saw during this operation,

"We dropped flares that lit up the local landmarks, by which the markers located the target. Cheshire's bomb sight was u/s so it was Munro who dropped two red spot fires on the roof. There were thirteen of us with 12,000 pound blockbusters and only one fell outside the compound. We dropped ours from 10,200 feet. The lack of searchlights, flak, and bandits made a most pleasant change and we were back home four hour after taking off." [33]

Joe dropped his bomb from 8800 feet. He reported that it appeared to fall fifty yards short of the red spot fire target marker and that the last bombs dropped caused large explosions. One bomb toppled and fell in the open countryside, but the rest went down onto the factory which was almost completely destroyed as was a large stock of completed engines.

Two nights later the squadron was operating again and this time fifteen aircraft were dispatched to the La Ricamerie needle-bearing factory at St-Etienne, near Lyon. About 10,000 bearings a month were being made there for aero engines.

It would be Joe's 45th operation. However upon reaching the target it was found to be obscured by 10/10ths cloud cover and it proved impossible to identify the target. On the instructions of W/C Cheshire the force returned to Woodhall Spa, landing very carefully with their huge bombs still on board. On 10/11 March sixteen squadron aircraft returned to the La Ricamerie needle-bearing factory. This time Joe was part of the target-marking effort, dropping a load of thirty pound incendiaries from only 100 feet. Conditions over the target were less than ideal with some cloud cover and the attacking crews had difficulty evaluating the attack. However a French report refers to the attack as, "a very precise bombardment. The dimensions of the rectangle in which the bombs fell was not more than 1150 feet by 320 feet" and a Bomber Command report later noted that, "Every building in the works except one was destroyed or damaged."

10	LANCASTER	Q ME559	SELF	F/O McLEAN P/O JOHNSON P/O RADCLIFFE F/S BATSON F/S EATON F/L RODGER	OPERATION'S 46TH LA RICAMARIE NEEDLE BEARING FACTORY – ST ETIENNE 30 LB INC. 100 FT.

On 15/16 March poor weather over an aircraft factory at Woippy, north of Metz, forced the abandonment of the raid and the 22 Lancasters, including Joe's, were forced to return to base with their bombs still aboard. During their return, F/O Duffy's aircraft was attacked by enemy fighters. Two were claimed as shot down by the rear gunner, Sgt. McLean, who sustained a slight wound to his hand during the exchange. As well, there was an 'intruder' over the Woodhall Spa aerodrome and the runway lights had to be turned out until it was certain it had left the area.

Joe was marking the target again the next night as 21 Lancasters attacked the Michelin tyre factory at Clermont-Ferrand. As was done at Limoges, Cheshire made three low passes over the factory to warn the French workers and give them time to escape,, which they did. After parachute flares lit up the target, Joe dropped two green target indicators and a load of incendiaries from 100 feet while flying through intense opposing fire from machine guns. He reported that the incendiaries were, "Seen to hit roof of east end of Central Shed" and that the, "Aiming point was obtained."

W/C Cheshire reported, "Bombing well concentrated; Smoke up to 6500 feet; Huge explosion in target area." The raid was referred to as a complete success with, "Hits on every building; Largest was hit by two heavy bombs; Half of the plant making inner tubes was destroyed."

The squadron's focus was on explosives factories for its next two raids. On 18/19 March Joe was flying one of thirteen aircraft that attacked a factory at Bergerac. Again Cheshire warned the French in and near the factory by making a number of low passes over the target. The initial markers were placed short of the target and according to Joe's report he was, "Instructed to overshoot spot fires by 150 yards" with his green target markers and incendiaries. All the bombs fell within the target area. Joe reported, "Sheds seen to be on fire; Large explosion on edge of factory area." The entire factory area was left in flames with many internal explosions taking place.

Nick Knilans had some interesting recollections about bombing this target from 8000 feet which he felt may not have been high enough,

The Michelin factory at Clermont-Ferrand following the raid. Note the destruction in the large building at centre with no evidence of damage to the adjacent areas.
Imperial War Museum

"We received a severe jolt when another crew hit an ammunition dump. The armourers had arranged for the 1000 pound bomb to hit first, setting off their 12,000 pounder just before it landed, creating a larger blast area. It worked to perfection." [34]

Two days later the explosives factory at Angouleme was targetted by the Lancasters of 617 Squadron. Joe dropped three target indicators as well as an 8000 pound bomb and reported that the last bomb seen to drop caused a large explosion. The bombing was again very concentrated and the factory was said to have been 'wrecked.' Air Commodore A.C.H. Sharp flew as an observer with one of the crews and wrote that, "I never thought I should be able to see night precision bombing of such accuracy." This was Joe's fiftieth operation.

An aero-engine factory in the Rhone Valley south of Lyon was targetted during the night of 23/24 March. 617 Squadron put up fourteen of the twenty aircraft. Identification of the target was difficult owing to the hazy conditions, the target marking was questionable, and the raid could not be assessed as no results were observed. Joe reported, "Bombed spot fires as instructed; No results observed." The returning aircraft were low on fuel having spent more time than anticipated over the target. As well the weather at Woodhall Spa was deteriorating so Joe and all but one of the other aircraft were diverted to Tangmere, a base located near the south coast, about fifteen miles east of Portsmouth.

Following the aircraft's return to Woodhall Spa, it was announced that the squadron was being divided into three flights with F/Lt. Shannon to be in charge of 'A' Flight, S/L Munro to be in charge of 'B' Flight, and F/Lt. McCarthy to command 'C' Flight. Both Shannon and Joe were being recommended for the rank of Squadron Leader.

Joe and the squadron returned to the aero-engine factory at Lyon again on the night of 25/26 March. Flares lit up the area but W/C Cheshire and Joe accurately marked some buildings that were similar to the target but were actually about 1000 feet short. Cheshire again dropped markers but these over-shot by 150 to 300 feet. Joe then dropped his last two spot fires dead on target and they could be seen burning inside the main shed. Cheshire ordered the main force to bomb Joe's spot fires but in the confusion almost all the bombs fell on the initial markers to the west of the target. Unfortunately only one bomber accurately bombed Joe's markers that had been placed on the factory.

This raid, his 52nd, was Joe's twentieth with 617 Squadron and it was determined to be the last of his second tour. W/C Cheshire wrote a very complimentary note in Joe's logbook to mark this milestone.

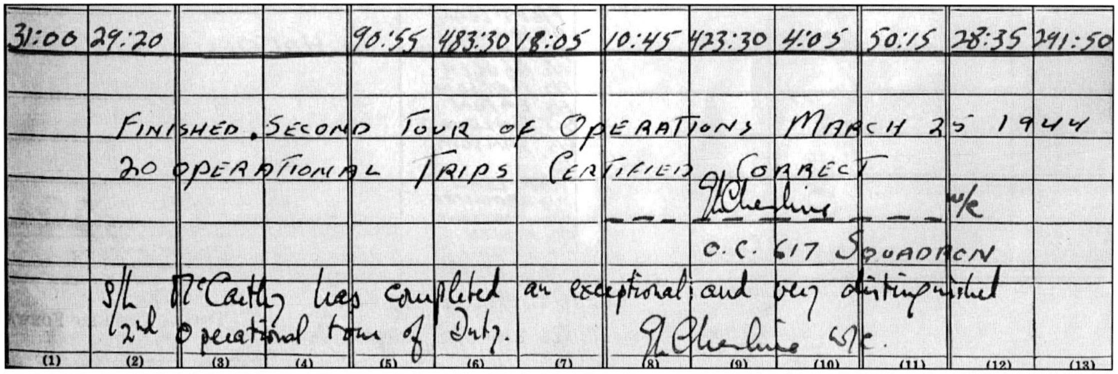

(1)	(2)	(3)	(4)	(5)	(6)	(7)	(8)	(9)	(10)	(11)	(12)	(13)
31:00	29:20			90:55	483:30	18:05	10:45	423:30	4:05	50:15	28:35	291:50

FINISHED SECOND TOUR OF OPERATIONS MARCH 25 1944
20 OPERATIONAL TRIPS CERTIFIED CORRECT
W/C
O.C. 617 SQUADRON
S/L McCarthy has completed an exceptional and very distinguished 2nd Operational tour of Duty.
W/C.

It was also the last of Joe's thirteen operations in Lancaster ME559. The aircraft eventually crash-landed in northern Russia on 12 September 1944 while en route to the first raid on the Battleship Tirpitz that 617 Squadron participated in. The bomber skidded on wet grass and crashed through a boundary fence at Kegostrov airfield. It has been reported that the Russians managed to repair the aircraft and that ME559 went on to serve with the Soviet Air Force flying with 16 Squadron of the White Sea Fleet.

At the end of March, as at the end of every month, the squadron's Flight Commanders had to sign the logbooks of all of the aircrew in their Flight and then the logbooks of all three Flights had to be signed by the Squadron Commander. It seems that this was a traumatic exercise for Joe McCarthy,

> *"Hell,' Joe expostulated to Dave (his friend and fellow Flight Commander, Dave Shannon), 'How I hate to sign those books! I'm here to fly, not give autographs.' But the main cause of Joe's distaste for the chore was the fact that he had a slow and laborious hand and it did take him a long time to get through the task . . . Joe was probably the most popular American in Britain at that time, and certainly his Flight aircrew thought the world of him, but it was their monthly treat to see this giant of a man literally running with sweat over the simple task of signing their books."* [35]

Joe's Signals Leader, Larry Curtis, was responsible for seeing to it that Joe signed the logbooks which Joe was doing by signing 'Joe McCarthy.' To make the exercise even more entertaining Larry,

"persuaded Joe that 'Joseph C. McCarthy' was a much more impressive signature and was really the form of signature the ordinary Britisher expected from an American. Joe complied, and only succeeded in adding to his nightmare!" [36]

Marking with Mosquitos

For some time Leonard Cheshire had been having discussions with AVM Cochrane regarding the difficulties involved with using the Lancaster, a large, somewhat unwieldy, four-engined heavy bomber, to do low-level target marking. Cheshire wanted to try the fast and agile twin-engined Mosquito. With these, he insisted, targets could be marked more accurately and with less risk when attacking heavily defended targets.

An example of engineering ingenuity inspired by the challenges of war, the de Havilland Mosquito's all-wooden design was a major advantage during a time of acute shortages of light metal alloys. Almost all of the aircraft was made of wood. The fuselage was a frameless shell of plywood made of balsa wood sandwiched between sheets of birch and the wings were made of wood as well. Powered by the same Merlin V-12 engine as the Lancaster, the sleek design, together with lightness and the lack of any defensive armament or armour, allowed the Mosquito to travel at speeds in excess of 400 mph to escape from enemy fighters.

During much of the war the Mosquito was the fastest aircraft in the sky on either side. It could deliver the same bomb-load to distant targets as the heavily armoured four-engined B-17 Flying Fortresses flown by the American Air Force. Although designed as a bomber, the Mosquito also served as a fighter. As well as defending Britain against enemy aircraft, Mosquito fighter squadrons conducted sweeps across Europe against the Nazi's night-fighters that were attacking Bomber Command's aircraft.

Following the problems with the target marking over Lyon, Cochrane agreed to

de Havilland Mosquito.

transfer a Mosquito to 617 Squadron for Cheshire to try out. Bill Hume recalled the day the first Mosquito arrived at Woodhall Spa,

"Cheshire had asked for a Mosquito so everybody was on the tarmac that day when it was coming in. It landed, taxied up and Cheshire, out he comes and he says, 'That's no good to me.' So the pilot, he was laughing, he says, 'Why?' 'Well I was told they had more guns; I want them (guns) here and I want them in there.' So they took it away and they came back with a loaded one. It had guns all over." [37]

Cochrane decided to have Cheshire and his Mosquito mark the target for a fairly large raid that involved aircraft from a number of 5 Group squadrons. On the night of 5/6 April, 144 Lancasters, including Joe and sixteen others from 617 Squadron, attacked an aircraft factory on the outskirts of Toulouse. This was the first Mosquito marking flight of the war and was also significant that 617 Squadron would be marking the target rather than the Pathfinder Force.

The raid began with flares being dropped to light up the area so that it would be easier for W/C Cheshire to do his marking. 617 Squadron pilot Nick Knilans was watching from his aircraft,

Right: Cheshire insisted on a Mosquito with lots of guns, like this version.

"Cheshire made two low-level passes over the factory roofs. I could see his Mosquito zooming about though a shower of light flak shells and searchlights. He dropped his red spot fires on the third pass. They were in the middle of the factory complex. He called in the bombers but a shortage of fuel meant he couldn't stay until the end. It didn't matter." [38]

Joe and Les Munro dropped additional red spot fires from 11,000 feet but Joe felt that they were not necessary, writing, "Bombed Red T.I. as ordered by Leader; Fair amount of smoke and fire; Own spot fires not required; Aiming point obtained." The main force Lancasters then proceeded to bomb almost perfectly. Reconnaissance photographs taken the next day showed a completely devastated site with only a few near misses. Within hours of the Toulouse attack, Harris advised that 5 Group could begin to operate as an independent force using its own marking techniques.

This was Joe's first flight in Lancaster LM492 which he would fly on eleven operations.

It was Joe's last trip with George 'Johnny' Johnson as his bomb aimer. Johnny had completed his operations. F/O W.A. 'Danny' Daniel became the crew's bomb aimer.

The night of 10/11 April saw seventeen Lancasters and one Mosquito attacking the airfield and signals equipment depot at St. Cyr, near Tours, France.

W/C Cheshire reported that he dove from 5000 feet to 1000 feet and that the, "Factory buildings were bombed in a dive attack" and that the "Red spot fires were dropped on northwest edge of factory buildings." Instructions were given to the main force correcting the error and the weight of the attack fell on the target which soon became obscured by thick smoke. Reconnaissance showed severe and concentrated damage.

Joe was carrying three flares and six red spot fires with which to back-up Cheshire's marking if necessary as well as an 8000 pound bomb. He reported that his spot fires weren't necessary as the aiming point was obtained.

On 13 April Joe flew to Earls Colne Airfield, an RAF station about forty miles north-northeast of London. It had been allocated for use by the United States Army Air Force. While there he and his crew were photographed with the crew of a U.S. B-26 Marauder. The aircraft in the photo were from the 456th Bomb Squadron, 323rd Bomb Group. It's not known why Joe and his crew were at Earls Colne but it did provide a 'photo-op.' It likely had something to do with the fact that Joe and fellow-American John Stirling, who featured prominently in the photo, had trained together at 12 EFTS at Goderich, Ontario.

It was back to war on the night of 18/19 April as Joe was flying one of 202 Lancasters that attacked the railway marshalling yards at Juvisy, just south of Paris. The raid was undertaken by 5 Group with W/C Cheshire and 617 looking after the target marking.

Left: The nose art that was likely on Joe's Lancaster LM492.
The McCarthy Family

Opposite: The following caption was printed when the photograph appeared in a newspaper: "CANADIANS, YANKS, AND BRITISHERS are in this group, pictured as the crew of a Lancaster bomber visited the crew of a U.S. Marauder in Britain." (l-r) J. Halton, Texas; R. Batson RAF; W. Brier, Alabama; L. Eaton RAF; Don MacLean RCAF of Toronto; L. Johnson RAF; John Bull Stirling, Maryland; J. McCarthy RCAF from New York; L. McNally, Connecticut; G. Wilcox, Texas; Bill Radcliffe RCAF of New Westminister B.C.
The McCarthy Family

Left: LM492 nose art.
Nose art replica painting by Clarence Simonsen

Q
131892

But now the squadron had four Mosquitos with which to do the work. Although Joe had a Mosquito flight in his logbook by the end of 1945 he was not one of the pilots chosen to fly the aircraft in combat with 617 Squadron. His son, Joe Jr., believes that this may have been because he was simply too big for the Mosquito's cramped cockpit.

The complexity of the raid on Juvisy is made clear by the following Bomber Command Report,

"The Mosquitos were to drop green target indicators as 'proximity markers.' Flare force aircraft were then to illuminate the aiming point at z-4 on orders from the Master Bomber. Two Mosquitos of 5 Group (led by W/C Cheshire) were then to mark the north aiming point, and two (led by S/L Dave Shannon) were to mark the south aiming point with red spot fires. The Mosquito leaders were to assess the accuracy of these markers and call in their backers-up (Joe was one of these) to drop more red spot fires.

"The Master Bomber (W/C Cheshire) was then to order the force to bomb one or both of the aiming points if the marking was sufficiently accurate to ensure a successful attack. If the marking was inadequate, he was to order the force to bring their bombs back. One aircraft was to act as a link between the Master Bomber and the main force, to retransmit his broadcast. The main force were to arrive at z+10.

"The markers were concentrated in the centre of the yard, and another exceptionally accurate attack was delivered. Immense damage was caused. Apart from innumerable hits on tracks and rolling stock, the engine shed, the carriage and wagon repair shop, and both trans-shipment sheds were all at least 80 percent destroyed. The Paris up-line flyover, the circulation roads flyover, and the road bridge west of the passenger station sustained several direct hits." [39]

Joe was carrying six red spot fires and a load of 1000 and 500 pound bombs which he was ordered to drop onto the markers that had been placed by the 617 Mosquitos.

Only a single Lancaster was lost from the force of over 200 aircraft; a remarkably low loss rate. This was in stark contrast to the significant losses that Bomber Command had sustained during the previous winter's attacks on Berlin and other German cities.

Arthur Harris had believed that a concentrated attack on the German capital might be enough to break German resistance. He boldly stated, "It will cost us between 400 and 500 aircraft. It will cost Germany the war." By this time he could deploy over 800 bombers

Mickey Martin's Lancaster 'P for Popsie' with a 617 Squadron Mosquito beyond.

on any given night, all of them equipped with new and more sophisticated navigational devices such as H2S radar. Between November 1943 and March 1944 Bomber Command made sixteen massed attacks on Berlin.

The so-called 'Battle of Berlin' clearly did not deliver the knockout blow that Harris had predicted and during the battle, Bomber Command lost 1047 aircraft with a further 1682 damaged. Over 7000 aircrew were killed or taken prisoner. The losses culminated in the raid on Nuremberg on 30 March 1944 when 94 bombers were shot down and 71 damaged, out of 795 aircraft. While the Battle of Berlin raged, the chances of a Bomber Command crew surviving a tour of thirty operations was significantly less than 25 percent.

During April 1944 Bomber Command's focus was changing to support preparations for the invasion of Europe by destroying railway facilities such as those at Juvisy and destroying the enemy's capability to deliver the V-1 flying bomb and other 'vengeance' weapons that were being developed by the Nazis.

On 20 April Joe was part of another large raid on a railway marshalling yard, this time at La Chappelle just north of Paris. 247 Lancasters and 22 Mosquitos (including four from 617 Squadron) from both 5 Group and the Pathfinders were involved. A Bomber Command report described the technique that was to be used,

"OBOE Mosquitos (Pathfinder Group) were to mark the aiming point with cascading green target markers at zero hour. From z+1 to z+5, Lancasters were to illuminate the target with flares, while two Mosquitos of 617 Squadron marked the aiming point visually with red spot fires. The Master Bomber was to assess the accuracy of these, and if necessary back them up with red spot fires of his own. Main force crews were to arrive over the target between z+15 and z+40 and were to bomb as instructed by the Master Bomber." [40]

This raid was different from previous ones in that the main force was split into two groups and bombed 25 minutes apart.

Again, Cheshire and the other 617 Mosquitos released their markers in a 'dive attack,' Cheshire beginning at 5000 feet and releasing at 1200 feet. Joe carried a regular bomb load of twelve, 1000 pound bombs on this raid which he released from 13,000 feet. He reported that he, "Bombed red spot fires and bend in river" and that his "Own bombs dropped right across red spot fires, Other bursts concentrated around markers." The raid was said to have been extremely accurate and concentrated.

Two days later the new techniques were brought to a heavily defended city in Germany, Brunswick, and Joe was on the Battle Order again.

After being well illuminated by flares, the initial target markers were accurately placed by the 617 Squadron Mosquitos. However, because of a thin layer of cloud that hampered visibility and faulty communications, most of the bombs were dropped on H_2S-aimed indicators that were dropped inaccurately and well southwest of the target.

W/C Cheshire reported, "Target marked with spot fires from squadron Mosquito aircraft; Main force instructed to bomb these markers but V.H.F. communication difficult; Four minutes after the original marking a Wanganui flare and green T.I. were dropped (by the Pathfinder Force) five miles to the southwest of the target; This attracted 50 percent of the Main Force who could not be directed away to the spot fires."

After a days rest, Joe and the squadron were part of another large raid against a German city on 28 April. The railway centre at Munich was the target and 260 bombers were involved.

This was a long trip. As part of the main force, Joe took off during daylight at 8:46 pm and flew across France and over the Alps into Switzerland as a diversion prior to turning north towards Munich. Cheshire and the other Mosquitos, being much faster, did not take off until just before midnight.

Again the marking by the 617 Mosquitos was accurate despite heavy flak and searchlights. Cheshire led the way releasing two red spot fires after a 'dive attack' from 12,000 to 3,000 feet at a speed that reached 480 mph. The bombing was accurate. Joe dropped six red spot fires and his bomb load from 18,000 feet.

Nine Lancasters were lost on the raid including one from 617 Squadron flown by F/Lt. J.L. Cooper. All but one of the crew survived and were taken prisoner. Joe landed at 6:16 am after flying for nine hours and thirty minutes. This was Joe's 58th operation and would be his last until 5/6 June, the night before D-Day.

Prior to the Munich raid on 28 April, Joe had been awarded a Bar to his DFC (the equivalent of a second DFC) with the citation,

"Since being awarded the Distinguished Service Order this officer has completed numerous sorties as captain of aircraft in which he has taken part in difficult and hazardous operations at low level. Squadron Leader McCarthy has displayed exemplary skill and courage which, combined with his unfailing devotion to duty, have contributed much to the success achieved." [41]

Operation Taxable

The squadron had been granted a week's leave following the Munich operation. Upon their return, intensive training for a different type of special operation occupied Joe and the Lancaster crews of 617 Squadron for the next five weeks. It was what Joe and his fellow squadron members must have perceived as extremely boring, given the action they were now used to. However exacting flying and navigation was required for their next challenge.

For the first time in the war the squadron objected strongly to an assignment but AVM Cochrane told W/C Cheshire to, "Do what you're told." Operation Taxable would be playing an important rôle in the invasion of Europe that was being planned for early June.

After the intense operational schedule his crews had become used to, Cheshire knew that they might not be pleased with this month of demanding training exercises. So he created a series of distractions for them during the month of May. A Squadron Sports Committee was formed under the direction of F/Lt. 'Bunny' Clayton and cricket matches and other events were held. As well there were route marches and escape training.

The Secretary of State for Air visited nearby Coningsby on 8 May. W/C Cheshire and his Flight Commanders, S/L's Munro, McCarthy, and Shannon, were invited to a dinner in his honour that evening.

Then on 16 May, the anniversary of the Dams Raid, a party was held in the Officers Mess at the Petwood Hotel to which all members of the crews who took part in the raid were invited. W/C Gibson was unfortunately unable to attend but most of the officers who had survived the attack and the following year of operations did. Several of the civilians from A.V. Roe and Vickers Ltd. who contributed to the raid's success attended as well. Three days later an all ranks Squadron Dance was held as a further celebration of the Dams Raid. W/C Gibson was able to join the squadron for this evening and it is said he was given a rousing reception. A cake was cut by Gibson and W/C Cheshire, both of whom made speeches.

This was the last evening that those who remained of the original Dambusters would spend with Guy Gibson as he was killed on operations just four months later. This would have been another blow to Joe. According to Joe Jr., "Dad had great confidence in, and really respected Guy Gibson."

Robert Cockburn was a physicist, a scientist who like Barnes Wallis, had an idea that required a special squadron. Testing of his theory had shown that a number of aircraft flying low over the sea in elongated, overlapping circuits parallel to the coast, gradually closing in toward the shore, and gradually increasing the amounts of 'window' (strips of aluminium foil that were excellent radar reflectors) dropped at precisely timed intervals would create the illusion on radar screens based on shore that a large number of ships were approaching.

Until now 'window' had been used solely for the purpose of saturating radar with enough false responses to prevent the operators from picking out target aircraft from the false radar returns. The idea of using it to give the impression that there was a convoy of ships where in fact the sea was empty was a new one.

Nothing could conceal the invasion fleet itself, but Cockburn thought that by creating a false pattern on the enemy's radar screens they could make the enemy think they were being attacked at more than one point simultaneously.

617 Squadron was tasked to create this diversion. A group of eight aircraft would fly the pattern and drop the 'window'. Then after three hours of this, a second group of eight aircraft would take over. This was the trickiest part of all because the replacement aircraft had to come in directly behind with split-second timing to carry on the diversion, creating no disruption to the enemy's radar images.

The aircraft had to be flown very accurately and it was a demanding task, but if done properly, the Nazis would be deceived into thinking that an invasion fleet was approaching the coast. To add further to the illusion, eight small Royal Navy gunboats would slowly move towards the shore and create lots of radio chatter.

The squadron would create this deception to the north of the invasion beaches and further north still, Short Stirling aircraft of 218 Squadron would do the same in what they referred to as Operation Glimmer. Thus three invasion fleets would appear on enemy radar screens during the night prior to the invasion. This would keep the them guessing, spread out their forces, and delay their deployment to the invasion beaches at Normandy.

F/Lt. Nick Knilans was at the briefing for the operation,

"This Dr. Cockburn guy came in and said he wanted us to simulate a convoy fourteen miles wide, crossing the English Channel at seven knots. Eight double crews (a normal crew plus an extra pilot and an extra navigator) and three 'Window Chuckers' would fly for four hours, then to be relieved by another eight crews. Each plane would fly 35 seconds on course, then a reverse course for 32 seconds. Then a slow turn back on the first course, meanwhile throwing out a load of Window (every four seconds but not on the turns). We could not vary our height (800 feet) or our speed by more than the smallest fractions." [42]

F/L Nick Knilans.
Imperial War Museum

After each of these eliptical routes was flown the aircraft would advance towards the coast far enough to keep in line with the convoy's speed of seven knots. To further complicate the operation, as the training proceeded it was determined that the size of the 'window' (the length of the aluminum foil strips) had to vary as the coast was approached. Six different sizes of 'window' were used.

If the 'window chuckers' miscounted or fumbled in some way, if the navigator was a little slow in signalling the beginning or end of a leg, or if the pilot was not precisely on course, the enemy radar operators would immediately note a response on their screens that could not possibly have come from a group of ships

F/Lt. Knilans continues,

"I had to do this for two hours, after which Jimmy Castagnola (Nick's fellow pilot) would take over. Joe McCarthy was to fly with his close pal Dave Shannon. They did everything together, including dropping a flare down the Wingco's chimney which got them on the night duty roster for quite a while.

"We practised precision flying by day and night, with the navigators timing us on stop watches. We were allowed no leave, but that wasn't so bad at the Petwood as there were some very nice WAAFs and lasses from the village. We were confined to camp on 4 June and told the next day we were on." [43]

In his book 'The Dam Busters,' Paul Brickhill provides interesting detail of the, 'dropping a flare down the Wingco's chimney' incident,

"Shannon and McCarthy were rarely seen apart; they drank together and dined together... One day they climbed to the roof of Squadron Headquarters to drop a Verey cartridge down the Adjutant's chimney. They knew that the innocent Humphries had a fire in the grate.

"A Verey cartridge in artful hands is like a semi-lethal firework. Exploding in a confined space it resembles a small but concentrated bombing raid, providing a monstrous crash, sheets of coloured flame, and clouds of choking smoke. Half the beauty of the thing is that it goes on for about fifteen seconds. They dropped it down

the chimney and started laughing as the waves of sound came rocking up from below.

'Unfortunately it was not Humphries' chimney, but the Commanding Officer's. "Cheshire scuttled out pursued by flashes and rolling fumes, ran onto the tarmac and spotted his two flight commanders hiding behind a chimney. With aristocratic dignity he said nothing, but for several nights Shannon and McCarthy found themselves doing duty officer together, an irksome task which kept them out of their beds and abstemiously patrolling the station buildings." [44]

Leonard Cheshire described what his aircrew were thinking as the 617 Squadron Lancasters took off into the night prior to D-Day to execute Operation Taxable,

"For once emotion was absent. The fear was not that they might fail in courage or lack determination but that someone, through mis-calculation or neglect, might destroy the simulation and needlessly jeopardise the lives of the soldiers in the ships." [45]

Above: Joe McCarthy at the Petwood.
Nell Rodger

Sixteen Lancasters, including Joe's, took part in Operation Taxable. It began about midnight and went on steadily and without pause throughout the night. Joe, together with his partner S/L Shannon and their crew, led the second group. They were airborne for four hours and forty minutes as Joe played his rôle in the invasion of Europe.

At first light the illusion was ending as the last Lancaster turned for home just eight mile short of the French coast. Other forces had been operating during the night as well and now bridges had been destroyed making the movement of enemy troops much more difficult. Meanwhile the real invasion force was nearing the coast many miles away.

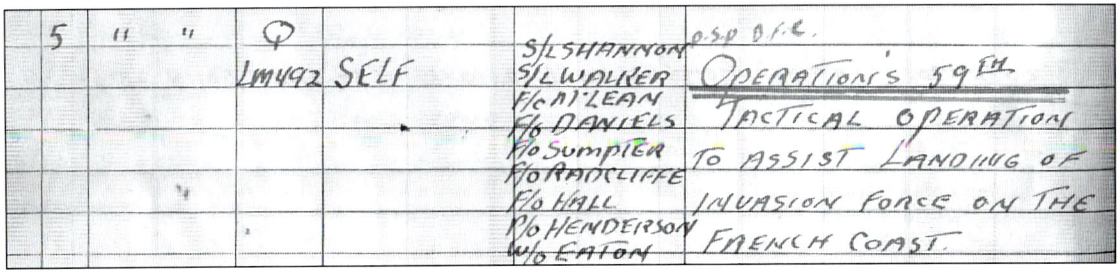

5	"	"	Q	LM492	SELF	S/L SHANNON S/L WALKER F/O McLEAN F/O DANIELS F/O SUMPTER F/O RADCLIFFE F/O HALL P/O HENDERSON W/O EATON	D.S.O. D.F.C. OPERATION'S 59TH TACTICAL OPERATION TO ASSIST LANDING OF INVASION FORCE ON THE FRENCH COAST.

Left: Joe's Operation Taxable logbook entry.
The McCarthy Family

Joe McCarthy and Dave Shannon.
The McCarthy Family

Tallboy

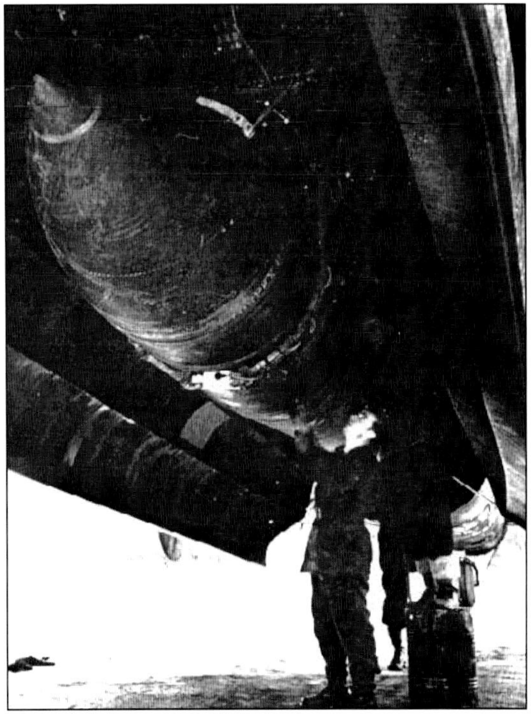

A Tallboy in a Lancaster's bomb bay.

As knowledge of the Nazi's V-1 Flying Bomb and V-2 Rocket programs became known to British intelligence, it was determined that these weapons were to be stored and in some cases launched from massive, concrete bunkers which could not be penetrated by existing weapons. As well, the enemy's U-Boat and E-Boat pens were being extensively reinforced with very thick concrete roofs and walls.

The 12,000 pound bombs that 617 Squadron had been using since the Dams Raid had very thin casings and would simply shatter when dropped on solid concrete. However Barnes Wallis had been thinking of these sorts of problems and developed plans for a very heavy, strong-cased and extremely streamlined bomb of similar weight that could be dropped accurately from great height immediately next to these hardened targets. The weapon would exceed the speed of sound prior to reaching the ground and impact with such energy that it would penetrate deeply underground prior to exploding after a pre-set time delay. A series of 'earthquake waves' would then collapse the nearby concrete structures and tunnels.

The bomb casing was made of special chrome molybdenum steel, cast in a single piece to ensure that it would survive the impact. Near the tip of the bomb this casing was over four inches thick. This was then filled with 5200 pounds of Torpex D1 explosive. The bomb was 21 feet long with fins that were placed at a five degree angle so that it spun as it fell. This improved the aerodynamics and thus the accuracy. When dropped from 18,000 feet it took 37 seconds to reach the ground where it impacted at 750 mph and, depending on the characteristics of the material it struck, penetrated to a considerable depth. By war's end 854 Tallboys had been dropped on a variety of targets including the Battleship Tirpitz, E-Boat and submarine pens, viaducts, tunnels, and canals as well as V-weapons sites.

A 12,000 pound Tallboy is hoisted from the bomb dump to its carrier at Woodhall Spa to be loaded into a 617 Squadron Lancaster for a raid on the V-weapon site at Wizernes, France.
Imperial War Museum

The success of Wallis' Upkeep weapon on the Dams Raid certainly added to his credibility and the development and testing of this new weapon proceeded without delay.

Named 'Tallboy,' the bomb was first manufactured during the winter of 1943-44. The Lancaster with its huge, uninterrupted bomb bay was the only aircraft capable of carrying it and the accuracy possible with the SABS bomb sight would be vital. During May 1944 the first Tallboys were delivered to 617 Squadron at Woodhall Spa.

The Saumur Tunnel

Following its extensive training for, and finally the execution of, Operation Taxable, 617 Squadron was back in the bomb dropping business just two days after D-Day. The first Tallboys were to be dropped on a railway tunnel near Saumur, some 125 miles south of the Normandy beachheads. Joe recalled that,

"Systematically the RAF and the French Underground had destroyed practically every railway line and damaged them so much that from Paris and the south you couldn't get a train running." [46]

But as the Allies landed at Normandy there was one route that had been untouched, a line that passed through the Saumur Tunnel.

The raid was prepared in great haste because a German Panzer unit and other reinforcements were expected to move through the tunnel by train from southwest France and enter the battle at Normandy.

The target was to be illuminated by flares dropped from four 83 Squadron Lancasters and then marked at low level by 617's Mosquitos. Again, W/C Cheshire led the way, diving from 3000 feet and releasing his four red spot fires from 500 feet at the tunnel's south entrance. The markers were placed accurately as were the Tallboys that followed. One actually pierced the roof of the tunnel and brought down a huge quantity of rock and soil. Other hits on the edge of the cut in the hillside 150 feet from the entrance

Tallboy craters at the entrance to the Saumur Tunnel. Joe thought his bomb made the crater directly on the tracks at left. Note the crater at right that actually pierced the tunnel just past the entrance.
Imperial War Museum

Joe was given credit for the Tallboy that pierced the roof of the tunnel as shown above. This photo was taken after the debris had been removed.

caused the side of the road cut to collapse and slide down over the tracks.

Joe dropped his Tallboy on Cheshire's markers from 10,500 feet and reported that the bombing was, "Well concentrated around the spot fire; All bombs seen to fall in a fifty yard radius; One direct hit on the marker itself." Later, he recalled,

"We (the squadron) put one on the top (of the tunnel). I was sure that mine was right on the railroad. Then there was one up a little bit closer than mine but on the railroad track and we destroyed that whole area (at the entrance to the tunnel). I found out later on that I got credit for the one on the top. I don't know how that happened. I don't think it was ours but I didn't see it go off." [47]

Thirty minutes later, F/Lt. Fawke placed three red spot fires with his Mosquito to mark the other end of the tunnel where it emerged from the hillside to cross the Loire River. He saw six Tallboys accurately dropped on his markers and some others about 450 feet away. The bridge over the Loire was also destroyed.

Later it was calculated that 10,000 tons of earth collapsed into the tunnel which had still not been cleared when the area was liberated in August 1944. All of the 617 Squadron aircraft returned safely to Woodhall Spa. It was Joe's sixtieth operation.

E-Boat Pens

The German navy's fast motor-torpedo attack boats were referred to by the Allies as 'E-Boats.' With a top speed of over forty knots, they were agile, larger, and more formidable than similar boats built by the British and Americans. A total of 230 were used in the Baltic, Mediterranean, and Black Seas, however, their main operational area was the English Channel where they regularly attacked coastal shipping with considerable success. E-Boats sank over forty warships including twelve destroyers and well over 100 merchant vessels.

For a time they controlled a significant portion of the Mediterranean Sea and a sizeable area of the English Channel. Convoys venturing from the London docks or the Firth of Forth were liable to be attacked.

As the war progressed things began to go badly for the E-boats and they sought refuge during the day in massive bunkers. These were built on the northeast coast of France at Cherbourg, Boulogne, and Le Havre. The boats would come out at night and wait in the darkness near convoy lanes. The Royal Navy destroyers found it very difficult to catch them before they slipped back into their protected docks.

The E-Boats based at Le Havre and Boulogne now posed a significant danger to the shipping that was supporting the invasion which was taking place only thirty miles away. In fact, their presence was one of the reasons for Operation Taxable.

In response to the invasion, there were now many more E-Boats and other light attack ships in the harbours than could be accommodated in the pens. These targets were among the most heavily defended in occupied France but there was a need to protect the Allied supply line to Normandy.

On 14 June 617 Squadron was part of Bomber Command's first large daylight raid in over a year. The target was the E-Boat base at Le Havre. 221 Lancasters took part and 617 Squadron sent three Mosquitos and 22 Lancasters loaded with Tallboys. They were escorted by Spitfire fighters, something that Bomber Command had not had the benefit of before and which must have given the airmen who were not accustomed to operating during the daylight, considerable comfort.

This photo of a German E-Boat was taken as it surrendered during May 1945.
Imperial War Museum

The raid was divided into two attacks, the first being on the docks, E-Boat pens, and harbour facilities. Cheshire's Mosquito again led the way on the first attack, this time diving from 11,000 feet to 700 feet through intense flak before releasing four red spot fires. Shannon and Fawke were prepared to mark as well but Cheshire felt that additional markers were not required, particularly in view of the intense flak that he felt fortunate to have survived. 617 Squadron's Tallboys followed with hits on the E-Boats in the harbour and several on the E-Boat pens including one bomb that penetrated the bunker whose re-inforced concrete roof and walls were eight to eleven feet thick.

Whereas previous attacks with 500 and 1000 pound bombs had left only blast marks, the Tallboy had made a hole in the roof that had a diameter of sixteen feet and displaced the roof's supporting walls.

Joe reported bombing from 16,000 feet and achieving a direct hit on a group of E-Boats.

Interior of one of the E-boat pens at Le Havre showing the collapsed roof caused by the Tallboys.
Imperial War Museum

The second attack came 2.5 hours later and focussed on shipping. Bomber Command reported that, "both were highly concentrated and great fires were started all over the dock area." Photos taken the next day showed that most of the E-Boats had been sunk. As well there was great damage to the roof of the pen, a large floating dock had been sunk, and a number of adjacent buildings had been severely damaged. One report stated that a total of 53 boats of various kinds were destroyed. Only a single E-Boat remained operational and the threat to the invasion beaches from Le Havre was completely removed by this raid.

Joe recalled the raid as follows,

"They used to put E-Boats as well as submarines in them and there was thick reinforced concrete on the top and the same on the walls. They had so many ships in there, E-Boats and others; they were lined up on the wharves. When we went in there to bombs the aiming point for about a dozen of us was where the E-Boats were. We had three of us aiming at the centre, the top of the first pen and we had sites all around the place.

"So as we came down from England we were out far enough that they could not see or hear us with radar. We turned to go east with a straight run in from about thirty or forty miles. We went in first, leading them. We had the heavy-duties (Tallboys) so that's why we went in first. We didn't have a formation. It was a gaggle. We had a freedom of movement but we stayed together to give protection and also to be able to turn and do what we wanted to do. We dropped but I couldn't see down too well but my bomb aimer and my rear gunner could. All of a sudden I hear this, 'Jesus Christ, there's one, two, three hits.' We got hits right on the edge of where these E-Boats were all lined up.

"HONOR"

Opposite: Ground crew preparing to place a Tallboy in the bomb bay of 617 Squadron Lancaster 'Honor'.

"Some of the boys had overshot and put their bombs down in the water just a short distance from the pens that we were hitting. Barnes Wallis had always said that the bomb was essentially excellent if you put it next to a concrete structure a dam or a bridge or something of that nature, because it would penetrate before it detonated and the earthquake shake would crack the concrete and cause it to collapse and that's what happened here.

"Besides us bombing some of the others that came through after us dropped in the water and formed a tidal wave, a humungous big tidal wave moving forward and this big wave went through the pen gates all the way into the thing, hit the back . . . and came back out again and completely scuttled anything that was in there. All these boats were wrecked. It wiped out the whole damn thing. That was something to live through. It was amazing." [48]

The following day Joe and his squadron were leading another raid, this time to the E-Boat pens at Bologna. There were 297 bombers involved but the weather was not as good as it had been at Le Havre and the 617 Squadron bomb aimers required a clear view. Upon his arrival over the target W/C Cheshire noted the cloud cover and did not drop his red spot fires. However the Pathfinders did drop some markers and Cheshire reported that they appeared accurate.

Ten of the squadron's 22 Lancasters returned with their Tallboys. Heavy flak was encountered and several of those that did drop down to a lower altitude below the clouds to bomb had difficulty during their bomb run. Although none of the 617 Squadron aircraft were lost, one of the bomb aimers was wounded by shrapnel. The aircraft from the other squadrons all dropped their bombs and there was said to have been great destruction in the port and general area.

Despite the cloud and flak the raid was thought to have been a success with 130 boats being reported destroyed and some of the Tallboys having struck and penetrated the E-Boat pen roofs which were eleven feet thick.

Following the two raids, the remnants of the French-based E-boat flotillas were forced to pull back to the Dutch port of Ijmuiden.

As for Joe this raid was the one during which he came closest to being shot down and not returning,

Les Munro.

'We had sent the bombers back because there wasn't enough height below the clouds to drop. Darby Munro had gone ahead of me surveying the weather to see what was up. He called me up and told me so I called them all up and sent them home. Then I contacted Darby again and I said, 'What are you doing?' He said, 'I'm going in.' I said, 'Where are you?' He said, 'I broke out at 11,500.' So I said, 'All right, good.' He gave me his heading and I dropped down fast. I came out (of the clouds) and started heading in. I never heard anything more from Darby because I was concentrating on my run in.

'Just as the bomb doors were opened, I was settling down and I had about thirty seconds to go until bomb release when 'Boom!' I got hit! They didn't hit me per se but the concussion was so close to me that it lifted me up and over on my back.

'When I was over on my back I just automatically closed the bomb doors because I had to come out of that. So I put my nose down to roll out but I didn't know how much damage I had. I could smell gas and I could smell cordite. I checked with everybody and nobody had got hit. I told them to cut back on the electricity; no sparks.

'Then the rear gunner came up and said, 'We've got something trailing behind us.' It was the rubber pieces (the seals) from along the bomb doors or what little was left of them. It (the Tallboy bomb) had ripped them both (the bomb doors) off the aircraft and they (the rubber strips) were hanging out my back end. The bomb had dropped. The bomb aimer had let it go when we were up-side down. So when I turned down the whole damn issue went through the doors and everything because I was upside down when he let it go and I had pulled the doors shut.

'We weren't that far from home base so we could just keep going. I gradually put the speed up. We were checking everything we had to see if we had to evacuate or what. The Lanc just kept on going and going and going so I saw the opportunity that we were going to make it. I said, 'Everybody get prepared, get your chutes on, get in your emergency positions. If we blow up, we'll blow up together.' I hit the button and gave my call sign. I said we were heavily damaged by flak and had to come straight in, 'No more contact-Give me the runway only!' We landed. The aircraft stayed together.

"We taxied around to my dispersal and I put it in nose first because I knew they were going to have to pull it out. We got out and it was peppered to living Jesus. I'd never seen anything like it. The whole surface of the wing and the bottom of the fuselage and where the bomb bay was. We had a piece of about twelve inches just cut right out of the main spar. We almost got a direct hit I'm sure. It must have been or it couldn't have taken that damn thing out.

"The engineering officer came up and I explained to him what had happened and he said, 'Do you mind if we push it out onto the grass?' So they pushed it off of the tarmac and onto the grass. I was draining gas, I was draining oil, I was draining glycol. We were just saturated. That (LM492) was my second new aircraft on the squadron. The first one Cheshire got beat up while I was on leave." [49]

V-1s, V-2s, and V-3s

The Tallboy and 617 Squadron's ability to deliver it had been clearly demonstrated and now Bomber Command's attention shifted to Hitler's 'V' or 'Vengeance'8 weapons. As well as the V-1 Flying Bomb that Joe and the squadron had attacked previously, it was now clear that the V-2 Rocket and the V-3 Long Range Guns would be operational soon. Bomber Command had attacked the German experimental rocket base at Pennemunde in August 1943 and this had caused a significant delay in the development of the V-2 program. But production was still going ahead, albeit at a reduced scale and in a number of dispersed locations.

The threat of the V-1 was immediate as the so-called ski sites had been seen in numerous locations across northern France. As well it was now known that larger, underground sites protected with reinforced concrete intended for underground storage were under construction. The first V-1 had fallen on London on 13 June, the day of the raid on the E-Boat pens at Le Havre.

Joe's fellow American pilot on 617, Nick Knilans, had an experience with the V-1 while on leave while in his London hotel. He undoubtedly shared this with Joe and his fellow pilots,

"I crossed the lobby and entered the elevator, asking the girl operator for the sixth floor. She and I were alone as we began our upward trip and we were almost there when we were severely jolted by something like an explosion without sound. The elevator dropped like a stone for forty feet before the emergency brake stopped it.

V-1 Flying Bomb assembly and launch bunker under construction at Siracourt, France.
Imperial War Museum

The operator and I said nothing. She just took me back up to my floor and opened the door to the hallway where a thick cloud of dust enveloped us. Every door had been blown off its hinges and was lying across the hallway carpet. Broken glass and rags were heaped around. In my room, the floor and the furniture were covered with bits of wood and glass from the blown in window. The V-1 had hit the top floor and killed some of the staff while I was in the elevator." [50]

During the last two week of June the squadron records refer to the targets as being "construction works" suggesting that it was not certain at the time exactly what the Nazis intended to use these for although it was clear they would be used for one or more of the Vengeance weapons.

On 19 June, after delaying a day waiting for suitable weather, 617 Squadron sent nineteen Lancasters and two Mosquitos on a daylight raid to attack a large, underground site on the edge of the forest of Éperlecques, one mile from Watten and about 15 miles southeast of Calais. The French living in the area had been told it was to be a power station. They likely would not have believed that it was in fact to be a giant, bomb-proof building from which to fire supersonic rockets.

The structure's reinforced concrete roof was 16.4 feet thick. It was thought that it was being used as a storage site for V-1s but it was also to become a liquid oxygen production facility for the V-2s. As well, features for the movement and launching of the rockets had been incorporated. The internal hall was 92 feet high and the entrance to it was to be through a massive door seven feet thick and filled with 215 tons of concrete. Had the complex been completed, it would have been capable of launching up to 36 V-2s each day.

V-2 Rocket.

The V-1 Flying Bomb could be seen and defended against by fighters and anti-aircraft guns but the V-2 was effectively invisible after it had been launched. The first Londoners knew about a V-2 was when it exploded.

The rocket was 46 feet in length and, fully loaded with fuel and warhead, weighed thirteen tons. From launch to the speed of sound took only thirty seconds. Its maximum trajectory height was between fifty and sixty miles for long-range targets. The warhead weighed one ton and was capable of causing considerable damage.

On 8 September 1944 the first V-2 hurtled down on London without warning and exploded with devastating effect. The campaign reached a climax during February 1945 when 232 hit southern England. In all 1115 struck southern England and of these 517 struck in the London area.

Although 2754 people were killed and about 6500 were injured the V-2 program did not change the course of the war as Hitler had hoped, but it would have had more of an effect had its development not be delayed and many of its vital facilities destroyed by Bomber Command.

W/C Cheshire dove from 10,000 feet to 3000 in his Mosquito and released his spot fires over the Watten site. He reported that they failed to ignite although S/L Shannon

This Tallboy was photographed immediately after its release from 617 Squadron Lancaster JB139 over Watten. The aircraft's pilot was F/O D.H. Cheney RCAF.
Imperial War Museum

returned to Woodhall Spa with his, reporting that they were not required. The Lancasters then bombed with Joe and two other pilots reporting seeing the markers and basing their bombing on them. Joe recorded in his logbook that he spent fifty minutes over the target before releasing his Tallboy from 17,500 feet which indicates that the cloud problems were likely significant. Shannon flew low over the target and reported five hits, the nearest being 150 feet from the aiming point with the average error being 300 feet. There are mixed reports regarding the damage caused, but it likely was not extensive.

On 20 June another large, concrete-covered V-weapons 'Construction Works' was the target, this one at Wizernes about nine miles south of Watten. 617 Squadron sent nineteen Lancasters and three Mosquitos but all were recalled due to heavy cloud over the target. Joe, now flying Lancaster 'W,' was on the Battle Order but did not take off due to engine trouble.

The operation was scheduled again for the following day but cancelled just one hour prior to take off. Then on 22 June, Joe was part of a planned raid that included seventeen 617 Lancasters and three Mosquitos. Again the target was Wizernes and again the weather was bad. The force took off but was recalled.

Finally on 24 June the squadron was successful in reaching Wizernes. Like Watten, Wizernes was a large site that had not been completed and in their reports, Joe and other

The enormous bunker at Watten (late 1944).
U.S. National Archives and Records Administration

pilots referred to the 'dome.' This was a huge concrete feature that rose above a large area that had been tunnelled out beneath a quarry. The weather was clear over the target. This had the benefit of allowing the Lancasters to release their Tallboys from high altitude to maximize their effectiveness. The disadvantage, as always, was that the good visibility made the bombers easier targets during the long run-up to the release point that was required by thc SABS bomb sight .

The Lancaster flown by F/Lt. Edwards was hit in the port wing by flak over the target area and went down out of control and in flames, exploding prior to striking the ground. As this was a daylight raid many of the 617 aircrew would have watched this happen. There were reports that four parachutes were seen. Later the squadron learned that F/Lt. Edwards and three of his crew had been killed. Of the four who parachuted, one died shortly after of his wounds and three became Prisoners of War.

The Watten site is a museum today.

W/C Cheshire was unable to release his two red spot fires but F/Lt. Fawke, after diving from 17,000 feet to 6,000 before releasing, placed his accurately on the aiming point. His Mosquito was hit several times by flak as he did so.

With the good visibility, the reports from the pilots were detailed, many claiming very accurate results and F/Lt. Reid reported that he, "Saw three bombs about fifty yards from the mouth of tunnel; Saw one bomb penetrate roof of tunnel and it seemed to burst inside; There was no smoke but the ground seemed to lift and erupt." As for Joe, he reported seeing "Four bursts some fifty to one hundred yards short of the dome" after he dropped his Tallboy from 17,500 feet. His logbook entry refers to the site as a 'rocket site,' indicating that he knew what was planned for the 'construction works.' It was his 65th operation.

The raid was a success with many of the Tallboys proving effective. Damage had been caused to the domed roof and to installations in it. One of the bombs had caused a large landslide that blocked the railway track and an entrance to the structure. Other bombs had destroyed secondary installations in the vicinity. Although damage had been inflicted the work at Wizernes continued. Another raid by 617 Squadron on 17 July would finish the job.

The significance of the Wizernes site was not fully understood at the time that it was attacked by Joe and his squadron. It was later described as one of the great civil engineering feats of the war. The dome was built first, 233 feet in diameter, 16.5 feet thick, and with a weight of 55,000 tons. Excavated beneath it was a rocket launching base with control apparatus and facilities to store, transport, fuel, and service the V-2s. A railway supply tunnel was to lead to all of the underground workings and to a large octagonal chamber beneath the dome. The octagonal chamber would have a diameter of 135 feet with a

The Wizernes dome was declared an historic site in 1985 by the French government.
Clare Bennett

height to the underside of the dome of eighty feet-seven stories high. The rockets were moved while upright through the preparation zone beneath the dome on wheeled bogies prior to emerging at the other side through steel doors that were five feet thick and 55 feet high into the open for launch. The design was such that forty to fifty V-2 Rockets could be launched each day.

The facility was, of course, built with slave labour. It was later determined that a similar structure was being built at Watten. Some 40,000 forced laborers worked on the German secret weapons sites in northern France, 6000 of them at the Watten site alone.

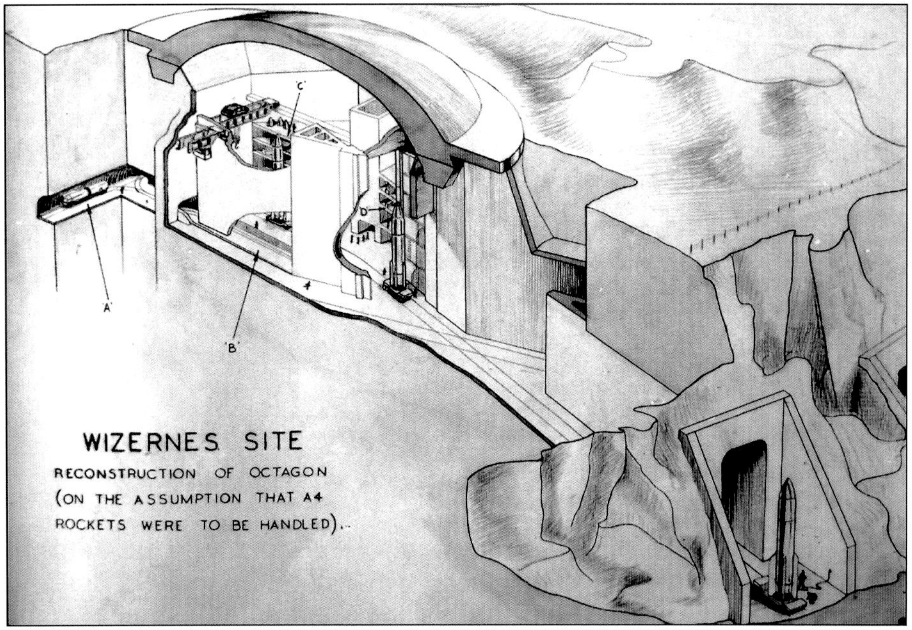

An artist's rendering showing what the Wizernes site would have looked like had it been completed.

The Wizernes site in late June. Although pitted with craters and the railway lines had been destroyed, construction work on the concrete dome (upper-left) and the underground workings continued until another Tallboy raid on 17 July when sixteen 617 Squadron Lancasters dropped Tallboys and all work at the site was stopped.
Imperial War Museum

The following day, 25 June, the squadron was ordered out again to a construction works at Siracourt, forty miles south-southeast of Calais. This one was a V-1 Flying Bomb assembly, storage and launching facility, a series of four huge bunkers. The exterior of the complex measured 120 feet by 700 feet and was 33 feet high. It was still under construction and had it been completed as planned would have been capable of launching two V-1s every hour of the day.

Despite his successful marking from the Mosquito aircraft which was much faster and more manoeuvrable than a Lancaster, Cheshire was still not satisfied and had been trying to obtain an even smaller and more nimble aircraft. The North American P-51 Mustang seemed ideal. It had a top speed of 440 mph, a much longer range than a Spitfire, and could carry two 1000 pound bombs under its wings.

Two crated Mustang IIIs had been delivered to the squadron at Woodhall Spa on 21 June. Much of the aircraft's components were covered with thick grease for shipping and, as well as assembling and ground-testing the Mustang, the ground crew had to remove all of this. Another problem was that, an 'ad hoc' bomb release had to be made as the American unit that came with the aircraft would not accept British bombs.

Cheshire had not been able to fly the aircraft prior to taking off to mark the target at Siracourt so his first flight in the Mustang would be an operational one that required low and very exact flying. It has been said that as he sat in the cockpit prior to taking off for Siracourt, he was reading the instruction book and somewhat concerned that he wouldn't have a navigator with him as he did when flying the Mosquito.

Cheshire identified the huge concrete structure and dove from seven thousand feet releasing his two red spot fires from 500 feet and accurately marking the target. Dave Shannon and Gerry Fawke followed up with more spot fires and smoke bombs from their Mosquitos. Seventeen Lancasters then dropped their Tallboys, Joe releasing his from 18,500 feet.

The pilots felt that the bombing was accurate, including Joe who reported that his Tallboy struck just 150 feet west of the markers and that he saw three others fall near the aiming point.

A Painting of Leonard Cheshire's 617 Squadron Mustang III.
Artist Mark Postlethwaite www.posart.com

Low-level oblique aerial photograph showing the flying-bomb assembly and launch bunker at Siracourt after 617 Squadron's attack on June 25, 1944.
Imperial War Museum

W/C Cheshire reported, "One direct hit which penetrated the roof of the building and caused a large explosion; One hit by the western wall of the building which blew the wall in; One very near miss that created a crater whose rim was raised up against the western wall; Several hits on the area to the east of the long building."

Later analysis showed that the site had certainly been struck, but that the damage was not as significant as first thought. Having said that, the raid was a success in that all future work on the site was stopped and it was never completed.

Joe's beloved Q-Queenie (LM492) had been repaired and Joe took it up for an 'Air Test' on 27 June. Three days later he flew the aircraft to the aerodrome at Silverstone for some reason. While there he was somehow able to get his hands on a Spitfire and take it up for a flight which, according to his logbook entry, he really enjoyed.

On 4 July Joe was again flying Q-Queenie on an operation, this one to a V-1 storage facility near Creil, northeast of Paris. The Flying Bombs were being stored in a large cave that had formerly been used by French farmers to grow mushrooms. The caves had been enlarged and reinforced by linings of concrete up to five feet thick and their entrances were fitted with steel doors. The plan was for 617 to bring down as much debris as possible at the entrance. A main force of 328 aircraft would then follow.

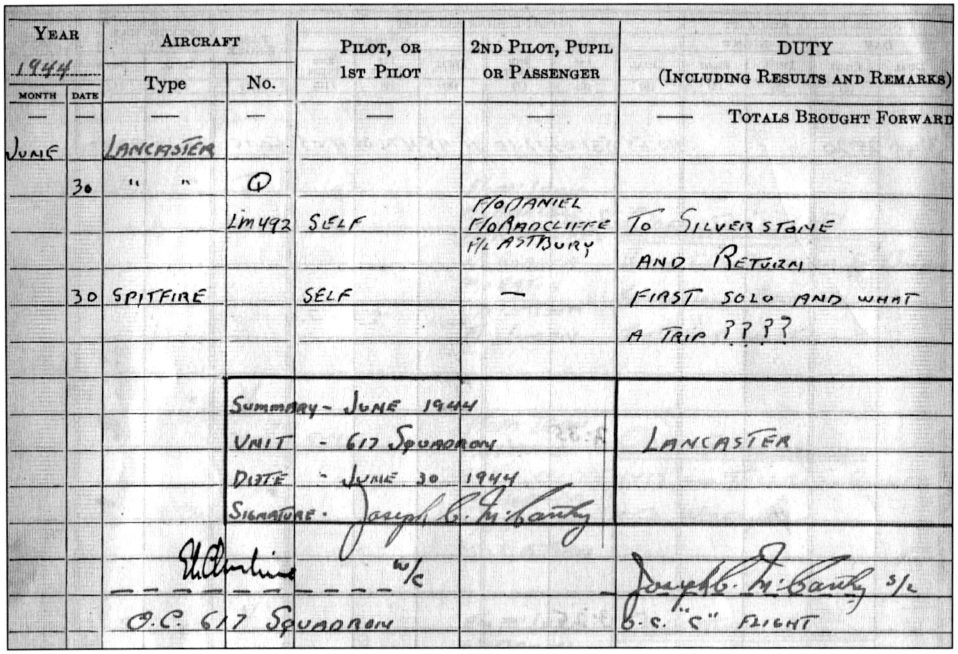

YEAR 1944 MONTH	DATE	AIRCRAFT Type	No.	PILOT, OR 1ST PILOT	2ND PILOT, PUPIL OR PASSENGER	DUTY (INCLUDING RESULTS AND REMARKS)
—	—	—	—	—	—	— TOTALS BROUGHT FORWARD
JUNE		LANCASTER				
	30	" "	Q			
			LM492	SELF	F/O DANIEL F/O RADCLIFFE F/L ASTBURY	TO SILVERSTONE AND RETURN
	30	SPITFIRE		SELF	—	FIRST SOLO AND WHAT A TRIP ????
			SUMMARY - JUNE 1944 UNIT - 617 SQUADRON DATE - JUNE 30 1944 SIGNATURE · Joseph C. McCarthy			LANCASTER
		[signature] W/C O.C. 617 SQUADRON				Joseph C. McCarthy S/L O.C. "C" FLIGHT

Joe's logbook entry recording his Spitfire flight.
The McCarthy Family

Cheshire dove his Mustang from 5000 feet and released his markers accurately from 800 feet. F/Lt. Fawke, flying a Mosquito, was not required to place his markers and the seventeen Lancasters were ordered to drop their Tallboys. Although some returned to Woodhall Spa with their bomb on board because the target was obscured by smoke most were accurately placed with one direct hit and another near-miss destroying the entrance to the tunnel. Joe dropped his from 18,500 feet, reporting that he, "Could not see the markers and bombed to the northwest of the concentration." The main force then dropped their bombs. None of the 617 Squadron aircraft were lost but enemy fighters arrived in time to attack the main force and twelve bombers were shot down.

Although he didn't know it at the time, this was Joe McCarthy's final wartime operation.

Two days later, Leonard Cheshire led the squadron on a successful attack on the V-3 site that was under construction at Mimoyecques near Marquise, France. Here there was a massive slab of concrete that protected a series of tunnels dug into the chalk which were to contain ten clusters of five, 400 foot long, smooth-bore long-range guns. Nothing would show above ground but the end of the gun barrels, all of which were aimed at London. Using slave-labour, the site was massive and complex. Had it been completed, it would have been capable of lobbing a 500 pound shell into London every minute. The raid caused significant damage as the 'earthquakes' caused great damage to the tunnels and the gun barrels. The

Low-level oblique aerial photograph of the bomb-cratered V-3 site at Mimoyecques. At upper centre is the concrete slab covering the guns which were to have fired on London.
Imperial War Museum

site was closed and all work had ceased when the Canadian Army arrived a month later.

This was Leonard Cheshire's 100th operation with Bomber Command.

Many of the 617 Squadron veterans, Leonard Cheshire in particular, were living on borrowed time. Prior to his 99th trip Arthur Pollen, Woodhall's intelligence officer, asked him how he felt about it. Cheshire replied, "You don't feel the strain Arthur, you keep on going more-or-less automatically and don't worry." Cheshire's right eye had begun to twitch and Pollen was concerned.

On 10 July W/C Cheshire was summoned to 5 Group Headquarters where Air Vice Marshal Cochrane told him,

'I've been looking at the records and I see you've done 100 now. That's enough. It's time you had a rest. I've got hold of Tait (G/C James 'Willie' Tait) to take over. It's no use arguing. Sorry but there it is. 100 is a good number to stop at. Shannon, Munro, and McCarthy will come off too. They've been going continuously for about two years and it's time they had a rest as well." [51]

With that, AVM Cochrane removed the commanding officer and the three flight commanders from the squadron. All protested and claimed that they could carry on, but Cochrane would not hear of it. He knew that it was time. Upon Cochrane's recommendation, Leonard Cheshire was awarded the Victoria Cross for his outstanding efforts.

Joe McCarthy photographed towards the end of WWII.
The McCarthy Family

Cheshire held Cochrane in the highest regards as well, later writing,

"In tracing the evolution of our low-level bombing technique don't under-estimate the contribution of Cochrane. He is the only senior officer with a really clear, unbiased brain that I have met. He followed our course with great attention to detail, was remarkably quick to grasp the fundamentals, and was seldom hoodwinked. If I ever asked for anything and he refused, he always gave me clearly his reasons . . . He is, of course, a strict disciplinarian, ruthless in dealing with inefficiency, and there is no doubt that he was the key figure behind all that 617 achieved." [52]

Upon reflection, Cheshire likely agreed with Cochrane's decision and gave some thought to some of the other veterans in the squadron. Just prior to Cheshire's departure from the squadron, Bill Hume, who had joined 617 Squadron immediately following the Dams Raid, recalls being ordered to report to Cheshire's office following his 49th operation. Bill was told that, "He'd done enough." He tried to convince Cheshire to let him do one more operation so that he could reach an even fifty. Cheshire replied curtly, "Believe me, that could be the one. So there's the door."

Having completed 67 operations, Joe McCarthy had flown about five times the average number of ops for a Bomber Command pilot. Statistically he should have been killed a long, long, time ago. It had been two years since that first operation to Düsseldorf in a Hampden on 31 July 1942 and he had been on operations virtually the entire time since.

On 20 July Joe was posted to 61 Base, the RCAFs training group at Topcliffe in Yorkshire. Joe's crewmembers were all taken off operations as well with the exception of bomb aimer Danny Daniel who would become the new C/Os bomb aimer. After being together for so long and having gone through so much together it must have been difficult for these men to go their separate ways. Navigator Don MacLean was posted to 1664 Conversion Unit, Len Eaton was awarded the Distinguished Flying Medal and sent to 84 OTU, mid-upper gunner Ron Batson was posted to 16 OTU, Flight Engineer Bill Radcliffe was posted to 1654 Conversion Unit, and rear gunner Dave Rodger was awarded the Distinguished Flying Cross. The citation reads,

"Flight Lieutenant Rodger has taken part in many operational sorties as rear gunner. His targets have included such defended objectives as Berlin, Hamburg and centres in the Ruhr. He has also participated in low level attacks on transformer stations, viaducts and other vital targets in France. His calm resolution in the face of the heaviest opposition has always been an inspiration to his crew." [53]

Dave Rodger DFC.

Rodger returned to Canada in September 1944 where he was married. He was released from the RCAF the following year.

W/C Willie Tait took over 617 Squadron and led it on many more successful operations including the sinking of the Battleship Tirpitz. Danny Daniel continued as part of W/C Tait's crew and according to Joe, it was his Tallboy that sunk the battleship. Following Tait, Canadian Johnny Fauquier became commanding officer and led many raids during which 617 Squadron's Lancasters dropped the massive Grand Slam bomb, similar to the Tallboy but weighing 22,000 pounds.

W/C Johnny Fauquier and a 22,000 pound Grand Slam.

Royal Canadian Air Force

(l-r) Bill Radcliffe, Joe McCarthy, and Don MacLean.
Nell Rodger

Part Seven

Non-combat Flying

"We had a policy that we don't let any Jerry show us how to fly an airplane. I had lots of people in the German Air Force who wanted to show me how to fly their Condor and I said, No, I'll just work with the ground crew and they'll tell me what it's all about and I'll fly it."

The Fighter Affiliation Unit at Dalton

Having spent the past two and one-half years as an RCAF officer serving with units of the RAF, Joe was reclaimed by the Royal Canadian Air Force and briefly posted to 6 Group Headquarters. Although operating as part of RAF Bomber Command, 6 Group was somewhat independent and largely made up of and commanded by Canadian airmen. Formed on 1 January 1943 it grew to fourteen squadrons.

On 1 August 1944 Joe was made commanding officer of a Royal Canadian Air Force fighter affiliation unit, 1695 Bomber Defence Training Flight, at Dalton in Yorkshire where he flew Hawker Hurricanes and Airspeed Oxfords.

The training at Dalton involved exposing bomber aircrew to mock attacks by friendly fighters to enhance their skills and teach them techniques to avoid and survive fighter attacks.

During September the King visited the nearly RCAF Station at Topcliffe to present decorations to RCAF aircrew. Joe had been awarded a Bar to his Distinguished Flying Cross on 28 April 1944 and travelled to Topcliffe where the decoration was presented to him by the King.

Joe's last flight at Dalton was on 9 November 1944. Less than a week later, he was back with the Royal Air Force.

King George VI presenting S/L McCarthy with the Bar to his Distinguished Flying Cross at Topcliffe.
The McCarthy Family

Joe McCarthy (centre) at the RCAF station at Dalton.
The McCarthy Family

The Royal Aeronautical Establishment at Farnborough

On 15 November 1944 Joe was posted to the Royal Aircraft Establishment at Farnborough to serve with the 'Experimental Flying Section.'

The variety of aircraft that he flew over the next few months is astonishing and speaks volumes as to his piloting skills and the confidence the RAF had in him. The types vary from operational bombers that were new to him, through a naval torpedo bomber designed to be flown from aircraft carriers, to a number of front-line fighter aircraft.

Between 22 and 30 November his logbook records flights in the North American B-25 Mitchell twin-engined bomber, Airspeed Oxford twin-engined trainer, Supermarine Spitifire fighter, North American Mustang fighter, Avro Anson, Handley-Page Halifax heavy bomber, and Martin B-26 Marauder medium bomber.

During December he flew the Lockheed Hudson light bomber, Armstrong-Whitworth Whitley twin-engined bomber, Douglas DC-3 Dakota transport, Fairey Swordfish torpedo bomber, North American Harvard advanced trainer, Consolidated B-24 Liberator heavy bomber, Douglas A-20 Boston light bomber, and Hawker Tempest fighter.

Then in January he flew the Vickers Wellington twin-engined bomber, de Havilland Mosquito fighter/bomber, and de Havilland DH.89 Dominie light transport.

Joe took off for his first trans-Atlantic flight on 20 February 1945, returning to Canada after a three year absence as a passenger in an RCAF B-24 Liberator. Following a stop at the Azores the aircraft flew for twelve hours and twenty minutes before landing at Moncton, New Brunswick and carrying on to Dorval near Montreal, Quebec. Later that day, Joe flew a Harvard to Newark, New Jersey where he spent some well-deserved time with his family.

Joe was soon back in Canada, flying a Hudson on 7 March and making six flights in a DC-3 Dakota during the following week.

On 31 March he was at the controls of a Lancaster again when he flew KB975, a brand new Canadian-built Mk. X across the Atlantic. Following a flight from Dorval to Gander in Labrador, Joe landed in Prestwick, Scotland following an 8 hour and 35 minute trans-Atlantic flight.

KB975 was one of 430 Lancasters manufactured in Canada, a tremendous achievement for a country still largely agrarian and just recovering from a decade of depression with very little experience in manufacturing aircraft. The challenge was immense. 500,000 manufacturing operations were involved in building a Lancaster which was made up of some 55,000 separate parts even when engines and turrets were only considered as one and small items such as rivets, nuts, and bolts were not included. Almost all were flown to Britain and assigned to 6 Group squadrons.

The Canadian-built Lancs served well, some 100 being lost in wartime service, approximately seventy missing in action and about thirty others crashing upon their return to England or in training. KB732 flew the most operations of any Canadian-built Lancaster, completing 83 operations during its tour of duty with 419 Squadron.

Lancaster Mk. X KB799, the one hundredth aircraft to roll off of the Victory Aircraft Limited assembly line.

Test Flying the Vickers Windsor

On 5 April 1945 Joe was seconded to Vickers-Armstrongs to test fly the Windsor Bomber. Again Joe was intimately involved with another of Barnes Wallis' ideas.

The Vickers Wellington was a twin-engined aircraft that was operational at the beginning of the war and served in a number of capacities throughout the conflict. Barnes Wallis had been the designer and had incorporated a geodetic framework that proved to be very successful. This geodetic design was utilized for the much larger, four-engined Windsor.

Designed as a high-altitude heavy bomber, the aircraft featured a pressurized crew compartment. Its geodetic fuselage and wing structures were covered by a stiff, light skin made with woven steel wires and very thin stainless steel ribbon which was doped with plastic. The Windsor had a wingspan of 117 feet, a cruising speed of 345 mph, and could fly at an altitude of 31,000 feet. The prototype flew on 23 October 1943 and a total of three were built. A unique feature of the aircraft was that it had four main-wheel struts, each extending from one of the engine nacelles.

Defensive armament included guns mounted in barbettes at the rear of each outboard nacelle.

Vickers Windsor.

These were to be remotely operated by a gunner in a pressurized compartment at the rear end of the fuselage.

The program was cancelled on 15 March 1946.

Syd Clay of Charlottetown, Prince Edward Island was a Sptifire pilot and recalls seeing the Vickers Windsor and meeting Joe McCarthy at RAF Pembrey in South Wales,

"A large four-engined aircraft joined the circuit. No one could identify it but it sported the RAF roundels so we all relaxed.

"Then, on the downwind leg preparatory to landing, a strange thing occurred. The pilot lowered the undercarriage and to our astonishment a wheel descended from each of the four nacelles. No one had ever seen anything like that before. A very smooth landing followed and immediately the aircraft taxied to a remote corner of the airfield and subsequent efforts to approach it were thwarted by armed guards, nor was there any sign of the crew.

"Naturally the Officers Mess was a-buzz that evening when our c/o entered accompanied by a very large Squadron Leader who had an impressive row of ribbons on his breast. It was then that we learned

At the Angle Aerodrome in Pembrokeshire, Wales. Joe is seated at right.

The McCarthy Family

the identity of the pilot of the strange aircraft. It turned out to be the Vickers Windsor.

"Why had it come to Pembrey? It was never divulged to us. We in the fighter flight had our hopes raised that we would be involved but those hopes were soon dashed.

"Shortly after dawn the following morning the Windsor roared off into the morning mists never to be seen again at Pembrey.

"However that brief episode, particularly meeting the fabled 'Dambuster,' stands out in my memories of the war." [1]

Joe had been flying the Mk. II version of the Vickers Windsor. His involvement with the testing of the aircraft ended on 25 May with what he referred to in his logbook as the, "First air test of the controls and a general acceptance check" of the Windsor Mk. III.

During his time test-flying the Windsor, Joe had been flying other aircraft as well including Spitfires, Wellingtons, and doing an armed 'Diving Trial' in a Hawker Typhoon ground-attack fighter.

The Foreign Aircraft Flight

Joe was then posted to the Foreign Aircraft Flight at Farnborough which was under the command of Squadron Leader H.J. King. Joe's logbook entry refers to it as the 'Enemy Aircraft Flight.' This group had the task of locating examples of a wide range of Luftwaffe aircraft types, ferrying them back to England, and evaluating them. Initially, this involved flying and driving around looking for aircraft in what was now a defeated and occupied Germany.

During his seven months with the Flight, Joe flew a total of twenty different former Luftwaffe aircraft-an amazing variety of fighters, bombers, and transports.

Joe recalled S/L King and the Flight's policy towards their former enemies and the flying of their aircraft,

"S/L King was a World War I officer and he was a Squadron Leader with me at that time. He was an elderly fellow and he was in charge of the flight when they decided that we should go and start picking up these German aircraft. After we started picking them up, King got sick and that's when they gave me the job to go over there.

"We had a policy even before King left that we don't let any Jerry show us how to fly an airplane. I had lots of people in the German Air Force who wanted to show me how to fly their Condor, their four-engined airplane, and I said, 'No, I'll just work with the ground crew and they'll tell me what it's all about and I'll fly it.' We were not going to have them put one step up on us. We were going to sit on them the way they were supposed to be sat on, so we did.

"A lot of the aircraft there we flew by ourselves without anybody telling us how to do it. The ground crew could tell us about gas tank switch-overs, RPMs and things of that nature. Speeds were questioned but once you got airborne you could notice the speed of take off. You'd climb to altitude and then you'd go through the stall phases and that would then give you an opportunity to work back the speeds. You'd put your wheels down and try that until it stalled and then put flaps down too at the same time and stall again. Then you'd have a series of speeds that you know that were safe before it started shaking, or dipping, or doing something like that. Then you'd go back to the circuit and try a few circuits and bumps, not actually touching down but getting enough of the feel of it. Then you'd come around, touch down, and land." [2]

A Messerschmitt Me 262 two-seat jet night-fighter was the first to be flown to Farnborough, arriving on 19 May 1945 after an overnight stop at Gilze-Rijen in the Netherlands. German aircraft would continue to be delivered until 18 January 1946 and a total of about 250 were brought to Farnborough.

Joe's first involvement with the Foreign Aircraft Flight was as the commanding officer of an RAF outpost in northern Germany. On 1 June 1945 he flew a Lancaster from Farnborough to Schleswig in northern Germany, 20 miles south of the Danish border and 60 miles north of Hamburg. His task was to coordinate the delivery of selected aircraft to Schleswig where they would be overhauled and prepared for delivery to Farnborough. Various staging points were established in Holland and Belgium where fuel and other support could be provided en route.

Joe recalled how his detachment operated,

"Initially we were supposed to go over there only for a day or two at a time but as they kept going around eventually we had to move over. They gave me the British ground crew that had been working on German aircraft and there were five pilots and myself. I had an aircraft with a radio in it. We'd use that

to communicate with our headquarters and they'd give us their instructions as to the locations and types of airplane that were already ear-marked. They were ear-marked because they knew that they were there and they weren't broken or bent.

"I would work with the British Army in regions that these aircraft were located in to see if the airport I wanted to go to was free. If it was free we'd go and get the airplane. In the meantime we'd picked up these caravans (trailers) that they pulled behind tanks. We had about four or five of those and we had trucks and we had jeeps and some German trucks so we had a caravan going. We looked like a bunch of Gypsies at times.

Siebel Si 204 at Flensburg.
William Sutherland

"The only thing that was bad about it was that on two occasions we had people killed by jumping up on an airplane when we got there, opening up the hood and then, 'Boom.'"[3]

The aircraft had been "booby-trapped" as the enemy was in the process of surrendering to the Allies.

The Siebel Si 204, a small twin-engined transport and trainer, was the first German aircraft that Joe flew. With S/L King as the pilot and Joe as co-pilot, the aircraft was ferried from Ecgbaek to Flensburg near the Danish border where hundreds of German aircraft had been assembled for disposal. Three days later, Joe flew the aircraft to Schleswig.

For the next seven months Joe's logbook documents almost daily flights and as many as five flights in a single day, in an astounding variety of aircraft.

Joe became very familiar with the Junkers Ju 352, first flying the type on 11 June and making a total of 22 flights in the aircraft.

Joe had flown numerous twin-engined aircraft and lots of four-engined aircraft but the Junkers Ju 352 Herkules was his first three-engined aircraft. The Ju 352 was powered by three BMW nine-cylinder radial engines. It was a large, transport aircraft with a

Junkers Ju 352 Herkules.

wingspan of 112 feet and was armed with a cannon and turret. Its wooden propellers featured reverse-pitch which reduced the length of runway required for landing by up to sixty percent. One was acquired by the Czechoslovakian government, restored, and then presented to Josef Stalin as a gift.

It was clear that immediately following the war Joe had no particular desire to befriend or work with the Germans he encountered though his work with the Foreign Aircraft Flight,

"The only one that I ever admired was a Major Kramer. He was flying 352s and he was in charge of the Germans that we had that we took out of the Prisoner of War camps. He went in and picked them up for us; the ones that were qualified. He was really influential with those German ground crews.

"He wasn't a boastful type. He was one of those individuals that you admired to a degree because he did have a rough time. As a matter of fact I was talking to him about 352s because I knew that he'd been flying them.

"We got talking about the Mediterranean and he said he used to fly across it to bring supplies to Rommel's troops. I asked him what he thought of the airplanes he flew. He said, 'Oh, it treat me

Focke Wulf Fw 200 Condor.

very good but I put them down in the Mediterranean five times.' I said, 'Why was that?' and he said, 'Your fighters.' He was a funny man. I liked him. He did wonders with the ground crew that we had." [4]

Once evaluated, the Ju 352 appears to have been used for various duties by the Flight. On 31 July S/L King flew the aircraft from Farnborough to Schleswig with Joe as co-pilot and twelve passengers. Three days later Joe flew the aircraft to Kiel to pick up a load of aircraft parts.

Joe made his first of eleven flights in the Focke Wulf FW 200 Condor on 19 June. Referred to by Winston Churchill as the 'Scourge of the Atlantic,' this long range reconnaissance bomber and military transport was a large aircraft which had a range of 2212 miles and could fly for fourteen hours. It clearly demonstrated its capabilities to the world when a specially modified Condor completed a non-stop flight from Berlin to New York on 10 August 1938 in 24 hours and 56 minutes.

Despite the fact that relatively few Condors were built, the aircraft caused great losses to British shipping while operating from bases in France. The Condor could also act as an airborne command post, directing U-Boats towards Allied shipping.

The Junkers Ju 290 was a four-engined, long-range maritime surveillance and transport aircraft that had a top speed of 273 mph and a range of 3821 miles. Joe made a total of nine flights in this type.

Hitler selected a Ju 290 to be his personal aircraft and appropriate modifications were

Joe relaxing in a Junkers Ju 290 en route to London.
The McCarthy Family

Junkers Ju 290.

1	J.U. 290	A.M. 6	SELF	F/O CLARK	LUBECK - FARNBOROUGH.
3	J.U. 290	A.M. 6	SELF	F/O CLARK	FARNBOROUGH - SCHLESWIG
4	OXFORD	346	SELF	F/L FOSTER F/L READING	HUSUM + FLENSBERG
4	M.E. 108		SELF	—	HUSUM - SCHLESWIG
6	CONDOR 200	A.M 97	SELF	F/O CLARK	FLENSBERG - SCHLESWIG. AIR TEST.
7	J.U. 290	A.M. 6	SELF	S/L M. BAINE F/O CLARK F/O GERRARD	SCHLESWIG - COPENHAGEN
8	JU. 290	A.M. 6	SELF	F/O CLARK	AIR TEST
9	J.U. 290	A.M. 6	SELF	F/O CLARK	COPENHAGEN - SCHLESWIG
9	J.U. 290	A.M. 6	SELF	F/O CLARK	SCHLESWIG - COPENHAGEN
16	J.U. 290	A.M. 6	SELF	F/O CLARK	COPENHAGEN - SCHLESWIG
11	ARADO 232	A.M.	SELF	GERMAN FLIGHT ENGINEER	FIRST HANDLING + PICK UP AT LECK
11	ARADO 232	A.M.	SELF	GERMAN FLIGHT ENGINEER	LECK - SCHLESWIG.
11	ARADO 232	A.M.	SELF	GERMAN FLIGHT ENGINEER	SCHLESWIG - FLENSBERG.
11	ARADO 232	A.M.	SELF	GERMAN FLIGHT ENGINEER	FLENSBERG - SCHLESWIG.
13	ARADO 232	A.M.	SELF	GERMAN FLIGHT ENGINEER	SCHLESWIG - GILIZ - RIJEN
13	CONDOR 200	A.M.	S/L KING ~~SELF~~	SELF	GILIZ-RIJEN - SCHLESWIG
14	JU- 52	A.M.	S/L SOMERVILLE	SELF	SCHLESWIG - GILIZ RIJEN
14	ARADO 232	A.M.	SELF	F/O WARREN GERMAN ENG. F/S MARTIN	GILIZ-RIJEN - FARNBOROUGH

Joe's logbook entries indicate a busy two weeks during July 1945.
The McCarthy Family

Arado 232.
William Sutherland

made to it including an armoured passenger compartment and an escape hatch that was fitted into the floor. A parachute was built into Hitler's seat and in an emergency he was to put the parachute on, pull a lever to open the hatch, and roll out through the opening. The aircraft was ready for Hitler's use by February 1945 but he never flew in it. Hitler's Ju 290 was destroyed in a bombing raid the following month.

On 11 July Joe flew the Arado Ar 232B and went on to complete six flights in the aircraft over the next three days. It is interesting to note in his logbook that on each flight there was a 'German flight engineer' aboard.

The aircraft was a large, four-engine, twin-boom, transport that had been nicknamed the 'millipede.' It had a complex arrangement of eleven pairs of small wheels that were used to support the fuselage during loading and unloading operations after the tricycle main landing gear had been partially raised by means of two hydraulic rams.

The aircraft was armed with a machine gun in the nose, one or two in the rear of the fuselage, and a 20 mm cannon in a powered dorsal turret.

On 1 August Joe and S/L King flew to Grove in Denmark aboard an Airspeed Oxford to pick up a Heinkel He 219 Owl. Following an air test at Grove, Joe flew the aircraft to

Schleswig. Six days later he repeated the flights with a second example of the He 219. On 19 August Joe flew an Owl to Farnborough

The Heinkel He 219 Uhu or 'Owl' was the Luftwaffe's most dreaded night-fighter. On its first operation of the war, Warner Streib destroyed five Berlin-bound Lancasters within thirty minutes. With a top speed of 416 mph, it was a deadly adversary against the Allied bomber forces but, fortunately for Bomber Command, only 268 Owls were produced.

Powered by two Daimler-Benz inverted V-12 liquid cooled engines that developed 1900 HP, the Owls were heavily armed with two 20mm cannons in the wing roots, two 30mm cannons in a belly tray in a belly tray, and two more cannons in a Shräge Musik mount that pointed upward.

On 6 September Joe made his first flight in what was likely the most exotic, challenging, and dangerous aircraft that he would ever fly, the Dornier Do 335. Joe had never noted any details regarding characteristics of the aircraft he flew in his logbook but in this case the entry included, 'Motors fore and aft." Nicknamed the 'Arrow,' the Do 335 was Germany's most advanced piston-powered fighter of the war with twin DB 603 engines that produced 2100 hp each. What made it unique was that the engines were in tandem, with one in the nose and the other in the tail. The Do 335 had an impressive maximum speed of 413 mph but a sustained speed of 477 mph could be reached with emergency boost. It was one of the fastest piston-engined fighters ever built.

When Joe flew the Do 335 it would have been a most exhilarating experience but there must have been thoughts of the ejection seat (which was a very new concept at this time) coupled with the knowledge that there was an entire engine and a very large propeller directly behind him. It may not have been that comforting to know that the upper tail fin and the rear propeller were equipped with explosive bolts to separate them from the fuselage to avoid impacting the pilot in the case of an ejection.

The prototype was not completed until early 1945 and it is thought that the Do 335 never entered combat although there were sightings of the strange aircraft. There was a report of four RAF Hawker Tempests intercepting, by chance, a lone Do 335 over northern Germany during April 1945. After detecting the RAF fighters, the Do 335 pilot reversed

Heinkel He 219 Uhu (Owl).

Dornier Do 335.

course and easily outran the Tempests despite their considerable speed that was comparable to that of the P-51 Mustang.

The young lady provides a sense of scale to the massive Dornier Do 335 twin-engined fighter.

The RAF was eager to evaluate the aircraft but the staff at Farnborough had learned that the Americans had acquired most of the Do 335s. It made sense then to send S/L McCarthy to Munich to negotiate with them. Upon his arrival on 6 September Joe learned that the Americans were willing to trade two Do 335s; a fighter and a two-seat trainer. With the permission of the Air Ministry, Joe offered ten Fw 190s and a deal was struck. Joe completed an air test on one of the 'Arrows' the following day and then flew it to Strasberg. The following day Joe flew the aircraft to Farnborough with stops en-route at Reims and Manston.

Later the aircraft came to a tragic end when, during a familiarization flight on 18 January 1946, the rear engine over-heated, caught fire, and the elevator controls burned through. The aircraft plunged vertically killing RAF Group Captain Alan F. Hards, the Commanding Officer of Experimental Flying at Farnborough. After this accident, severe restrictions were placed on the flying of ex-Luftwaffe aircraft at Farnborough.

Joe's one and only crash-landing occurred while flying in a twin-engined Junkers Ju 188 on 14 September. The aircraft was an improved version of the Ju 88, one of the Luftwaffe's most versatile and effective aircraft. Operating as a light bomber and as a night-fighter it was most effective and shot down thousands of Allied bombers. In fact it had been a Ju 88 that had attacked Joe's Lancaster almost three years earlier on one of his first operations. The Ju 188 became operational too late in the war to have any significant impact.

Joe described the accident,

"I was flying it and there was only one seat with a walkway beside it on the right. Dick was watching me fly it and I was showing him how to do things like take offs and landings. He was a twin-engined Mosquito boy so he was a good pilot. I liked him very much.

"So I got out of the seat and I was letting him fly. He'd only been flying about five minutes when we lost the starboard motor. He didn't know what to do because he didn't know all the gas things (tank switching procedures) and I didn't know much about it myself. I was leaning over switching tanks and trying to get that damn thing on when the port one went and that's when we went into the boondocks-we went into a field.

"He did a real good belly landing but after we hit the ground I went through the glass. He stopped and I didn't (no harness). I fractured my wrist and hurt my back and my face was all ripped on the left side when I hit the corn field. The Germans sent the ambulance out and got us.

"(Soon) I was back on the base and fine, except for my arm. So I just kept flying because we had lot of work to do. There were a lot of planes that I could fly and I could teach these other guys what to do." [5]

Joe continued to fly German aircraft until 20 December 1945 but beginning in mid-October there were more and more flights with RAF aircraft and fewer German types. Three of the aircraft he flew during this period that were new to him were the Supermarine Walrus, a biplane amphibian with pusher propeller capable of being launched from a ship by catapult and the American designed B-25 Mitchell and B-17 Fortress.

On 16 November 1945 S/L McCarthy flew his first jet, a Gloster Meteor.

Junkers Ju 188.

Gloster Meteor.

"There was another Flight at Farnborough that got all the jet flying so us Goggins on the other flight had to beg, borrow, and steal. So when the jets were not being flown by that group and an opportunity came along I grabbed it so I could say I'd flown a jet.

"It was so nice flying along and not hearing anything. It was beautiful. It was just like sailing."[6]

Joe's last flight with the Foreign Aircraft Flight, with the Royal Air Force and in Europe, was in an Airspeed Oxford on 21 December 1945. The RCAF had a need for an experienced test pilot and Joe was returning to Canada.

At this point in his career, S/L Joe McCarthy had accumulated over 1600 hours on some fifty different aircraft types, including the following:

At the end of October 1945, Joe stapled this list into his logbook.

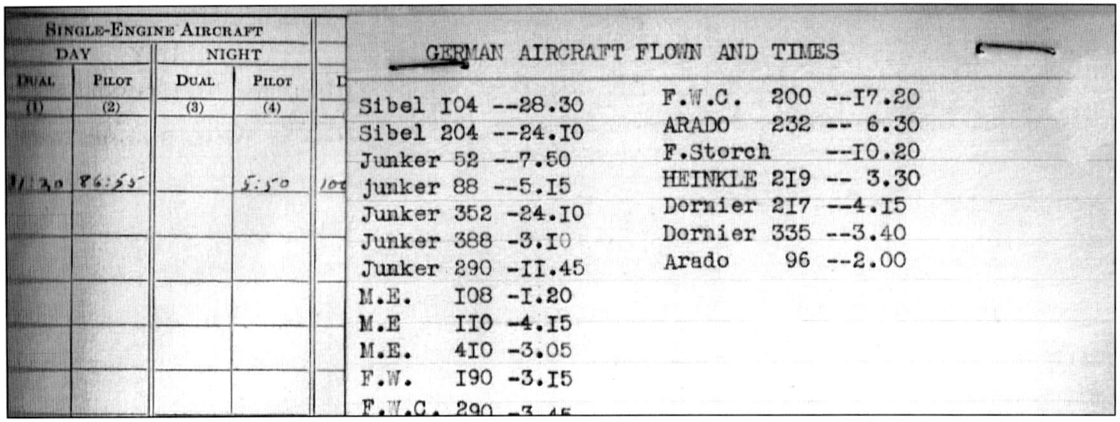
Single-Engine Aircraft
Day | Night
Dual (1) | Pilot (2) | Dual (3) | Pilot (4)

GERMAN AIRCRAFT FLOWN AND TIMES

Sibel I04 --28.30
Sibel 204 --24.I0
Junker 52 --7.50
junker 88 --5.I5
Junker 352 -24.I0
Junker 388 -3.I0
Junker 290 -II.45
M.E. I08 -I.20
M.E II0 -4.I5
M.E. 4I0 -3.05
F.W. I90 -3.I5
F.W.C. 290 -3.[illegible]
F.W.C. 200 --I7.20
ARADO 232 -- 6.30
F.Storch --I0.20
HEINKLE 2I9 -- 3.30
Dornier 2I7 --4.I5
Dornier 335 --3.40
Arado 96 --2.00

Arado Ar 232: 6 hrs. 30 min.

Armstrong-Whitworth Whitley: 1 hr 45 min.

Avro Manchester: 25 hrs.25 min.

Avro Lancaster: 1058 hrs. 35 min.

Avro Anson: 171 hrs. 25 min.

Dornier Do 335: 3 hrs. 40 min.

Gloster Meteor: 3 hrs.

Hawker Tempest: 1 hr 20 min.

Junkers Ju 290: 11 hrs. 45 min.

Junkers Ju 352: 24 hrs. 10 min.

Martin B-26 Marauder: 23 hrs.

Messerschmitt Bf 109: 1 hr. 20 min.

Messerschmitt Me 410: 3 hrs. 5 min.

Supermarine Spitfire: 15 hrs.

Vickers-Armstrong Windsor: 10 hrs. 30 min.

As for his favourite bomber, there was no hesitation when Joe's nephew asked him that question,

"The Lancaster-no doubt about that. The aircraft was fantastic. It could take a beating and still fly. It was strong and fast. You could come home on one and a half engines."[7]

Joe's favorite bomber-The Avro Lancaster.

Part Eight

With the RCAF in Canada

"About halfway through my tour, W/C Joe McCarthy arrived. He was a lot of fun as the C/O. He never tried to impress anyone with his rank and position. He was the C/O and everyone knew it. He didn't go around reminding everyone."

RCAF Test and Development Unit

After crossing the Atlantic in a BOAC Liberator Joe reported to No. 1 Repatriation Depot at Lachine, Quebec during February 1946. He was then officially posted to the RCAFs 'Test and Development Unit' at the RCAFs base at Rockcliffe, near Ottawa. Soon afterwards there were two significant changes to his status.

Following the war the Government of Canada made the decision that non-Canadians in the RCAF must become Canadian citizens if they wished to continue with their career in Canada's air force. Joe had made the decision to remain with the RCAF and subsequently revoked his American citizenship and became a Canadian which he remained for the rest of his life. The second change to Joe's status occurred on 17 March when Joe and Alice were married in Alice's hometown of Detroit, Michigan. It had been a long time since they had met in Goderich during the autumn of 1941. They had seen each other during February 1945, but it was another year until Joe returned to Canada to live.

Later in March Joe was sent to the Winter Experimental Flight at the RCAF base at Namao, near Edmonton, Alberta. Here he was involved in the trials of the National Research Council's flying-wing glider known as the 'Pterodactyl.' The basic principle had stimulated aircraft designers in Germany, Britain, and the United States for some time as the idea of the entire surface of an aircraft providing lift with no drag-producing parts seemed ideal. Canada's NRC became involved in 1942 and the first flight tests took place in April 1946.

The Pterodactyl Flying-wing.

The wing was all-wood construction with the frame covered by moulded plywood. The glider's pilot and navigator sat side-by-side under separate canopies. It featured a retractable undercarriage and hydraulically operated brakes. The wing was outfitted with extensive test instrumentation and was finished in a high-visibility, yellow paint scheme.

Joe's duties with this project are not clear but on 24 and 25 April he towed the glider to altitude using a twin-engine DC-3 Dakota tow plane. Eventually the glider was successfully towed across the country for further test flights in Arnprior, Ontario. The NRC's flying-wing glider program was eventually cancelled in 1948.

During the summer of 1946, Joe performed displays at air shows, flying a Lancaster on 9 July in Calgary and then travelling to Winnipeg where he flew a Lancaster display on 12 July and a Halifax display the following day. This was the only Halifax ever to fly in Canada and had been based at Namao for winter trials together with a Spitfire, Tempest, Mosquito, Lancaster, and a Lincoln, the aircraft that was designed to be the successor to the Lancaster.

Later in the summer Joe became involved with the Hadrian Glider. The RCAF had experimented with a few troop gliders during the war and acquired 26 Hadrians in 1946. The air force was testing a United States Air Force Hadrian that was powered by twin Ranger engines as used in the Fairchild Cornell trainers that operated at numerous BCATP EFTSs.

Joe flew the 'powered glider' during August of 1946. However interest waned and by the mid-1950's they had all been sold for scrap.

Handley-Page Halifax RG814 vin Canada.

Opposite: Hadrian Glider with two Ranger Engines.
The McCarthy Family

Despite these interesting assignments, Joe's primary focus while at Rockcliffe was the testing and acceptance of the air force's first North Stars.

The North Star was the RCAFs first major post-war acquisition. It was acquired to fulfill a heavy transport rôle and, like the Lancaster, was powered by the Rolls-Royce Merlin V-12 engine.

The RCAF North Stars had a stormy start to their careers because of their perceived obsolesence even when purchased. However, Air Transport Command operated the aircraft worldwide and they gained fame during the Korean airlift of the early 1950's when Canada found itself at war again. RCAF North Stars flew 599 round trips to Japan in support of the Canada's Korean War effort and later supported peacekeeping missions and humanitarian relief work in other parts of the World. In 1949 an RCAF North Star was the first aircraft to fly a non-stop, trans-Canada flight. It took off from Vancouver on 15 January and landed the next morning in Halifax after 8 hours and 32 minutes aloft. North Stars were the backbone of Air Transport Command from 1947 until the 1960's when the Canadair Yukons took over. Joe was checked out on the aircraft on 13 August.

On 26 August 1947 Joe accepted North Stars 17501 and 17502 as airworthy subject to completion of equipment checks and they were delivered to 426 Squadron. A total of 25 were taken on strength by the RCAF and Joe did many of the acceptance flights during his time at Rockcliffe.

During February and March 1948 Joe was a passenger during helicopter flights at Rockcliffe. This would have been the Sikorsky Dragonfly which in 1947 became the first helicopter to enter service with the RCAF.

AUG - 23 - 1946 # 514037 (RCG) ROCKCLIFFE - TEST + DEVELOPE. FLIGHT
"POWER GLIDER HADRIAN" TWO RANGER 160 H.P. MOTORS.
LINK LINER

Canadair North Star.

Don Vance

Trenton, Chatham, and Grostenquin

During September 1948 Joe spent some time at the RCAF Staff College in Toronto.

In June 1949 he was appointed Officer Commanding the Acceptance and Ferry Flight for No. 6 Repair Depot at Trenton. Then in July 1949 he became responsible for the acceptance flights of Lancaster and Mitchell B-25 bombers that had been modified by AVRO and de Havilland in Toronto. His logbook shows numerous flights in Beech-18 Expeditors, Dakotas (DC-3s), and North Stars.

Beginning in the late 1940's over 100 Canadian-built Lancasters that had been placed in storage following the war were modified to nine different configurations for post-war service. Although most served in maritime reconnaissance rôles, others were modified to perform rôles such as armed reconnaissance (carrying depth charges), aerial photography, search and rescue, navigational training, and as test beds for jet engine testing. Aerial photography taken from Lancasters even added new territory to the map of Canada that previous surveys had overlooked.

During May 1950 Joe was posted to 1 Instrument Flying School at Centralia, Ontario where he flew Beechcraft-18 Expeditors. Then in July he was back at Trenton flying Dakotas and North Stars again.

During his time at Trenton, Joe also ferried P-51 Mustangs and T-33 jets from the United States to serve with the RCAF.

Although Joe had been through numerous emergencies and threatening situations while in the cockpit, he experienced a quite unique one while at Trenton. His reaction, which quite likely involved his size and strength, earned a, 'Pilot's Commendatory Endorsement' from his commanding officer. The document reads,

"As pilot of a Service aircraft on 13 July 1951, S/L J.C. McCarthy DSO DFC and Bar displayed remarkable skill in landing the aircraft while having to contend with the unconscious interference of his passenger in the co-pilot's seat. The interference of the passenger was caused by an epileptiform seizure which was contracted by him whilst in the air. This situation left the pilot alone

Joe McCarthy jr. was born during the time Joe and Alice were stationed at Rockcliffe.
The McCarthy Family

with an aggressive person on board who was completely disoriented and extremely agitated, thereby hampering the pilot's control of the aircraft in flight.

By his coolness in this emergency and by superior flying ability, S/L McCarthy avoided a possible serious accident."

Commanding Officer 6 RD; Trenton
14 August, 1951 [1]

RCAF Chatham was the base where F-86 Sabre pilots were being trained and in March 1952, Joe was appointed the base's Chief Administrative Officer. Although Joe never flew the F-86 Sabre, in May he became the commanding officer of 1 (Fighter) Operational Training Unit.

The Canadair F-86 Sabre was built in Montreal and during Joe's time at Chatham the air force was very busy creating operational Sabre squadrons for service in Europe as the Cold War heated up.

In July 1953 and following his promotion to the rank of Wing Commander, Joe was posted to Grostenquin in France where he had similar duties at 2 Fighter Wing. He was then posted back to Trenton in August 1954.

In preparation for his next major assignment, Joe then spent four months at 1 Flight Instructor School flying the North American Harvard advanced trainer.

Penhold

In 1949, as the Cold War deepened, Canada signed an agreement whereby the RCAF would train aircrew for NATO member countries. By the time this arrangement was terminated in 1958, 5575 had been trained in Canada. Separate agreements with individual countries after 1958 saw even more pilots trained at Canadian bases. Although on a smaller scale, this was quite reminiscent of the BCATP during World War II.

Penhold, Alberta, had been the site of 36 Service Flying Training School under the BCATP' and had evolved into 4 Flying Training School where

No. 4 FTS Harvards at Penhold in 1956.
Harvard Historical Aircraft Society

Canadian and NATO pilots from other countries were flying Harvard aircraft. Joe was posted there on January 1955 to serve as the commanding officer of the school.

The Harvard was an American design, known in that country as the AT-6 Texan. It was first produced in 1939. Well suited to its training rôle, it was a high performance aircraft which had enough bad habits to teach inexperienced pilots to respect the even more powerful fighters they would soon be flying. Strong but unforgiving it required a delicate touch to maintain the proper attitude upon take off and landing.

The distinctive snarl of the Harvard is produced by its high-powered engine together with the nine foot propeller which, when in fine pitch at high rpm, approaches supersonic speeds.

During WW II the Harvard served as an advanced trainer at Service Flying Training Schools where pilots who had learned to fly on Tiger Moths or Cornells were prepared to fly fighters such as the Spitfire.

Harvard Mk. IV 20419 currently on display at the Bomber Command Museum of Canada was flown by W/C McCarthy while at Penhold.

Beginning in 1940, 2800 wartime Harvards were built by Noorduyn in Montreal and during the early 1950's, another 550 were built by Canadian Car and Foundry in Fort William, Ontario.

During May 1955 Joe travelled to London for a special reunion of the Dambusters and the Royal Premiere of the highly successful film that starred Michael Redgrave as Barnes Wallis and Richard Todd as Guy Gibson. 'The Dambusters' remains one of the most enduring of war films for its understated account of the raid and the drama that arose from the combination of heroism with technical ingenuity.

Ron Fentiman served with Joe as a flight instructor during his time at Penhold. He recalls Joe's involvement with a horse named Mae,

'The Officers' and WO & Sgts' Messes at Penhold followed the tradition of alternating being host for an inter-mess visit at New Years. On 1 Jan 1955 it was the Officers' turn to host the WOs & Sgts who purchased an old mare; 'Mae', and one of their number rode her to and into the Officers' Mess where

Joe shaking hands with Barnes Wallis at the Royal Premiere celebrations. Ken Brown (left) and Don McLean are to the left of Joe. Note the model of the dam in the foreground.
The McCarthy Family

(l-r) Duke of Gloucester, Joe, Revie Walker, Don MacLean, and Ken Brown.
The McCarthy Family

Mac and W/C McCarthy departing the Officers' Mess en-route to the Sergeants Mess at RCAF Station Penhold.
Ron Fentiman

W/C McCarthy 1956.

the horse was presented to the Officers. I was not present for that occasion, having arrived at Penhold as a brand new 'C' category instructor in August.

"The Officers arranged with a local farmer to board Mae and on 1 Jan 1956 the process was reversed. Our WingCo Flying, Joe McCarthy, rode her into the WO & Sgts' Mess where she was gifted back. I don't know what became of Mae as I was posted later that month to RCAF Station MacDonald to instruct on T-33s.

"W/C McCarthy was a fine leader and a hell of a good sport!" [2]

Following his service at Penhold, Joe took a course on B-25 Mitchells in Saskatoon and spent time at Summerside, Prince Edward Island as well.

Bill McKenzie recalls flying with Joe shortly after he left RCAF Station Penhold,

"When Joe McCarthy left RCAF Stn. Penhold in October 1958, I had him as a student at 1 Advanced Flying School at RCAF Station Saskatoon during a very short refresher of ten hours on the B-25 before he went to No. 2 (Maritime) Operational Training Unit at Summerside, Prince Edward Island. We only did four trips and incidently two of those flights were on B-25 5244 which is now in the National Aviation Museum in Rockcliffe. I received no advance notice about his flying background but to say he was an exceptional pilot was an understatement.

"When simulating a single engine on Joe, the instructor had to use either the mixture or the fuel valve to cut the engine. Because he was so big and strong when he had those hands on the throttles, I couldn't retard either one unless he agreed to reduce his grip on one of the throttles. As I recall Joe was a most jovial and personable individual and a very serious, meticulous, and professional pilot." [3]

B-25 5244 over Saskatchewan.
Bill McKenzie

No. 407 Squadron

During the immediate post-war period coastal defence was the responsibility of the Royal Canadian Navy. However by the end of the decade there was a growing threat posed by Soviet submarines in Canada's Pacific waters. 407 Squadron, which had operated with distinction as a Coastal Command squadron with the Royal Air Force from 1941 until 1945, was reformed on 1 July 1952 at RCAF Station Comox on Vancouver Island.

The squadron was designated as a maritime reconnaissance (MR) unit and was the first operational squadron on the west coast since the end of the war. As well as maritime reconnaissance and patrol with a focus on anti-submarine warfare, the squadron was tasked with long-range search and rescue, convoy escorts, and radio counter-measures.

Lancaster with a Neptune beyond.

Opposite: Neptune 24102 over the Pacific while serving with No. 407 Squadron.

Canadian-built Lancasters had been converted to fulfill this rôle and had operated with 407 Squadron, but were in the final stages of being phased out when W/C McCarthy arrived to become the new Commanding Officer in May 1959. Joe's logbook shows only four flights in Lancasters, all shortly after his arrival at the squadron. Interestingly, one of the aircraft he flew with 407, KB889, is now restored and on display at the Imperial War Museum's Duxford facility.

The aircraft flown by the squadron during Joe's command was the Lockheed P2V-7 Neptune. Initially they were equipped with twin piston engines however beginning in April 1959 the Neptunes were modified to carry additional turbojet engines mounted on each wing beyond the piston engine. Although the primary rôle of the Neptune was anti-submarine warfare, anti-shipping was also considered an important ability. Neptunes served with RCAFs maritime squadrons from 1955 until they were replaced by the Canadair Argus in 1968.

Marty Plumstead was a pilot with the squadron and remembers when Joe McCarthy arrived to take command,

"About halfway through my tour, W/C Joe McCarthy arrived. He was a lot of fun as a C/O. He never tried to impress anyone with his rank and position. He was the C/O and everyone knew it. He didn't go around reminding everyone. He still had that American accent too and I remember that my name came out 'Motty'. Coby, the Squadron Ops Officer, was a pretty irreverent guy. He used to call McCarthy, 'Tex.' McCarthy must have liked it because I never heard of him correcting Coby." [4]

As happened at Penhold in the incident with Mae, there was a similar rivalry at Comox as Joe Jr. related,

ROYAL CANADIAN AIR FORCE
102
MARITIME AIR COMMAND
24102

G/C Miller (left) and Joe welcoming Cdr. Parker Cooper to Comox.
The McCarthy Family

"The squadron had gone down to the U.S. Naval Air Station at Alameda, near San Francisco, to work with an American Neptune squadron and Dad and the C/O, Commander Parker Cooper, became pretty good friends. Later, the C/O flew up to Comox on a Friday to spend the weekend. Dad met them after they landed.

"Upon leaving the airplane Cooper said that they had brought something that they wanted to present to the squadron and wondered about a safe place to keep it. Joe asked where it was and was told it was in the bomb bay of the aircraft. Joe said, 'It's on my line. It'll be safe right where it is.' It was arranged that the presentation would take place at a Mess Dinner on Saturday night.

"On Saturday morning the phone rang and I answered it. The C/O of the American squadron was calling and said that he needed to talk with Dad. Cooper told Dad that the thing they were going to present to the squadron was missing. Joe asked, 'What is it?' but Cooper didn't really want to say. So Dad called one of his Sergeants and told him something was missing.

The Sergeant of course asked, 'Well what is it that's missing? and Dad could only reply, 'I don't know.' The Sergeant said, 'Well if you don't know what it is I'm going to have a hard time finding it.' Dad sort of picked up that maybe this guy knew a little more than he was letting on. The Sergeant said,

'Well let me check into it and I'll see what I can do.'

"About 3:00 in the afternoon, Dad gets a call and it's this Sergeant and he says, 'I think everything's taken care of. Where do you want it?' Dad says, 'Well it has to be presented in the Officers' Mess tonight.' The Sergeant said, 'Okay, it'll be there.'

"Well sure enough they get to the Mess and here's this thing sitting up ready to be presented with sheets over it so you couldn't see what it was. After dinner, the C/O gets up to do the presentation, reaches up and removes the sheets, and it's a set of fibreglass US Navy wings. These were very large, in the six to eight foot range, and had been made to honour the Fiftieth Anniversary of US Naval aviation.

"They were most impressive but when they got close they noticed a little brass plaque on the top of the wing that read, 'Presented First in the Sergeants' Mess' and included the previous day's date." [5]

Joe Jr. recalls another incident that took place during June 1960 in which his Dad became very upset with the military bureaucracy and got some quick results,

"They took three or four airplanes down to Alameda in California and were going to fly over to Hawaii to do some exercises with aircraft and ships of the American Navy. At that time somebody in the Canadian government or military had decided that they could save money by using re-furbished spark plugs instead of buying new ones.

"Dad took off for Hawaii but about an hour out he lost an engine. So he came back and had to fly around on the jets to lighten the aircraft before landing. Another of the aircraft was getting ready to leave so Dad took that one and about two hours out had an engine failure in that one and had to bring it back. "

A third aircraft flown by F/Lt. Hutchison took off and lost an engine just past the point of no return. They had the jet engines but didn't have the fuel to run the jets the whole way. They lightened the aircraft by jettisoning all non-essential equipment and declared an emergency. They were met by air-sea rescue who followed them into Hilo Airport because it was closer than the military airfield. When they landed in Hawaii they only had ten to fifteen minutes of fuel left and had come very close to losing the aircraft over these plugs.

S/L McCarthy in his office at Comox.
The McCarthy Family

Joe outside the theatre at Comox.
The McCarthy Family

"I know that Dad sent out messages to basically God and the World about this because he was very hot. He called headquarters, Lockheed, Pratt & Whitney who built the engines, the spark plug people, and anyone else he could think of."

"About thirty hours later brand new sparkplugs were air-shipped to Hawaii for all of his aircraft." [6]

Joe Jr. never saw his father angry or violent, explaining that, "The look was the thing. When he was not pleased or unhappy about something he didn't hide it and at 6'3" and with that big chest his message was impressively delivered."

The Congo

Britain granted independence to its former colony of Congo on 30 June 1960, however within weeks a section of the country known as Katanga separated and order broke down as various factions went to war and army units mutinied. During July 1960 Canada was called upon to support a United Nations operation to attempt to restore peace and order to the new, but strife-torn republic.

North Star 17517 is marshalled at Ndjili Airport in Leopoldville, Congo. This was the last vist to the Congo of a 426 Squadron North Star. Note the Canadair Yukon beyond at right.

The crisis in the Congo caused the deaths of some 100,000 people. It led to the assassination of Prime Minister Patrice Lumumba as well as to a traumatic setback to the United Nations following the death of U.N. Secretary General Dag Hammarskjöld in a plane crash as he sought to mediate. The situation was very complex and the leadership in the area was in turmoil until some stability returned with the rise to power of Joseph Mobutu in 1965.

The U.N. requested that Canada provide staff to operate and control air movements within the Congo. In addition to controlling the airspace the RCAF was ordered to provide air transport between the outside world and Leopoldville.

On 18 July 1960 the first cargo-laden North Star left Trenton and on 9 August a twenty day airlift of Canadian troops and equipment began. During 1961 the North Stars were replaced by the Canadair Yukon, a larger and faster transport aircraft with greater range and payload. One of the first Yukon crews to land was confronted by armed Congolese guards as they climbed down the ramp from their aircraft which was impounded and searched. The Congolese had never seen a Yukon before and thought it was a Russian aircraft.

Following his service at Comox, Joe proceeded to United Nations Headquarters in Leopoldville, Congo during May 1962. He had been appointed Chief Air Operations

Joe McCarthy directing traffic in the Congo.
The McCarthy Family

Officer and his task was to coordinate all transport flying for UN operations in that war-torn country. This was a massive operation and Joe was very busy during this six month assignment. He did very little flying himself, and when he did, it was as the pilot of a DC-3.

It must have been a very demanding time for Joe. At one time thirteen different aircraft type from various contributing nations were being used in the turbulent country. As well, living and operating in the heat and steaming jungle of Congo would have been a significant additional challenge for Joe and the other Canadians stationed there.

The RCAFs Air Transport Command flew 392 trips to the Congo. 2000 tons of freight and 12,000 passengers had been transported when the last Yukon left Leopoldville for Trenton in June 1964.

An unusual aspect of Joe's duties was that Congolese Army Chief of Staff and future President Joseph Mobutu would only fly on a United Nations aircraft if Joe was aboard with him as a guarantee that it would not be blown up.

Armed Forces Defence College

During January 1963 Joe was sent to the Armed Forces Defence College in Norfolk, Virginia where he took a four month course prior to playing a rôle in the office of the Commander in Chief (West Atlantic) who coordinates Canadian/American joint operations in the western Atlantic Ocean.

As Joe began to play a more senior rôle he flew less often although during June 1963 he made three flights in a T-28 Trojan.

Bill Rowbotham was an RCAF Squadron Leader and at this time was an exchange pilot serving with an American Navy Neptune squadron based at the Naval Air Station at Norfolk. He wrote of his recollections of Joe and those times in Norfolk,

"I was able to assist Joe, Alice, and family locate housing near to where I lived in Virginia Beach when they were transferred to Norfolk. I had not met Joe prior to that time, although he was known to me by reputation. In all my conversations with people that worked with or for Joe, I have always gained the

impression of the great respect and fond memories that they held for him. The RCAF was a small enough organization (the pilot group an even a smaller one) that the people who stood out were widely 'known' by their leadership qualities, deeds, and abilities etc. Joe was a terrific individual who was widely liked and held in high esteem by all.

"I recall a chance meeting and introducing Joe to my US Navy crew and other members of the Squadron in the Breezy Point Officers Club in Norfolk. We all chatted and had a few drinks. They were all quite impressed by his friendliness and ease of manner for one of his rank while socializing with much younger and junior officers. They had no clue as to his wartime experience until later.

"The cold war was on hot and heavy in the early sixties, especially with the US Navy. I was away on deployments and for over half of the time we were keeping an eye on Soviet 'at-sea' activities. You may recall the Cuban Missile Crisis of Nov-Dec 1962. We all, in our various positions, Headquarters Staff or operational flying, were very involved in that type of occurrence on a continuing basis.

"Our families met on several social occasions, had enjoyable times together, and Joe looked in on my family quite regularly during the times that I was deployed to see if there was anything he could do to assist.

"I was promoted to Squadron Leader in the fall of 1967 while serving on the Maritime OTU at Summerside. Joe, then Base Ops Officer at Greenwood, called me at home in the wee early hours of a Saturday morning to congratulate me on the promotion. (The promotion list was announced at a Friday evening party in the Mess at Greenwood but not until Saturday morning at Summerside.) He was the first to inform and congratulate me. It speaks highly of his wonderful nature and concern for others. I certainly appreciated that call from him." [7]

Greenwood

In September 1966 Joe received his last posting with the Royal Canadian Air Force when he was appointed Base Operations Officer at Greenwood, Nova Scotia. This was a busy time at Greenwood with the Canadair Argus being Canada's off-shore Maritime Patrol aircraft. Its primary focus was the containment of the USSR's vast cold war submarine fleet. Joe's first flight in the aircraft was on 20 September.

When the Argus entered service in 1957 it gave the RCAF the most advanced anti-submarine aircraft in the world. It carried the latest in anti-submarine electronics and an armament load (torpedoes and depth-charges) of almost four tons. Normally the crew consisted of three pilots, three navigators, two flight engineers, and seven electronic equipment operators. Fully loaded it could fly from Newfoundland to Ireland, patrol for 8 hours, return from this 1500 mile transit, and still have an hour of reserve fuel on board.

RCAF Argus at Greenwood.
Royal Canadian Air Force

The Argus served until 1982 when it was replaced by the CP-140 Aurora.

The amalgamation of Canada's three traditional armed services was first suggested in 1964. The public explanation for the reorganization was that unification would achieve cost savings and provide improved command and control. The idea met with strong opposition from serving personnel in the army, navy, and air force who felt that loyalty to each service was vital. But with the passage of the Armed Forces Reorganization Act in early 1968, Joe became a Lieutenant Colonel rather than a Wing Commander and the aircraft no longer carried the markings of the Royal Canadian Air Force.

This was likely seen by Joe as an appropriate time to retire and his last flight with the Canadian Armed Forces was as co-pilot of Argus 20738 on a flight from Norfolk to Greenwood on 9 April 1968.

Canadian Armed Forces Argus 738 The aircraft Joe flew on 9 April 1968.

Royal Canadian Air Force

Epilogue

Joe took the Princess of Acadia from Digby to St. John and drove to his home in Virginia. He worked in real estate and lectured at the United States Air Force Air War College and Maxwell Air Force Base prior to retiring.

Joe McCarthy passed away on 6 September 1998.

"Apropos Joe McCarthy: I got a very nice letter from someone living in the U.S.A. who signed himself Joe McCarthy following the publication of 'A Thousand Shall Fall' back in 1979.

I naturally responded, thanking him for his kind words. Thereafter, every Christmas, without fail, I would get a Christmas card from a gentleman named Joe McCarthy in the U.S. I responded, of course, so we exchanged cards for quite a few years.

It was not until he died, several years ago, and his wife wrote to me and sent along a newspaper obit, that I realised I'd been corresponding all those years with our Joe McCarthy, one of our famous Dam Busters.

I could have kicked myself for not inquiring earlier; but in his letters and cards he never said a single word about having been involved in the Dams Raid. I had had a vague idea that he had served as an airman, but nothing more.

I felt badly when I learned his identity; I'd have liked to have paid him some of the compliments he'd well and truly earned.

If you do any writing about him or put up any inscriptions, I hope you will mention his exceptional modesty. I still feel like kicking myself."

-Murray Peden DFC

Chronology

1919-08-31	-Born at St. James, New York
1941-05-05	-Enlists in RCAF; posted to 1 Manning Depot, Toronto, Ontario
1941-06	-Posted to 1 ITS, Toronto, Ontario
1941-08	-Posted to 12 EFTS, Goderich, Ontario
1941-09	-Posted to 5 SFTS, Brantford, Ontario
1941-12-18	-Awarded RCAF Pilot's Wings; Commissioned with rank of Pilot Officer
1941-12	-Reported to 1 'Y' Depot, Halifax, Nova Scotia for embarkation to U.K.
1941-01	-Reported to 3 Personnel Reception Unit, Bournemouth
1942-02	-Posted to 12 AFU, Spitalgate
1942-03-29	-Posted to 1518 Beam Approach School
1942-04	-Posted to 12 (P) AFU, Grantham
1942-05-19	-Posted to 14 OTU, Cottesmore
1942-07-31/01	-Op. 1; Düsseldorf
1942-09-06	-Posted to 97 Conversion Flight, Coningsby
1942-09-11	-First flight with Bill Radcliffe, Ron Batson, and R. Muskett
1942-09-13	-First flight with Len Eaton
1942-09-16	-First flight with W. Brayford
1942-09-29	-Posted to 97 Squadron, Woodhall Spa
1942-10-02/03	-Op. 2; Krefeld (Second Dickie flight)
1942-10-05/06	-Op. 3; Aachen; first flight with A. Westwell
1942-10-22/23	-Op. 4; Genoa
1942-11-06/07	-Op. 5; Genoa
1942-11-08/09	-Op. 6; Gardening
1942-11-13/14	-Op. 7; Genoa
1942-11-17/18	-Op. 8; Gardening
1942-11-22/23	-Op. 9; Stuttgart
1942-11-28/29	-Op. 10; Turin
1942-12	-Promoted to Flying Officer
1942-12-04/05	-Op. 11; Gardening
1942-12-06/07	-Op. 12; Manheim
1942-12-08/09	-Op. 13; Turin
1942-12-09/10	-Op. 14; Turin
1942-12-21/22	-Op. 15; Munich; first flight with George 'Johnny' Johnson
1943-01-08/09	-Op. 16; Duisburg
1943-01-16/17	-Op. 17; Berlin
1943-01-17/18	-Op. 18; Berlin; first flight with Dave Rodger
1943-01-30/31	-Op. 19; Hamburg
1943-02-02/03	-Op. 20; Cologne

1943-02-04/05 -Op. 21; Turin

1943-02-11/12 -Op. 22; Wilhelmshaven

1943-02-21/22 -Op. 23; Bremen

1943-02-25/26 -Op. 24; Nuremberg

1943-02-26/27 -Op. 25; Cologne

1943-02-28/01 -Op. 26; St. Nazaire

1943-03-01/02 -Op. 27; Berlin

1943-03-03/04 -Op. 28; Hamburg

1943-03-08/09 -Op. 29; Nuremberg

1943-03-09/10 -Op. 30; Munich

1943-03-11/12 -Op. 31; Stuttgart

1943-03-12/13 -Op. 32; Essen

1943-03-22/23 -Op. 33; St. Nazaire; first flight with Don MacLean

1943-03 -Promoted to Flight Lieutenant

-Awarded Distinguished Flying Cross

1943-03 -Posted to 617 Squadron, Scampton

1943-06-16/17 -Op. 34; Sorpe Dam

1943-06-27 -Awarded Distinguished Service Order

1943-07-15/16 -Op. 35; San Polo D'Enza (landed at Blida)

1943-07-24/25 -Op. 36; Leghorn (took off from Blida)

1943-07-29/30 -Op. 37; Milan (nickel raid) (landed at Blida)

1943-08-30 -617 Squadron moved to Coningsby

1943-09-16/17 -Op. 38; Antheor Viaduct

1943-12-20/21 -Op. 39; Supply drop from Tempsford*

1943-12-22/23 -Op. 40, V 1 Site

1943-12-30/31 -Op. 41; V-1 Site

1944-01-09 -617 Squadron moved to Woodhall Spa

1944-01-21/22 -Op. 42; V-1 Site

1944-01-25/26 -Op. 43; V-1 Site

1944-03-02/03 -Op. 44; Albert

1944-03-04/05 -Op. 45; St. Etienne

1944-03-10/11 -Op. 46; La Ricamerie

1944-03-15/16 -Op. 47; Woippy

1944-03-16/17 -Op. 48; Clermont-Ferrand

1944-03-18/19 -Op. 49; Bergerac

1944-03-20/21 -Op. 50; Angouleme

1944-03-23/24 -Op. 51; South of Lyon

1944-03-24 -Promoted to Squadron Leader

1944-03-24 -Appointed O/C 'C' Flight

1944-03-25/26 -Op. 52; South of Lyon

1944-04-05/06 -Op. 53; Toulouse

1944-04-10/11 -Op. 54; St. Cyr; first flight with W.A. 'Danny' Daniel

1944-04-18/19 -Op. 55; Juvisy

1944-04-20/21 -Op. 56; La Chappelle

1944-04-22/23 -Op. 57; Brunswick

1944-04-28 -Awarded Bar to Distinguished Flying Cross

1944-04-28/29 -Op. 58; Munich

1944-04-05/06 -Op. 59; Operation Taxable

1944-04-07/08 -Op. 60; Saumur Tunnel

1944-06-14 -Op. 61; Le Havre

1944-06-15 -Op. 62; Bologne

1944-06-19 -Op. 63; Watten (Éperlecques)

1944-06-22 -Op. 64; Wizernes

1944-06-24 -Op. 65; Wizernes

** Sources do not agree as to whether Joe flew on the first "Supply drop from Tempsford" operation on 1943-12-10/11. If he did, the entry was not recorded in his logbook and so is not included in this chronology.*

1944-06-25	-Op. 66; Siracourt
1944-07-04	-Op. 67; Creil
1944-07-10	-Taken off Operations
1944-07-20	-Posted to 61 Base RCAF, Topcliffe
1944-08-01	-Appointed O/C 1695 Bomber Defence Training Flight; Dalton
1944-11-15	-Posted to Royal Aircraft Establishment; Farnborough
1945-04-05	-Seconded to Vickers-Armstrong
1945-05	-Posted to Foreign Aircraft Flight
1946-02	-Posted to RCAFs Test and Development Unit; Rockcliffe, Ontario
1949-06	-Appointed O/C Acceptance and Ferry Flight; Trenton, Ontario
1952-03	-Appointed Chief Administrative Officer; RCAF Chatham
1952-05	-Appointed O/C 1 (Fighter) OTU; Chatham, Ontario
1953-07	-Promoted to Wing Commander
	-Posted to 2 Fighter Wing; Grostenquin, France
1954-08	-Posted to 1 Flight Instructor School; Trenton, Ontario
1955-01	-Appointed O/C 4 Flying Training School; Penhold, Alberta
1959-05	-Appointed O/C 407 Squadron; Comox, B.C.
1962-05	-Appointed Chief Air Operations Officer; United Nations Headquarters; Leopoldville, Congo
1963-01	-Armed Forces Defence College; Norfolk, Virginia
1963-05	-Posted to Office of Commander in Chief (Western Atlantic); Norfolk, Virginia
1966-09	-Appointed Base Operations Officer; Greenwood Nova Scotia
1968-04	-Retired to Virginia Beach, Virginia
1998-09-06	-Died at Virginia Beach, Virginia

Decorations, campaign stars, medals and other awards

Distinguished Service Order; Distinguished Flying Cross and Bar; 1939-45 Star; Aircrew Europe Star with France and Germany Clasp; Italy Star; Defence Medal; Canadian Volunteer Service Medal and Clasp; War Medal 1939-45; United Nations Medal with Congo Clasp; Canadian Forces' Decoration and Clasp; Operational Wings and Bar; Pilot's Flying Badge

Aircraft Flown

Airspeed Oxford
Arado 96
Arado 232
Armstrong-Whitworth Whitley
Avro Anson
Avro Manchester
Avro Lancaster
Beechcraft-18 Expeditor
Belanca Skyrocket
Boeing B-17 Flying Fortress
Canadair CP-107 Argus
Canadair North Star
Canadair T-33 Silver Star
Consolidated B-24 Liberator
Consolidated PB-Y Canso
de Havilland Chipmunk
de Havilland Dominie
de Havilland Dove
de Havilland Mosquito
de Havilland Tiger Moth
de Havilland Vampire
Dornier 217
Dornier 335
Douglas A-20 Boston
Douglas DC-3 Dakota
Fairey Swordfish
Fieseler Fi 156 Storch
Fleet Finch
Focke-Wulf 190
Focke-Wulf 200 Condor
Focke-Wulf 290
Gloster Meteor
Grumman Goose
Hadrian Powered Glider
Hawker Hurricane
Hawker Tempest
Hawker Typhoon
Handley-Page Halifax
Handley-Page Hampden
Heinkel 219 Owl
Junkers Ju 52
Junkers Ju 88
Junkers Ju 188
Junkers Ju 290
Junkers Ju 352
Herkules Junkers Ju 388
Lockheed Hudson
Lockheed P2V Neptune
Lockheed Ventura
Martin B-26 Marauder
Messerschmitt Bf 108
Messerschmitt Bf 110
Messerschmitt Bf 410
Miles Martinet
Noorduyn Norseman
North American Harvard
North American B-25 Mitchell
North American P-51 Mustang
North American T-28 Trojan
Siebel Si 104
Siebel Si 204
Supermarine Spitfire
Supermarine Walrus
Vickers Wellington
Vickers Windsor

End Notes

INTRODUCTION

1. Lawlor, Bill. Interview with Joe McCarthy (video).1997.

PART ONE

1. McCarthy, Joe Jr. (Interview-audio). 2010.

PART TWO

1. Walsh, Tom. Big Joe-The American Dambuster. Airforce Magazine. Fall 2008.
2. Turner, Gilbert Letter to Joe McCarthy. 16 May 1968.
3. idem
4. McCarthy, Joe Jr. (Interview-audio). 2010.
5. A.M. 'Milt' Harradance is 1 in the centre row. Milt became an illustrious criminal lawyer and judge in the City of Calgary. He maintained his interest in aviation by owning and flying a de Havilland Vampire, P-51 Mustang, and F-86 Sabre Jet.
6. Sutherland, Fred. (Interview-audio). 2010.

PART THREE

1. Campbell, J.A. The Airborne Years. Self-published.
2. Bomber Command Museum of Canada.
3. Peden, Murray. A Thousand Shall Fall. Stittsville: Canadas Wings. 1979.
4. Halliday, Hugh. Honoursand Awards. Air Force Association of Canada.
5. Bailey, D. A Collection of Wartime Letters by Bill Radcliffe.
6. idem
7. Bailey, Dorothy (Personal communication).
8. Tickler, F/Lt. Eddie. Bomber Command Museum of Canada.
9. McCarthy, Joe. Letter to Mr. Backhouse. (Date unknown).

PART FOUR

1. Bailey, Dorothy. A Collection of Wartime Letters by Bill Radcliffe.
2. Lawlor, Bill. Interview with Joe McCarthy (video).1997.
3. Bailey, Dorothy. A Collection of Wartime Letters by Bill Radcliffe.
4. Harvey, J. Douglas. Boys, Bombs, and Brussels Sprouts. Toronto: McClelland and Stewart. 1981.
5. Bailey, Dorothy. A Collection of Wartime Letters by Bill Radcliffe.

6. Royal Air Force-Combat Report.
7. The airmen in the photo are (l-r) C Watson, J Zunti, J Rees, JSaxton, P Fryer, F Baker, and W Coates. ED430 went on to have a long career with Bomber Command. After serving with No. 97 Squadron, it went on to fly with No. 50 and 622 Squadrons as well as No. 3 Lancaster Finishing School. It survived the war and was scrapped on 7 February 1947. Sadly the young airmen in the photo were killed while serving with No. 50. They did not fly ED430 while they were with No. 97 but they too were posted to No. 50 Squadron and may have flown the aircraft there. They were lost 22/23 November 1944 during a raid to Berlin.
8. Godfrey, Arthur. Bomber Command Museum of Canada.
9. McCarthy, Joe. Letter to Mr. Backhouse. (Date unknown).
10. McCarthy, Joe Jr. (Interview-audio). 2010.
11. Halliday, Hugh. Honours and Awards. Air Force Association of Canada.
12. Arthur, Max. Dambusters. London: Virgin. 2008.
13. Halliday, Hugh. Honours and Awards. Air Force Association of Canada.
14. McCarthy, Joe Jr. (Interview-audio). 2010.

PART FIVE

1. Holting, Pierre. Venture-The Dams Raid. Canadian Broadcasting Corporation (audio). 1961.
2. Bashow, David. No Prouder Place. St. Catherines: Vanwell. 2005.
3. Holting, Pierre. Venture-The Dams Raid. Canadian Broadcasting Corporation (audio). 1961.
4. Humphries, Harry. Living with Heroes –The Dam Busters. Norwich: Erskine. 2003.
5. Arthur, Max. Dambusters. London: Virgin. 2008.
6. Munro, Les. A Kiwi with the Dambusters. Aviation Classics Magazine. 2009.
7. Brown, Ken. Dambusters Fiftieth Anniversary Address. Bomber Command Museum of Canada (video).1993.
8. Gibson, Guy. Enemy Coast Ahead. London: Michael Joseph. 1946.
9. Bashow, David. No Prouder Place. St. Catherines: Vanwell. 2005.
10. Wilson, Kevin. Bomber Boys –The RCAF Offensive of 1943: London: Weidenfeld & Nicholson. 2005.
11. Williams, Frank C. The Raid on the Dams. Airforce Magazine. July, October 1985; January 1986.
12. United States Air Force Air Warfare College. Interview with Joe McCarthy. National Air Force Museum of Canada (video). 1991.
13. Brown, Ken. Dambusters Fiftieth Anniversary Address. Bomber Command Museum of Canada (video). 1993.

14. Gibson, Guy. Enemy Coast Ahead. London: Michael Joseph. 1946.
15. Holting, Pierre. Venture-The Dams Raid. Canadian Broadcasting Corporation (audio). 1961.
16. idem
17. idem
18. Weeden, Gordon. Unearthing Family History. Legion Magazine. Nov-Dec 2009
19. Arthur, Max. Dambusters. London: Virgin. 2008.
20. United States Air Force Air Warfare College. Interview with Joe McCarthy. National Air Force Museum of Canada (video). 1991.
21. Wilson, Kevin. Bomber Boys –The RCAF Offensive of 1943: London: Weidenfeld & Nicholson. 2005.
22. Brown, Ken. Dambusters Fiftieth Anniversary Address. Bomber Command Museum of Canada (video). 1993.
23. Williams, Frank C. The Raid on the Dams. Airforce Magazine. July, October 1985; January 1986.
24. Brown, Ken. Dambusters Fiftieth Anniversary Address. Bomber Command Museum of Canada (video). 1993.
25. Wilson, Kevin. Bomber Boys –The RCAF Offensive of 1943: London: Weidenfeld & Nicholson. 2005.
26. idem
27. idem
28. Hallam, Vic. Lest We Forget –The Dambusters in the Derwent Valley.
29. idem
30. idem
31. Arthur, Max. Dambusters. London: Virgin. 2008.
32. United States Air Force Air Warfare College. Interview with Joe McCarthy. National Air Force Museum of Canada (video). 1991.
33. Bashow, David. No Prouder Place. St. Catherines: Vanwell. 2005.
34. United States Air Force Air Warfare College. Interview with Joe McCarthy. National Air Force Museum of Canada (video). 1991.
35. idem
36. idem
37. Wilson, Kevin. Bomber Boys –The RCAF Offensive of 1943: London: Weidenfeld & Nicholson. 2005.
38. United States Air Force Air Warfare College. Interview with Joe McCarthy. National Air Force Museum of Canada (video). 1991.
39. Humphries, Harry. Living with Heroes –The Dam Busters. Norwich: Erskine. 2003.
40. Holting, Pierre. Venture-The Dams Raid. Canadian Broadcasting Corporation (audio). 1961.
41. Wilson, Kevin. Bomber Boys –The RCAF Offensive of 1943: London: Weidenfeld & Nicholson. 2005.
42. Holting, Pierre. Venture-The Dams Raid. Canadian Broadcasting Corporation (audio). 1961.
43. Johnson, George 'Johnny'. Imperial War Museum 0179 70 (video).
44. Holting, Pierre. Venture-The Dams Raid. Canadian Broadcasting Corporation (audio). 1961.

45. United States Air Force Air Warfare College. Interview with Joe McCarthy. National Air Force Museum of Canada (video). 1991.
46. Humphries, Harry. Living with Heroes –The Dam Busters. Norwich: Erskine. 2003.
47. Williams, Frank C. The Raid on the Dams. Airforce Magazine. July, October 1985; January 1986.
48. McCarthy, Joe. Letter to Mr. Backhouse. (Date unknown)
49. United States Air Force Air Warfare College. Interview with Joe McCarthy. National Air Force Museum of Canada (video). 1991.
50. Holting, Pierre. Venture-The Dams Raid. Canadian Broadcasting Corporation (audio). 1961.
51. United States Air Force Air Warfare College. Interview with Joe McCarthy. National Air Force Museum of Canada (video). 1991.
52. Munro, Les. A Kiwi with the Dambusters. Aviation Classics Magazine. 2009.
53. Holting, Pierre. Venture-The Dams Raid. Canadian Broadcasting Corporation (audio). 1961.
54. Brown, Ken. Dambusters Fiftieth Anniversary Address. Bomber Command Museum of Canada (video).1993.
55. Wilson, Kevin. Bomber Boys –The RCAF Offensive of 1943: London: Weidenfeld & Nicholson. 2005.
56. idem
57. Gibson, Guy. Enemy Coast Ahead. London: Michael Joseph 1946.
58. Thorning, Arthur G. The Dambuster who Cracked the Dam. Barnsley: Pen and Sword. 2008.
59. Wilson, Kevin. Bomber Boys –The RCAF Offensive of 1943: London: Weidenfeld & Nicholson. 2005.
60. Millberry, Larry. The Royal Canadian Air Force at War 1939-1945. Toronto: Canav. 1990.
61. Holting, Pierre. Venture-The Dams Raid. Canadian Broadcasting Corporation (audio). 1961.
62. McCarthy, Joe Jr. (Interview-audio). 2010.
63. United States Air Force Air Warfare College. Interview with Joe McCarthy. National Air Force Museum of Canada (video). 1991.
64. Wilson, Kevin. Bomber Boys –The RCAF Offensive of 1943: London: Weidenfeld & Nicholson. 2005.
65. idem
66. Holting, Pierre. Venture-The Dams Raid. Canadian Broadcasting Corporation (audio). 1961.
67. Lawlor, Bill. Interview with Joe McCarthy (video). 1997.
68. Wilson, Kevin. Bomber Boys –The RCAF Offensive of 1943: London: Weidenfeld & Nicholson. 2005.
69. Euler, Helmuth. The Dams Raid –Through the Lens. London: Battle of Britain International. 2001
70. United States Air Force Air Warfare College. Interview with Joe McCarthy. National Air Force Museum of Canada (video). 1991.
71. Wilson, Kevin. Bomber Boys –The RCAF Offensive of 1943: London: Weidenfeld & Nicholson. 2005.
72. United States Air Force Air Warfare College. Interview with Joe McCarthy. National Air Force Museum of

Canada (video). 1991.

73. Wilson, Kevin. Bomber Boys –The RCAF Offensive of 1943: London: Weidenfeld & Nicholson. 2005.
74. Holting, Pierre. Venture-The Dams Raid. Canadian Broadcasting Corporation (audio). 1961.
75. United States Air Force Air Warfare College. Interview with Joe McCarthy. National Air Force Museum of Canada (video). 1991.
76. Williams, Frank C. The Raid on the Dams. Airforce Magazine. July, October 1985; January 1986.
77. Sutherland, Fred. (Interview-audio). 2010.
78. Williams, Frank C. The Raid on the Dams. Airforce Magazine. July, October 1985; January 1986.
79. Sutherland, Fred. (Interview-audio). 2010.
80. idem
81. Flower, Stephen. Barnes Wallis' Bombs. 2002. Stroud: Amberley. 2010.
82. United States Air Force Air Warfare College. Interview with Joe McCarthy. National Air Force Museum of Canada (video). 1991.
83. Wilson, Kevin. Bomber Boys –The RCAF Offensive of 1943: London: Weidenfeld & Nicholson. 2005.
84. Brown, Ken. Dambusters Fiftieth Anniversary Address. Bomber Command Museum of Canada (video). 1993.
85. idem
86. idem
87. Holting, Pierre. Venture-The Dams Raid. Canadian Broadcasting Corporation (audio). 1961.
88. idem
89. Bashow, David. No Prouder Place. St. Catherines: Vanwell. 2005.
90. Holting, Pierre Venture-The Dams Raid. Canadian Broadcasting Corporation (audio). 1961.
91. Williams, Frank C. The Raid on the Dams. Airforce Magazine. July, October 1985; January 1986.
92. Arthur, Max. Dambusters. London: Virgin. 2008.
93. Euler, Helmuth. The Dams Raid –Through the Lens. London: Battle of Britain International. 2001.
94. Holting, Pierre. Venture-The Dams Raid. Canadian Broadcasting Corporation (audio). 1961.
95. Euler, Helmuth. The Dams Raid –Through the Lens. London: Battle of Britain International. 2001.

PART SIX

1. Humphries, Harry. Living with Heroes –The Dam Busters Norwich: Erskine. 2003.
2. Hume, Bill (Interview-audio). 2010.
3. idem
4. idem
5. Humphries, Harry. Living with Heroes –The Dam Busters. Norwich: Erskine. 2003.
6. Harris, Sir Arthur. Bomber Offensive. London: Greenhill. 1947.
7. Hume, Bill (Interview-audio). 2010.
8. McCarthy, Joe Jr. (Interview-audio). 2010.
9. Humphries, Harry. Living with Heroes –The Dam

Busters. Norwich: Erskine. 2003.

10. Hallam, Vic. Lest We Forget –The Dambusters in the Derwent Valley.
11. Humphries, Harry. Living with Heroes –The Dam Busters. Norwich: Erskine. 2003.
12. Sutherland, Fred. (Interview-audio). 2010.
13. Humphries, Harry. Living with Heroes –The Dam Busters. Norwich: Erskine. 2003.
14. Sutherland, Fred. (Interview-audio). 2010.
15. idem
16. idem
17. idem
18. Humphries, Harry. Living with Heroes –The Dam Busters. Norwich: Erskine. 2003.
19. Lawlor, Bill. Interview with Joe McCarthy (video). 1997.
20. Johnson, George 'Johnny'. Imperial War Museum 0179 70 (video).
21. Lawlor, Bill. Interview with Joe McCarthy (video). 1997.
22. idem
23. Humphries, Harry. Living with Heroes –The Dam Busters. Norwich: Erskine. 2003.
24. Lawlor, Bill. Interview with Joe McCarthy (video). 1997.
25. idem
26. Humphries, Harry. Living with Heroes –The Dam Busters. Norwich: Erskine. 2003.
27. idem *Although Humphries states that Joe took part in the operation, there is no corresponding entry in his logbook. Bateman reports that Joe did not fly in the first operation from Tempsford but it is clear that he flew to Tempsford with the others and, according to Humphries, was very involved in the operation.
28. Hume, Bill (Interview-audio). 2010.
29. Johnson, George 'Johnny'. Imperial War Museum 0179 70 (video).
30. Humphries, Harry. Living with Heroes –The Dam Busters. Norwich: Erskine. 2003.
31. Bomber Command Museum of Canada.
32. Brickhill, Paul. The Dam Busters. 2nd ed. 1972. London: Pan Books. 1983.
33. Thorburn, Gordon. No Need to Die –American Flyers in RAF Bomber Command. Sparkford: Haynes. 2009.
34. idem
35. Bennett, Tom. 617 Squadron –The Dambusters at War. Wellingborough: Patrick Stephens. 1986.
36. idem
37. Hume, Bill (Interview-audio). 2010.
38. Thorburn, Gordon. No Need to Die - American Flyers in RAF Bomber Command. Sparkford: Haynes. 2009.
39. Royal Air Force-Bomber Command Report.
40. idem
41. Halliday, Hugh. Honours and Awards. Air Force Association of Canada.
42. Thorburn, Gordon. No Need to Die - American Flyers in RAF Bomber Command. Sparkford: Haynes. 2009.
43. idem
44. Brickhill, Paul. The Dam Busters. 2nd ed. 1972.

London: Pan Books. 1983.
45. Cheshire, Leonard. I led D-Day Hoax. Sunday Graphic Newspaper. 2 December, 1945.
46. Lawlor, Bill. Interview with Joe McCarthy (video).1997.
47. idem
48. idem
49. idem
50. Thorburn, Gordon. No Need to Die - American Flyers in RAF Bomber Command. Sparkford: Haynes. 2009.
51. Brickhill, Paul. The Dam Busters. 2nd ed. 1972. London: Pan Books. 1983.
52. Bennett, Tom. 617 Squadron - The Dambusters at War. Wellingborough: Patrick Stephens. 1986.
53. Halliday, Hugh. Honours and Awards. Air Force Association of Canada.

PART SEVEN

1. Clay, Syd (Personal communication)
2. Lawlor, Bill. Interview with Joe McCarthy (video). 1997.
3. idem
4. idem
5. idem
6. idem
7. idem

PART EIGHT

1. Royal Canadian Air Force-Pilot's Commendatory Endorsement (14 August 1951)
2. Fentiman, Ron (Personal communication).
3. McKenzie, Bill (Personal communication).
4. Plumstead, Marty (Personal communication).
5. McCarthy, Joe Jr. (Interview-audio). 2010.
6. Rowbotham, Bill (Personal communication).
7. Peden, Murray (Personal communication).

Bibliography

BOOKS

Arthur, Max. Dambusters. London: Virgin. 2008.

Barris, Ted. Behind the Glory. Toronto: MacMillan. 1992.

Bashow, David. No Prouder Place. St. Catherines: Vanwell. 2005.

Bateman, Alex: No. 617 'Dambusters' Squadron: Osprey, 2009.

Bending, Kevin. Achieve Your Aim. 1st ed. 2005. Bognor Regis: Woodfield. 2006.

Bennett, Tom. 617 Squadron - The Dambusters at War Wellingborough: Patrick Stephens. 1986.

Bishop, Arthur. True Canadian Heroes in the Air. 1992. Toronto: Key Porter. 2004

Boyle, Andrew. No Passing Glory-The Full and Authentic Biography of G/C Cheshire VC DSO DFC.

Braddon, Russell. Cheshire VC. London: Evans Brothers. 1954.

Brickhill, Paul. The Dam Busters. 2nd ed. 1972. London: Pan Books. 1983.

Brown, Eric. Wings of the Luftwaffe. Great Britain: Pilot Press. 1977.

Campbell, J.A. The Airborne Years. Self-published.

Chorley, W.R. Bomber Command Losses. Earl Shilton: Midland Counties. 1992-2007.

Cooper, Alan W. Beyond the Dams to the Tirpitz. London: William Kimber. 1983.

Cooper, Alan W. The Men who Breached the Dams. London: William Kimber. 1982.

Douglas, W.A.B. The Creation of a National Air Force. Toronto: University of Toronto Press. 1986.

Euler, Helmuth. The Dams Raid - Through the Lens. London: Battle of Britain International. 2001.

Falconer, Jonathan. The Bomber Command Handbook 1939-1945. Stroud:Sutton. 1998.

Flower, Stephen. Barnes Wallis' Bombs. 2002. Stroud: Amberley. 2010.

Foster, Charles. Breaking the Dams. Barnsley: Pen and Sword. 2008.

Freeman, Roger A. Bases of Bomber Command –Then and Now. London: Battle of Britain International. 2001.

Fydenchuk, W. Peter. Immigrants of War: WPF. 2008.

Gibson, Guy. Enemy Coast Ahead. London: Michael Joseph. 1946.

Hallam, Vic. Lest We Forget –The Dambusters in the Derwent Valley.

Halley, J.J. The Lancaster File. Tonbridge: Air Britain. 1985.

Harris, Sir Arthur. Bomber Offensive. London: Greenhill. 1947.

Harvey, J. Douglas. Boys, Bombs, and Brussels Sprouts. Toronto: McClelland and Stewart. 1981.

Hillier, S.J. Willingborough: The History of 617 Squadron "The Dambusters 1943-1945.

Humphries, Harry. Living with Heroes –The Dam Busters. Norwich: Erskine. 2003.

Middlebrook, Martin. The Bomber Command War Diaries.

New York: Viking. 1985.

Millberry, Larry. Sixty Years. Toronto: Canav. 1984.

Millberry, Larry. The Royal Canadian Air Force at War 1939-1945. Toronto: Canav. 1990.

Moyes, Philip. Bomber Squadrons of the RAF and their Aircraft. London: MacDonald. 1964.

Murray, Iain R. Dam Busters-1943 Onwards. Haynes: Sparkford. 2011.

Peden, Murray. A Thousand Shall Fall. Stittsville: Canadas Wings. 1979.

Procter, Tom. 407 Squadron History. Comox: 407 Maritime Patrol Squadron. 2000.

Reynolds, Peter. The Dambusters at 60. Lincoln: Lincolnshire Echo. 2003.

Skaarup, Harold A. RCAF War Prize Flights, German and Japanese Warbird Survivors. Lincoln: iUniverse. 2006.

Sweetman, John. Bomber Crew. 2004. London: Abacus. 2005.

Sweetman, John. The Dambusters Raid. 2nd ed. 1990. London: Cassel. 1999.

Thorburn, Gordon. No Need to Die - American Flyers in RAF Bomber Command. Sparkford: Haynes. 2009.

Thorning, Arthur G. The Dambuster who Cracked the Dam. Barnsley: Pen and Sword. 2008.

Ward, Chris. 617 Dambuster Squadron at War. Barnsley: Pen and Sword. 2009.

Wilson, Kevin. Bomber Boys –The RCAF Offensive of 1943: London: Weidenfeld &Nicholson. 2005.

PERIODICALS

Cheshire, Leonard. I led D-Day Hoax. Sunday Graphic Newspaper. 2 December, 1945.

Coughlin, T.G. Candid Congo. Roundel. Jan./Feb. 1964.

Munro, Les. A Kiwi with the Dambusters. Aviation Classics Magazine. 2009.

Walsh, Tom. Big Joe-The American Dambuster. Airforce Magazine. Fall 2008.

Weeden, Gordon. Unearthing Family History. Legion Magazine. Nov-Dec 2009.

Williams, Frank C. The Raid on the Dams. Airforce Magazine. July, October 1985; January 1986.

INTERVIEWS/PERSONAL COMMUNICATIONS

Bailey, Dorothy (Personal communication)

Clay, Syd (Personal communication)

Fentiman, Ron (Personal communication)

Hume, Bill (Interview-audio). 2010.

McCarthy, Joe Jr. (Interview-audio). 2010.

McKenzie, Bill (Personal communication)

Peden, Murray (Personal communication)

Plumstead, Marty (Personal communication)

Rowbotham, Bill (Personal communication)

Sutherland, Fred. (Interview-audio). 2010.

DOCUMENTS

Bailey, Dorothy. A Collection of Wartime Letters by Bill Radcliffe.

Bomber Command Museum of Canada. Various archival files.

Halliday, Hugh. Honours and Awards. Air Force Association of Canada.

McCarthy, Joe. Letter to Mr. Backhouse. (Date unknown)

Turner, Gilbert Letter to Joe McCarthy. 16 May 1968.

Royal Air Force:

97 Squadron Operational Record Books.

617 Squadron Operational Record Books.

Bomber Command Reports.

Combat Reports.

Royal Canadian Air Force

Pilot's Commendatory Endorsement (14 August 1951)

AUDIO/VIDEO TAPES

Brown, Ken. Dambusters Fiftieth Anniversary Address. Bomber Command Museum of Canada (video).1993.

Holting, Pierre. Venture - The Dams Raid. Canadian Broadcasting Corporation (audio). 1961.

Johnson, George 'Johnny'. Imperial War Museum 0179 70 (video).

Lawlor, Bill. Interview with Joe McCarthy (video). 1997.

United States Air Force Air Warfare College. Interview with Joe McCarthy. National Air Force Museum of Canada (video). 1991.

WEBSITES

97 Squadron Association. Petwood Hotel.

Royal Air Force.

Royal Canadian Air Force.

Acknowledgements

I would first like to thank Joe McCarthy Jr. for supporting me in the writing of his father's biography and for his cooperation and assistance by allowing me access to his father's logbook, photographs, videotapes and other documents. Joe Sr.'s nephew, Bill Lawlor, recorded a wonderful video interview with Joe that the family made available to me.

A special thanks to Shere Lowe whose interest in her father's rôle in the Dams Raid as part of F/Lt. Hopgood's crew led her to our museum. She donated a copy of an historic CBC audio recording that included extensive interviews with her father (John Fraser), Joe McCarthy, and others.

Being able to spend time with Fred Sutherland and Bill Hume who served with Joe McCarthy on 617 Squadron provided 'first-person' information as well as an opportunity for me to gain some direct appreciation of the history that they lived through on 617 Squadron with Joe.

Artists Mark Postlethwaite and Clarence Simonsen have permitted their work to be part of the book and this is very much appreciated.

Organizations such as the Royal Canadian Air Force, the Royal Air Force, and the Imperial War Museum, and individuals including Nell Rodger, Ian Leech, William Sutherland, Rob Taerum, Fred Sutherland, Bill Hume, Dorothy Bailey, Bill Mackenzie, and Clare Bennett have made photographs available to me. Thanks to Carl Orde who assisted by improving the quality of many of the photos.

Dorothy Bailey contacted the Bomber Command Museum of Canada to offer photos and tell us about her panda bear that had accompanied her father, Joe, and the crew on all their operations. As well, she made available the collection of her father's wartime letters. Thank you Dorothy.

A special thanks to Tony Bunker and Tony Peatman who spent a day with my wife Leslie and I, arranging visits to RAF Scampton and its museum, RAF Coningsby, the former RAF Woodhall Spa, the 617 Memorial at Woodhall Spa, and most especially bought us a pint at the Petwood Hotel. Their kindness in helping me to visit these places is appreciated.

Many of those who served with Joe in the post-war RCAF assisted by sharing their memories and stories. Thanks to Bill McKenzie, Ron Fentiman, Marty Plumstead, Max Maxted, Duke Dawe, and Jim Thoreson.

Long-time Bomber Command Museum of Canada member Peter Whitfield made extensive use of his numerous contacts to answer many questions that came up during the final stages of completing the book. Thank you Peter.

A special thanks to my former colleague, Sheila Mackin, for her editing and other suggestions.

I very much appreciate Fred Sutherland reading the manuscript and offering his comments and suggestions. Fred 'was there' and his comment after reading the book that, "In fact it was like being transported back 68 years to 1943" was most encouraging.

And finally, I am very fortunate to have had the Foreword written by someone else who 'was there' and in this case in the aircraft with Joe during forty of his operations. Thank you George 'Johnny' Johnson.

The Author

A geophysicist, teacher, and interpretive guide in the Canadian Rockies, Dave Birrell was a founding director of the Nanton Lancaster Society which developed and operates the Bomber Command Museum of Canada.

One of hundreds of volunteers, he has been primarily involved with the development of the display material in the museum, the maintenance of the library and archives, and with the research and organization associated with the museum's special events.

Dave is also the author of 'Baz,'-the Biography of Ian Bazalgette VC, 'People and Planes-Stories from the Bomber Command Museum of Canada,' 'FM159-The Lucky Lancaster,' 'Calgary's Mountain Panorama,' 'Fifty Roadside Panoramas in the Canadian Rockies,' numerous mobile device applications regarding the Canadian Rockies, and the website 'www.peakfinder.com.'